Teacher Interviews:

How to Get Them and How to Get Hired!

Robert Pollock

A

Advanta Press · Martinsville, NJ

Advanta Press books may be purchased for educational or reference use.

Library of Congress
Cataloging in Publication Division
101 Independence Ave., S.E.
Washington, D.C. 20540-4320
Library of Congress Control Number: 2001118203

ISBN 978-0-9712570-0-9

Dedicated to the memory
of my wife

Debra Ann Pollock

Contents

dedication   *iii*
acknowledgements   *v*
about the author   *vii*

1   A PASSION TO TEACH! 9

2   WRITING AN EFFECTIVE COVER LETTER 23

3   BUILDING THE DYNAMIC RESUME 37

4   HOW TO BUILD AN INTERVIEW PORTFOLIO 51

5   DRESSING FOR A SUCCESSFUL INTERVIEW 57

6   GENERAL INTERVIEW TECHNIQUES 67

7   THE ELEMENTARY SCHOOL INTERVIEW 101

8   THE MIDDLE SCHOOL INTERVIEW 121

9   THE HIGH SCHOOL INTERVIEW 149

10   LANGUAGE ARTS QUESTIONS 165

11   MATHEMATICS QUESTIONS 183

12   SCIENCE QUESTIONS 205

13   SOCIAL STUDIES QUESTIONS 227

14   SPECIAL EDUCATION INTERVIEWS 239

15   HANDLING YOUR OFFER 267

16   PUTTING IT ALL TOGETHER 281

APPENDICES 291

ACKNOWLEDGEMENTS

In acknowledging any accomplishment I might have, I must first recognize the true inspiration of my life, my wife Debbie who passed away in 1998. It was she who continuously encouraged me to do something "special" and to work toward my personal best. Debbie was always at my side, no matter how difficult the challenge, to provide her encouragement, energy, and love. Her memory and spirit are with me always, certainly during the writing of this book.

Special thanks must also go to my two children, Robert and Kimberly, for their support and patience during the writing and editing of this book. They often had to give up our valuable time together while "Dad worked on his book." At the same time, a special thank you is extended to Debbie's mother, Mrs. Genevieve Castro who often watched the children and took care of many household responsibilities as the work progressed. My uncle, Archie W. Pollock served as my proofreader and advisor as the book took shape. As a public school administrator and educator for 31 years, his advice and counsel were vitally important and appreciated.

Many administrators, teachers, college students, colleagues and friends contributed ideas, questions and pertinent information. Conversations with them provided key additions to elements of the interview process.

I must also thank Carol Wilson, Director of the Principals' Center for the Garden State for her advice and help in the publishing of this book. Her sound guidance and advice were instrumental.

I must finally recognize the hundreds and hundreds of applicants who allowed me the opportunity to interview them for teaching positions. Formulating questions and listening to their answers provided a key ingredient for this book.

Before concluding, I want to salute all of you who will be undergoing interviews for a professional position in the coming weeks and months. You are the reason for this book. I wish you well. If you are just beginning your career, I welcome you to one of the finest of all professions – teaching!

ABOUT THE AUTHOR

Bob Pollock first started interviewing when he was an assistant principal at Jackson High School in Jackson, New Jersey. During his years as the vice-principal for curriculum and instruction, he interviewed over one hundred applicants for teaching positions and headed twenty-three teams in screening applications for the many openings in the school.

In 1988, Dr. Pollock moved to the middle school level where he served as a principal for 11 years in both Jackson and Bernardsville, New Jersey. During this time, Bob began to develop an interview format to identify specific traits through sets of penetrating questions. Hundreds more candidates appeared and he developed a system to screen the applications that flooded the district for each teacher opening. Over time, this process became more deliberate and objective.

When Dr. Pollock moved to the college level as an adjunct professor at The College of Saint Elizabeth in Convent Station, New Jersey, students beginning their search for the right teaching position continued to ask for advice on the interview process. To answer these increasing requests, he began to write down suggestions. The number and length of these writings steadily increased and before long a manual for seminars began to emerge.

Bob was prompted to place his interview information in a book because of the many requests for advice and his personal observations of how little most teachers understood about the process associated with finding and securing the right teaching position. Gathered from years of successful work with candidate interviews, he is now sharing this wealth of information with you. It is inside information as viewed from the other side of the desk – observations you can only receive from someone who has occupied the interviewer's chair. In this book he offers a collection of battle-tested, successful techniques that will help you prevail in your search for a rewarding teaching career.

1
A Passion to Teach!

Allow me to open this book by congratulating you on your decision to be a teacher. For every person, the decision to pursue a teaching career comes at different times and for different reasons. Whatever your reasons, I can assure you of one thing: you *will* be a positive force in the lives of hundreds of children. The ideas you convey, motivation you provide, confidence you instill, and model you set will carry well beyond the classes you teach. Your work will affect the quality of life for literally thousands of people. I know this sounds lofty, but I assure you it is true. Often, events that seem of almost no consequence to you can be of extraordinary importance to others. You think this far-fetched? Consider the case of Mrs. Mildred Hondorf, a music teacher from Des Moines, Iowa. She tells her story the following way.

I've always supplemented my income by teaching piano lessons – something I've done for over 30 years. Over the years I found that children have many levels of musical ability. I have never had the pleasure of teaching a protégé though I have taught some talented students. However, I have also had my share of what I will call "musically challenged" pupils.

One such student was Robby. Robby was 11 years old when his mother, a single mom, dropped him off for his first piano lesson. I prefer that students (especially boys!) begin at an earlier age, which I explained to Robby.

Robby said it had always been his mother's dream to hear him play the piano. I took him as a student. Robby began with his piano lessons and from the beginning I thought it was a hopeless endeavor. As much as Robby tried, he lacked the sense of tone and basic rhythm needed to excel. But he dutifully reviewed his scales and some elementary pieces that I require all my students to learn. Over the months he tried and tried while I listened, cringed and tried to encourage him. At the end of each weekly lesson he'd always say, "My mom's going to hear me play someday." But it seemed hopeless. He just did not have any inborn ability.

I only knew his mother from a distance as she dropped Robby off or waited in her aged car to pick him up. She always waved and smiled but never stopped in. Then one day Robby stopped coming to our lessons. I thought about calling him but assumed, because of his lack of ability, that he had decided to pursue something else. I also was glad that he stopped coming. He was a bad advertisement for my teaching!

Several weeks later I mailed to the students' homes a flyer on the upcoming recital. To my surprise Robby (who received a flyer) asked me if he could be in the recital. I told him that the recital was for current pupils and because he had dropped out he really did not qualify. He said that his mom had been sick and unable to take him to piano lessons but he was still practicing.

"Miss Hondorf...I've just got to play!" he insisted. I don't know what led me to allow him to play in the recital. Maybe it was his persistence or maybe it was something inside of me saying that it would be all right.

The night for the recital came. The high school gymnasium was packed with parents, friends and relatives. I put Robby last in the program, just before I was to come up and thank all the students and play a finishing piece. I thought that any damage he would do would come at the end of the program and I could always salvage his poor performance through my "curtain closer."

Well, the recital went off without a hitch. The students had been practicing and it showed. Then Robby came up on stage. His clothes were wrinkled and his hair looked like he had run an eggbeater through it. "Why didn't he dress up like the other students?" I thought.   "Why didn't his mother at least make him comb his hair for this special night?" Robby pulled out the piano bench and he began.   I was surprised when he announced that he had chosen Mozart's Concerto #21 in C Major.   I was not prepared for what I heard next. His fingers were light on the keys; they even danced nimbly on the ivories. He went from pianissimo to fortissimo...from allegro to virtuoso. His suspended chords that Mozart demands were magnificent! Never had I heard Mozart played so well by someone his age. After six and a half minutes he ended in a grand crescendo and the audience was on their feet in wild applause.   Overcome and in tears I ran up on stage and put my arms around Robby in joy.

"I've never heard you play like that Robby! How'd you do it?"

Through the microphone Robby explained: "Well, Miss Hondorf...remember I told you my mom was sick?   Well, actually she had cancer and passed away this morning. And well.... she was born deaf so tonight was the first time she ever heard me play. I wanted to make it special."

There wasn't a dry eye in the house that evening.   As the people from Social Services led Robby from the stage to be placed into foster care, I noticed that even their eyes were red and puffy and I thought to myself how much richer my life had been for taking Robby as my pupil.   No, I've never had a prodigy but that night I became a protégé...of Robby's. He was the teacher and I was the pupil.   For it is he that taught me the meaning of perseverance, and love, and believing in yourself, and maybe even taking a chance in someone and you don't know why.

This is especially meaningful to me since after serving in Desert Storm Robby was killed in the senseless bombing of the Alfred P. Murrah Federal Building in Oklahoma City in April of 1995, where he was reportedly....playing the piano.

How many people were affected by Mrs. Honsdorf's decision to work with Robby? How far will her reach extend? No one will ever know, but many will never be quite the same again. It is this dimension of our profession that provides each of us the passion to teach. When we are there to see the struggling student finally reach success, we are uplifted. When a student learns something new and provides us a smile that fills the room, we are filled with joy.

For each of us, someone has made a special impact on our life and significantly influenced the person we have become. Listen to Jane Lee, a geologist in San Antonio, Texas talk about her art teacher Mrs. Bee.

I'll never forget my art teacher, Mrs. Bee. I met her thirty four years ago when entering fourth grade. Most kids love to go to art class, and I was no exception. Her projects were creative and practical at the same time. Though I didn't become a professional artist, I received from her a few of life's important lessons, lessons that went far beyond the colorful walls of her classroom. Mrs. Bee believed in me. She challenged me to try new things and explore my creative abilities. She complimented me but also gave constructive criticism when I needed it. She held high expectations for me, and because she believed in me, I always tried to do more than was expected. She also taught me to finish what I started. The life lessons Mrs. Bee taught me may not have made me a famous artist, but they helped me in so many other ways. (McGuire and Abitz, 2001)

The power of this story is that it is so familiar. Mrs. Bee is not uncommon. In fact, there are thousands of Mrs. Bees. For almost every one of us, there is a Mrs. Bee who taught us more than just a subject. They taught us how to live and how to be a better person. For those of us in the teaching profession we must always remember the amount of power we hold. It is a power that reaches across generations and beyond even our own existence. It is from this desire to be such a positive influence in the lives of children that many of us derive our passion to teach. Yet, we must each remember that with this capacity to influence comes an awesome responsibility. We must remain conscious of the potential impact we might have on the young minds that sit before us each and every day. Our students will not all be easy to inspire and love.

There is a story written by Elizabeth Silance Ballard about a young boy named Teddy and his experience with his teacher, Miss Thompson. It has been told many times, but I am including it here because it so passionately describes how a singular teacher can make such a difference in a young person's life. I tell it too, because every person who enters the teaching profession must remember Miss Thompson's experience when they encounter that child who is difficult to teach, unlikable, and easy to discard. The story is entitled, ***Three Letters From Teddy.***

Teddy's letter came today and now that I've read it, I will place it in my cedar chest with the other things important to my life.

"I wanted you to be the first to know." *I smiled as I read the words he had written, and my heart swelled with a pride that I had no right to feel. I have not seen Teddy Stallard since he was a student in my fifth-grade class, 15 years ago.*

It was early in my career and I had only been teaching for two years. From the first day he stepped into my classroom, I disliked Teddy. Teachers (although everyone knows differently) are not supposed to have favorites in a class, but most especially they are not to show dislike for a child, any child. Nevertheless, every year there are one or two children that one cannot help but be attracted to, for teachers are human, and it is a human nature to like bright, pretty, intelligent people, whether they are 10 years old or 25. And sometimes, not too often fortunately, there will be one or two students to whom the teacher just can't seem to relate.

I thought myself quite capable of handling my personal feelings along that line until Teddy walked into my life. There wasn't a child I particularly liked that year, but Teddy was most assuredly one I disliked. He was dirty. Not just occasionally, but all the time. His hair hung low over his ears, and he actually had to hold it out of his eyes as he wrote his papers in class. (And this was before it was fashionable to do so!) Too, he had a particular odor about him that I could never identify. His physical faults were many, and his intellect left a lot to be desired also. By the end of the first week, I knew he was hopelessly behind the others. Not only was he behind, but he was just plain slow! I began to withdraw from him immediately.

Any teacher will tell you it's more of a pleasure to teach a bright child. It is definitely more rewarding for one's ego. But any teacher worth her credentials can channel work to the bright child, keeping him challenged and learning while she puts her major effort on the slower ones. Any teacher can do this. Most teachers do it, but I didn't. Not that year. In fact, I concentrated on my best students and let the others follow along as best they could. Ashamed as I am to admit it, I took perverse pleasure in using my red pen; and each time I came to Teddy's papers, the cross-marks (and they were many) were always a little larger and a little redder than necessary.

"Poor work!" I wrote with a flourish. While I did not actually ridicule the boy, my attitude was obviously quite apparent to the class, for he quickly became the class "goat," the outcast - the unlovable and the unloved. He knew I didn't like him, but he didn't know why. Nor did I know - then or now - why I felt such an intense dislike for him. All I know

is he was a little boy no one cared about, and I made no effort in his behalf. The days rolled by and we made it through the Fall Festival, the Thanksgiving holidays, and I continued marking happily with my red pen. As the Christmas holidays approached, I knew Teddy would never catch up in time to be promoted to the sixth-grade level. He would be a repeater. To justify myself, I went to his cumulative folder from time to time. He had very low grades for the first four years, but no grade failure. How he had made it, I didn't know. I closed my mind to the personal remarks:

First grade: "Teddy shows promise by work and attitude but has a poor home situation."
Second grade: "Teddy could do better. Mother terminally ill. He received little help at home."
Third grade: "Teddy is a pleasant boy. Helpful, but too serious. Slow learner. Mother passed away end of year."
Fourth grade: "Very slow, but well behaved. Father shows no interest."

"Well, they passed him four times, but he will certainly repeat fifth grade! Do him good!" I said to myself.

And then the last day before the holiday arrived. Our little tree on the reading table sported paper and popcorn chains. Many gifts were heaped underneath, waiting for the big moment. Teachers always get several gifts at Christmas, but mine that year seemed bigger and more elaborate than ever. There was not a student who had not brought me one. Each unwrapping brought squeals of delight and the proud giver would receive effusive thank-you's.

His gift wasn't the last one I picked up; in fact, it was in the middle of the pile. It's wrapping was a brown paper bag, and he had colored Christmas trees and red bells all over it. It was stuck together with masking tape.

"For Miss Thompson - from Teddy," it read. The group was completely silent, and for the first time I felt conspicu-

ous, embarrassed because they all stood watching me un-wrap that gift. As I removed the last bit of masking tape, two items fell to my desk; a gaudy rhinestone bracelet with several stones missing and a small bottle of dime-store co-logne - half empty. I could hear the snickers and whispers, and I wasn't sure I could look at Teddy.

"Isn't this lovely?" I asked, placing the bracelet on my wrist. "Teddy, would you help me fasten it?" He smiled shyly as he fixed the clasp, and I held up my wrist for all of them to admire. There were a few ooh's and ahhs, but as I dabbed the cologne behind my ears, all the little girls lined up for a dab behind their ears. I continued to open the gifts until I reached the bottom of the pile.

We ate our refreshments, and the bell rang. The chil-dren filed out with shouts of "See you next year!" and "Merry Christmas!" but Teddy waited at his desk. When they had all left, he walked toward me clutching his gift and books to his chest. "You smell just like Mom," he said softly. "Her bracelet looks real pretty on you too. I'm glad you liked it." He left quickly, and I locked the door, sat down and wept, resolving to make up to Teddy what I had deliberately de-prived him of - a teacher who cared. I stayed every after-noon with Teddy from the end of the holidays until the last day of school. Sometimes we worked together. Sometimes he worked alone while I drew up lesson plans or graded papers.

Slowly but surely he caught up with the rest of the class. Gradually there was a definite upward curve in his grades. He did not have to repeat the fifth grade. In fact, his final averages were among the highest in the class, and although I knew he would be moving out of the state when school was out, I was not worried for him. Teddy had reached a level that would stand him in good stead the following year, no matter where he went. He had enjoyed a measure of success and as we were taught in our teacher training courses: "Suc-cess builds success."

I did not hear from Teddy until seven years later, when his first letter appeared in our mailbox.

"Dear Miss Thompson,
I just wanted you to be the first to know. I will be graduating second in my class next month.

Very truly yours,
Teddy Stallard."

I sent him a card of congratulations and a small package, a pen and pencil gift set. I wondered what he would do after graduation. Four years later, Teddy's second letter came.

"Dear Miss Thompson,

I wanted you to be the first to know. I was just informed I'll be graduating first in my class. The university has not been easy, but I liked it.

Very truly yours,
Teddy Stallard."

I sent him a good pair of sterling silver mono-grammed cuff links and a card, so proud of him I could burst! And now - today - Teddy's third letter.

"Dear Miss Thompson,

I wanted you to be the first to know. As of today I am Theodore J. Stallard, M.D. How about that!!?? I'm going to be married in July, the 27th, to be exact. I wanted to ask if you could come and sit where Mom would sit if she were here. I'll have no family there as Dad died last year.

Very truly yours,
Ted Stallard."

I'm not sure what kind of gift one sends to a doctor on completion of medical school and state boards. Maybe I'll just wait and take a wedding gift, but my note can't wait.

"Dear Ted,

Congratulations! You made it, and you did it yourself! In spite of those like me and not because of us, this day has come for you. God bless you. I'll be at that wedding with bells on!"

(Reprinted from Home Life, March 1976)

What an emotional and wonderful story of a teacher and student who found and brought out the best in one another. Miss Thompson left an indelible mark on the life of Teddy, but Teddy changed Miss Thompson forever. Her gift from Teddy was one that carried her through a lifetime and you will find events and students who similarly fill the treasure chest of pleasant memories in your life. There are so many moments that make teaching one of the most rewarding professions on earth and you will enjoy them all. But first, we must find just the right position.

You are ready to take that important step right now. You have a degree. You know your subject. You have the skills and know you will be a great teacher! BUT, if you fail to get the desired interview and make a dynamic impression, that passion may have little opportunity to evidence itself.

We need great teachers. The profession needs men and women just like you to come into its classes and work with the fine young people who will be tomorrow's leaders. We need those who embody a passion to teach. It is said that without our profession, none of the other professions can exist. The truth of that statement is what makes your decision to teach so important. Equally important is your ability to obtain that teaching position in the district and discipline to which you aspire. A teacher does his or her best work when he or she is in a position where he or she can feel professionally fulfilled. The teaching job market has many vacancies and you will have to choose wisely. More than that, you must prepare for the interviews that can lead to obtaining that truly special position. This is not easy.

THE MYTH OF TEACHER SHORTAGES: Recently, you have been reading of a teacher shortage and how some schools are finding it difficult to staff certain classes. This is true. Schools often encounter fewer applicants in areas such as Foreign Language, Technology, Science, Mathematics and Special Education. This reality leads teachers to believe they only need apply and principals will be vying for their services. This is just not the case. If you are not concerned about the kind of school in which you will work and are willing to relocate, the surplus can work to your advantage. In all other cases, heed the following warning. **BEWARE:** *Do not confuse a teacher shortage to mean an absence of competition.* Good schools and positions *always* have multiple applications. Granted, there is more competition in some districts than others, but there is always competition. You need strategies that will place you in front of that competition. You need sharp answers that will be noticed by the committee. You need the skills provided by this book.

Over the years, prospective teachers have asked me what they could expect in an interview. What questions could they anticipate and how could they prepare? I recall a student who was trying desperately to enter the teaching field and, after sending out 71 resumes, had not received one interview. I asked to see her resume and cover letter. Both were neatly written and prepared with care, but they were quite routine and uninspired. The cover letter also contained a fatal error that would almost surely put her application in the "no interview" pile. Together we reworked both documents and readied them for a second round of mailings. From this second, more strategic mailing, she received two interviews and we met again to prepare for her interview. My phone soon rang and she exclaimed, "I got the job! I got the job! They hired me!!" She was an excellent candidate who had great potential. She was truly passionate about wanting to teach, but until she secured an interview where her skills could be properly displayed, she was just one application in a large pile of others.

This book will help prevent such a poor initial response from happening to you. It will provide answers to the many questions you have about interviews. Each chapter provides valuable, inside information that is rarely taught in college. Specific information on teacher interviews is difficult to find. Libraries provide little help regarding teacher interviews and the Internet lists only a few related sites. Most books on the topic are directed toward the business world and hold only passing relevance to your needs. This book, on the other hand, is *only* for prospective teachers and focuses entirely on proven ways to secure a teaching position.

When you finish, you will have cover letters and resumes that will put you in the top group nearly every time. You will know how to prepare and dress for that important interview. You will have an interview portfolio ready to make the final sale. You will know what questions are likely to be asked and how to make impact responses. You will know how to handle your offer and what traps to avoid. Finally, when you begin your next search, you will have a complete game plan to attack the job market. You will also have this book to review and study until you own both the knowledge and confidence necessary to go into the right schools with the right answers. You will maximize your potential for success and minimize your chances of committing that fatal error. Remember, most people competing for the position *will not* have read this book. You will be the person with the knowledge and that will give you the advantage!

A friend of mine once told me how lucky I was to have secured a post in a very prestigious school district. I remember thinking at the time that luck had little to do with the success. Daryl Royal, the famous football coach at the University of Texas defined luck as that time when opportunity and preparedness meet. I had diligently prepared for my interview and the work paid dividends. In that respect, I was lucky.

The passion to teach is already inside your heart, but you need to secure a position you truly want and work in the district that best meets *your* needs. To reach that goal, you need to prepare for the interviews you will receive. Study this book and take the necessary steps to secure that desired position – THEN TEACH WITH A PASSION!!

My Favorite Teacher

Our bus always arrived by 7:25 and today was a long ride into school. In this part of New Jersey, we get a lot of snow, but today it was just snow, rain, and ice. My father called them "gunk storms." As I got out of my bus, there was the familiar figure of Mr. Gunderson standing at the end of the ramp with his umbrella. I remember thinking to myself how difficult it must be for a teacher to stay happy when he had to stand in this weather. Not Mr. Gunderson. He was *always* happy; especially when we were around him.

"Hi John. Hey, where are those boots? I bet your mother didn't see you leave the house without them. You go stand over there and I'll spank you for her. Ha, ha, ha."

"June, did you get that part in the play? You did!!! Well, good for you. I'll be there, (Think you can score me a couple of free tickets?), ha, ha, ha.

Mr. Gunderson knew everyone and something about each of us. He loved to talk to us about life and what we were going to do after we left school. He would always tell us to go do something great because he wanted to be able to say he knows great people and then laugh. I think this is why every kid in that school loved Mr. Gunderson. He didn't just like you, he really loved you — even the bad kids; something he said didn't exist.

You worked if you were in Mr. G's class. He wasn't perhaps the most innovative teacher I ever had, but he was certainly the most caring. I got so much more than just science from sitting with Mr. G. in his lab. He taught me that attitude, work ethic, and your approach to life is more important than just intellect. I will never forget my favorite teacher – Mr. Gunderson

2
WRITING AN EFFECTIVE COVER LETTER

The first document any school administrator will see from you is likely to be your cover letter. It is the first impression made on the reader who will decide your fate. As you can only make one first impression, it is essential that your cover letter present you as a first rate candidate who is professional, well qualified and worth the time of an interview. The cover letter provides the reviewer his or her first image of your ability to communicate and present ideas. I cannot tell you how many times I received cover letters so poorly done I did not even want to read the individual's resume. At the end of this chapter, you will know exactly how to construct that eye-catching cover letter and maximize the chances your resume will be carefully read and given strong interview consideration. In addition, there are several sample cover letters you can use as starting points for your own letter. We will talk more about that later.

PARTS OF A COVER LETTER

The cover letter can be divided into a few simple parts, each set off as a paragraph. One key to effective writing is the ability to be concise! Understand that the person "paper screening" applications for this position might have from 50 to 500 resumes under review. That is correct, 500! He or she may take as little as thirty seconds to examine your resume and cover letter. Do you now see the need for a high impact cover letter? A two or three page cover letter is rarely read and often makes a poor impression. You must decide what information is essential and focus your writing energy to create a strong impact in a short space.

Before going further, I must tell you there are entire books on just the subject of writing cover letters. You can find them in any bookstore or library and they are excellent. Nonetheless, in the field of education, there are only a few styles that enjoy consistent success. The key components of these letters are outlined in this chapter and their use will help you design straightforward, effective cover letters.

A good place to begin is to look at the basic parts of a cover letter. Each part is developed in a single paragraph of just a few sentences.

First: Establish your interest in the position.

Briefly explain how you know about the position, why you are qualified and your interest in the advertised opening. You want the reader to see you are excited about both the position and the prospect of working in his or her district or school.

Second: Establish a match between the district's identified employment characteristics listed in the ad and your credentials.

This is vitally important. Over seventy percent of the cover letters a district receives contain a fatal flaw that eliminates them from consideration. This flaw must be avoided at all cost.

FATAL FLAW OF COVER LETTERS: *The cover letter fails to clearly show how the candidate meets the stated requirements for the position.*

That is correct. The most frequent reason applications do not survive the paper-screening process is the applicant's failure to establish how his or her credentials fit the criteria established for the position. Your cover letter must clearly and boldly establish your qualifications. Martin Yate's book, <u>Knock Em Dead</u> offers one of the more effective ways to make this connection, yet I rarely see the technique in use. Yate calls this concise outline of connections **the executive summary** (Yate, 1999). By using Yate's simple strategy, your cover letters will clearly and forcefully establish you as a match for the advertised position. Here it is.

Review the advertisement to identify each and every requirement listed. A typical ad might stipulate such things as:

- *NJ Elementary School Certificate Required*
- *Knowledge of Current Reading Pedagogy*

- *Previous Experience Working with Elementary Students*
- *Ability to Work With Diverse Groups*

Next, quickly show the employer how you meet each of these criteria. If a candidate does not clearly identify how he or she meets the necessary requirements, he or she runs the risk of being screened out on the first review. Understand that when someone is reviewing a few hundred resumes, it does not take much to have an application that appears unqualified placed in the "no-interview" pile. Your cover letter will avoid this mistake by creating a two-column table that will allow you to match each requirement with specific qualifications. Here is an example:

POSITION REQUIREMENTS	*CREDENTIALS*
NJ Certified Elementary Teacher	• *I hold NJ Elementary Teaching Certificate*
Knowledge of current reading pedagogy	• *Taught in both whole-language and literature based reading programs.* • *Strong training in phonics and traditional reading instruction.*
Experience teaching elementary students	• *Teaching experience at 3rd grade at Trenton Elementary School.*
Ability to work with diverse groups	• *Received strong background in urban education principles from The College of New Jersey.* • *Experience teaching Hispanic, African-American and other ethnic groups.* • *Student taught in multicultural classes in Ewing, NJ.*

This block form is effective because it is so visually convincing. In a glance, the reader can see all of the criteria and how your qualifications match.

If you do not like the appearance of the table, you can achieve the same effect by using two columns and bullets. The information is the same, but you create a different visual affect.

BUT, what if you lack one or more of the criteria listed by the ad? Are you already out of the mix? Not necessarily. In this case, however, you are better advised to state your qualifications in paragraph form because this allows you to selectively highlight strengths and downplay points where your background is less than a good match. You need only insure that your positive attributes stand out sufficiently to prevent any chance the reader will miss them as he or she rapidly scans your letter. For example, suppose your teaching experience was in a school where diversity was not a characteristic of your classes. A paragraph format will allow you to minimize that area of your background and focus on other strengths. Look at this illustration.

In reviewing your advertisement, I noted how my background and credentials match your needs. I currently hold a **New Jersey Elementary School Certificate** *and have completed all the requirements necessary to teach. More importantly, my teaching experience has provided a* **strong background in both whole language and phonics** *reading instruction. I am familiar with* **diagnostic and remedial methodology** *which enables me to work with students who have a diverse range of abilities. My* **teaching experience at the Upper Snoot Academy** *has provided valuable experience in dealing with elementary school children. I intend to enroll in two urban education courses to further enhance my abilities as a teacher for all students.*

You can see how both formats clearly identify you as a fully qualified candidate. By demonstrating the one-to-one match between the ad requirements and your background, you maximized the probability of an interview. Other applicants may have failed to make this connection clear and committed a deadly error.

Third: Request an interview

Once your credentials are established, build on that idea to request an interview and an opportunity to explore your qualifications in depth. In this paragraph, be sure to re-indicate your high interest in the position and a need for further discussion of your candidacy. Provide an indication of the best time for someone to reach you and any pertinent information on your availability. Here is a sample of how this might sound.

> *As you will see in my resume, I have many of the qualities you require for this position. Your advertised position is precisely what I seek and I would like to meet with you to discuss my candidacy in full. I know that it is often the match between a person's qualifications and a district's specific needs that determine a candidate's final suitability. I am available for an interview at your convenience. Should you need to speak to me by phone, I am home most evenings after 5:00 PM or you can leave a message on my machine, (732) 555-1234 at any time. I will return your call as soon thereafter as possible. I look forward to hearing from you in the near future.*

This closing paragraph tells the interviewer you are qualified, available for an interview and when you can be best reached. It will get results and you have done everything necessary to establish your candidacy.

THE DO'S AND DON'TS OF WRITING THE COVER LETTER

Now that you know what needs to be included in your cover letter, you should consider a few other items of importance. Attention to these items will help prevent other deadly mistakes and provide important hints on style.

- • *DO* personalize the letter to the district and include the name of the person to whom you are speaking. A blanket or form letter can be spotted from a mile away and lacks impact. Avoid the deadly, "To Whom It May Concern" salutation at all cost. Do your homework and find out the name of the principal or superintendent.

- **DO** use short hard-hitting paragraphs written in simple, straightforward language. This is not the place to demonstrate your vocabulary and facility with a thesaurus. Excess verbiage only makes your cover letter sound contrived and unnatural. The intent of this letter is to make the reader say, "Here is someone we should see."

- **DO** present a positive image. It is unwise to complain about previous employers, supervisors, principals or other situations that were not to your liking. This comes off as sour grapes and underscores a possibility that perhaps *you* were less than a team player.

- **DO** WORD PROCESS YOUR LETTER! This is not a personal note to a pal; it is a business letter. Handwritten letters can be difficult to read and do not provide the professional appearance you are trying to create. **CAUTION:** *When you use a word processor to send numerous letters, be sure to check your date, personal references, and any dated material to insure they are correct.* There is nothing more damaging than letters with the wrong names of people, districts or dates in the text. It can kill your candidacy before it gets started.

- **DO** place your name, address and phone number at the upper right-hand corner for easy access.

- **DO** use a slightly heavy bond (24 lb holds up well) paper in a light shade. Off-white, buff or cream work well, but white is considered the standard. You can get these from any office supply store. Lightweight, white duplicating paper will look like all the rest. Why not stand out a little?

- **DO** identify your ability to work on extra-curricula activities. The details can be saved for the resume, but a one-sentence indication that you are qualified and interested in working beyond the classroom will be noted and well received. Most candidates leave this out and your attention to the matter may provide just the edge you need!

- **DON'T** get folksy or cute. I have seen letters that included a quiz, down-home humor and other casual, off-message paragraphs. Believe me, this is not appreciated and places you in an unprofessional light. The reader has no time for games or humorous side-trips.

- **DON'T** offer any indication of weaknesses or negative points. For example, if your teaching experience in language arts is different than what the district seeks, don't mention it. Find the areas where you meet the district needs and underscore those.

- **DON'T** make boastful statements such as, "I know exactly how to make your fifth grade team the most successful team in the school." Such statements are rarely well received. Moreover, they may antagonize someone and you need to avoid that possibility.

- **DON'T** use clichés. Avoid statements like, "You'll never find a better candidate than me" or "I'm a real child-centered teacher" or the proverbial, "I'm a genuine team player." These statements are overused and generally ignored by the reader.

To demonstrate how you might write a good cover letter, I've taken an actual ad and written a corresponding sample letter. In addition, you may wish to review the books in the library on this topic and, although most of them are written for business, you can read and adapt their examples for your use.

Middle School Social Studies
Upper Utopia School District
Upper Utopia, NJ 09999

September opening. Must have NJ
certification, knowledge of team process
and NJ Core Standards. The district is
suburban with a strong commitment to
student achievement. All inquiries to Dr.
Ruth Jones. No phone inquiries.

Look at what this ad tells us about the district and what it
seeks in its candidate. First, the *opening is for September.* Can you
be available then? If you are just finishing college or between positions, the answer is probably yes. You will want to focus on that. If
you are under contract and will need to provide notice, you will not
focus on that until the interview.

Certification is always a must. Preferably you already have
certification, however, if you are applying out-of-state, you will need
to make a statement about your qualifications for a state certificate
and the status of your application. This is an essential area to address. It is the number one criteria used to eliminate unqualified
candidates. It will not be appreciated if you reach an interview and
then disclose you do not yet hold a certificate to teach in that state.
NOTE: *If you are applying to schools in any state where you are not
yet certified, the minimum requirement is that you have already established that you can be certified and an application has been submitted.*

"Knowledge of team process" means that you have worked on a teaching team with two or more teachers to organize instruction for a
group of students. If you have this experience, underscore it and
provide a brief example of how that team may have worked. You
might address such things as interdisciplinary units, the planning

process or other team activities. If you have not been on a team, you can speak to your understanding of the principle and how you have worked with other teachers on team-type projects. You want to emphasize that you understand the philosophy.

"Knowledge of NJ Core Standards," is a very specific set of State requirements but you can substitute any state's graduation require-ments in this phrase. As these requirements are generally accom-panied by competency tests, it is essential that you know the spe-cific expectations in your subject area. If you do not already know this information, you need to get a copy of your state's requirements before you go to the interview. This is another "must." and will be discussed with more detail in later chapters.

"Strong commitment to student achievement" suggests the district gives significant attention to student scores on the various achieve-ment tests to measure student learning. It may also suggest stu-dents are expected to achieve above average class grades. High fail-ure rates are never acceptable. Your letter should identify how you will focus on student learning and attainment.

The ad finally provides *the name of the person to whom ap-plications should be addressed* and alerts you to avoid directly phon-ing the district. This is common in districts where they receive a large number of applicants. FOLLOW THE DIRECTIONS. You can be sure the secretaries will take note of your name should you ignore the ad and call for an interview.

Now that we have distilled the key information from the ad, we can prepare a cover letter for **a well-suited applicant.** Our second letter will be for someone who may lack one of the criteria.

James T. Hopeful

38 Deer Path Lane	Work (908) 555-1212
Clearbrooke, NJ 07777	Home: (908) 555-8513

May 14, 1999

Dr. Ruth Jones
Upper Utopia School District
Upper Utopia, NJ 09999

Dear Dr. Jones,

I noted with great interest your ad in the *Newark Star Ledger* for a middle school Teacher of Social Studies. As you will see in my resume, my qualifications well suit me to the advertised position and I would like to personally speak with you about how I might fit your school team.

The following summary highlights some of my qualifications for this position:

September opening for middle school social studies	I hold a BA from The College of New Jersey and possess an Elementary Teaching Certificate with emphasis in Social Studies. Available September.
Knowledge of team process	My student teaching experience was at the Hopewell Middle School where I was an active member of the sixth-grade team. As part of that team I assisted in the planning of units, design of field experiences and running team meetings.
Knowledge of NJ Core Standards	I have reviewed and constructed numerous lessons to teach key indicators of the Core Standards and Proficiencies in Social Studies.
Strong Commitment to Student Achievement	Student mastery is a primary criterion by which each of my lessons is evaluated. Alignment to required proficiencies is made during planning and each student's progress is continuously evaluated against those desired outcomes. My class performance on the ITBS was two stanines above the national average

I am a highly motivated teacher who has a proven record of results with children. I am anxious to work on building initiatives and school committees as well as extra-curricular activities. I am available for an interview and can be reached at the above address and phone. I look forward to meeting with representatives of your district to explore my candidacy.

Sincerely,

James T. Hopeful

Enclosure

James T. Hopeful

38 Deer Path Lane
Clearbrooke, NJ 07777

Work (908) 555-1212
Home: (908) 555-8513

May 14, 1999

Dr. Ruth Jones
Upper Utopia School District
Upper Utopia, NJ 09999

Dear Dr. Jones,

I noted with great interest your ad in the *Newark Star Ledger* for a middle school Teacher of Social Studies. As you will see in my resume, my qualifications well suit me to the advertised position and I would like to personally speak with you about how I might fit your school team.

The following are highlights of qualifications that match your requirements:

- I hold a BA from the College of New Jersey and possess an Elementary Teaching Certificate.
- I have worked with colleagues on grade level projects and read numerous articles on middle school teams.
- I have been part of several in-service workshops regarding NJ Core Standards and incorporated them in my teaching.
- Student mastery is an important part of all lessons. Students are continuously monitored and provided before or after school assistance if they require additional support.

I am a highly motivated teacher who has a proven record of results with children. I am anxious to work on building initiatives and school committees as well as extra-curricular activities. I am available for an interview and can be reached at the above address and phone. I look forward to meeting with representatives of your district to explore my candidacy.

Sincerely,

James T. Hopeful

Enclosure

As you can see, the letters are very similar, but the second one is less targeted than the first. Did you see the differences? The first letter provided direct work experience while the second was more general. The second letter is from a person who has not worked on a teaching team, but the item is addressed in other ways. Both letters provide assurance that the prospective candidate meets the stated requirements and would be a good interview candidate.

It cannot be too strongly stressed that anything you place in your letter must be accurate and verifiable. If you say you know the Core Standards, you will need to be fully conversant on them at the interview. If you say you worked on a team, then that *must* be the case.

A last word of advice is to have your cover letter read by at least one other person to insure it is clear and well written. If you can find someone who is qualified to check grammar, that is always a good idea. Double-check all spelling and make sure you sign the document. Now you are on your way with everything you need to write a cover letter that will get notice. Write it and good luck!

CONCLUDING THOUGHTS

Now you know how to construct a high impact cover letter that will present you as someone who is professional and potentially meet the needs of the school. There are an infinite number of phrases and ideas you can include and you must choose those that accurately reflect your background and style. For this reason, I strongly suggest that you do not just reproduce the sample copies provided in this chapter and send them off as your own. Use the information as a starting point, but tailor the sentences and paragraphs to reflect your own professional background and ideas.

Keep in mind what we said was the real purpose of the cover letter. It only needs to establish your credentials to a sufficient degree that the reader moves on with interest to your resume. A cover letter is crafted so that it clearly and quickly identifies how you meet the district and school needs. The resume will build on this foundation and solidify your place in the interview pool.

A final word is to consider writing a separate, tailored cover letter for each district. As mentioned in the chapter, a blanket letter is easily identifiable and will do little to enhance your standing with the reader. The cover should reflect the district's needs and your specific qualifications. If the advertisement did not specifically mention the school's position requirements you may have to conduct some research to identify their interests. We will discuss how that can be done in the next chapter. You now have everything necessary to produce a hard-hitting document so put this information to work and start writing!

A Teacher's Story

As a teacher of fourth grade, I always anticipate the group of students that I will be getting and get excited with what I expect to accomplish with them. I always expect students coming into a grade level to be prepared for that grade, especially when it deals with reading. The students read everything orally in my class.

We were reading the book "Fourth Grade Nothings" to take a break from the normal textbook. I had just gotten a new student, when it was his turn to read I asked him to read a couple of paragraphs. With his head lowered, he said, "I can't read." I thought I had mistaken what he said, so I asked him to read again. I found out the child could not read even all of the sight words. So I went and stood beside him and helped him with the words that he could not pronounce which were a considerable sum. I taught him how to decode and break words into syllables, the different vowel sounds and etc. When I couldn't help him the way I needed to, I asked another teacher to help him in her spare time. She did so without question. The day this child held up his hand to read and read almost like a trooper I teared up. When he finished and turned to me with a huge smile and said, "Mrs. Newcome, I can read, I can read," I blubbered like a child. He left not long after that to go to a community in another county. When he gave me the biggest hug and said, "I will always remember what you have given me," I blubbered again.

By
Linda Newcome

3
BUILDING THE DYNAMIC RESUME

The cover letter wets the reader's initial appetite to know more and examine the resume. The resume explains your experience, what kinds of classes you taught, your school involvement, and any co-curricular activities you directed. The resume will help make the final sale to secure a place on the interview list.

SOME GENERAL CONSIDERATIONS

The main objective of your resume

Your first objective is to make the interview list. To accomplish that, the resume must sufficiently sell your skills and future potential. The resume should tell your story in a way that the reader can see how you would be an asset to his or her school. Many resumes simply recite the employment history and give a list of miscellaneous accomplishments with no particular focus. This is a major mistake. Your information needs to concentrate on strengths the district values. This emphasis will move you ahead of the plain vanilla, historical resumes that seem to populate most application piles. Remember; the reader needs to see how you will improve his or her school and make a better candidate than others.

Do your homework and match your resume to the district needs

The most effective resumes focus on the elements of a candidate's background the district will see as important. The difficult piece is how to identify those district priorities. Often you will not be able to speak directly with someone in a leadership position prior to an interview. However, there are ways to obtain the necessary information from other sources. Most districts publish an annual report or newsletter. In New Jersey there are state report cards and QAAR reports. These documents have valuable information about schools. Individual schools might publish a newsletter or brochure. Some schools even have their own web page. If you can get a few of these items, they will tell you about the activities of students, various grade-level projects, and important school programs. After you identify the district priorities, select corresponding elements from your background for use in constructing your resume.

To help your resume speak directly to the school needs, add bullets and highlights to specific qualities of your background that target school priorities. Pertinent activities can be listed in the historical data section of the resume. We will discuss how this can be accomplished later in the chapter.

Make the resume compact and powerful

There is nothing that will dim your chances for an interview more than a fifteen-page blockbuster resume. The reviewer only wants to know what makes you a potential fit for the advertised position. He or she does not have time to wade through your life history and pull out the important information. The most powerful resumes I have seen filled only two sides of a single sheet of paper. **WARNING:** *Do not reduce the print to less than 10 points in order to squeeze in information.* This will overcrowd your resume and make it difficult to read.

SUGGESTIONS THAT ADD POWER

- *Eliminate the job objectives portion of the resume.* You may read other opinions on this topic. Some books on the subject suggest that you lead with your employment objective, but in my view this is not necessary on resumes for teaching positions. It occupies precious space that would be better used to tell your story. The reader knows your application is for a specifically advertised position and an objective that trumpets, "I am looking for a rewarding teaching position" will do little to place you at the head of the line.

- *Use language that will create impact:* Wherever you communicate a special accomplishment, it is made stronger when you cite the <u>evidence</u> of that work. For example, which of the following statements is more effective?

> *"Average student achievement in my reading classes rose by 1.4 years in 1998-99."*
> OR
> *"Improved student ability to read."*

Obviously the first example makes a much stronger statement. These entries should use action verbs wherever possible. Words like "implemented, designed, and employed" effectively underscore your deeds and accomplishments.

- ***Avoid the use of personal pronouns:*** Repeating the phrase, "I did this," and "I did that . . ," becomes redundant and reduces overall impact. The reader will make the logical assumption that you are speaking of your own deeds. Personal pronouns can also make your application sound boastful whereas a list of work and accomplishments usually does not.

- ***Eliminate unnecessary information:*** Do not bother to tell the reader about a hobby or how you spent last summer unless you feel the item has some relationship to your qualifications. Experience you gained working in a real estate office for the last two years does not qualify you for a teaching position. In fact, references to numerous business positions, no matter how good you think they were, can have the negative effect of making a reader wonder if you are serious about a teaching career. Avoid business references unless they have a clear connection to the teaching position for which you are applying.

- ***Don't overstate your case!*** Honesty is not the best policy on your resume – it is the only policy. If one fabrication or half-truth is discovered at the interview, you will not likely survive as a candidate. You might be forgiven almost anything else, but dishonesty will not be tolerated. Even if the interviewer does not initially catch the dishonest statement, it may cost you the

job if it is discovered later. Believe me, you already have sufficient positive qualities to be an attractive candidate.

- *Pay attention to details:* Use proper grammar, correct spelling, and correct syntax. I once reviewed applications for the
position of superintendent in which an applicant had misspelled
the word "superintendent." The result was swift and predictable. Check your dates to insure they are correct and there is no
overlap of time that places you in two locations simultaneously.
Errors such as these can reduce your chances of moving to the
interview round.

APPEARANCE COUNTS

- *Never, ever send a handwritten resume.* If you have weak
computer skills, let someone prepare your resume professionally. Word processing is the standard. In fifteen years of hiring,
I never saw a handwritten resume move past the first review.

- *Make the resume easy to read and follow.* Use standard
margins, do not make paragraphs too long, and allow for space
between sections. Keep in mind your resume is likely to be read
in sixty seconds or less. Lengthy paragraphs with crowded information will often remain unread. Use bold face type where
there is something the reader must see. **CAUTION:** *Bold type
can be effective when wisely placed, but it can also be easily overused.* If your resume is longer than one page, place your name
on every page.

- *Don't skimp on the stationery.* I recommend you use a white,
ivory, or buff paper of bond quality. The slightly heavier 24#
weight will stand up to harsh handling and still look good, but
take care not to use a paper that is too heavy because it may not
copy well. When you move to the interview stage the district is
likely to duplicate your resume and a heavy bond may not provide the crisp, clear copies you would like. Never use bright or
phosphorescent paper. The reader should not require sunglasses
to review your resume. Such paper may stand out, but it does
not present a professional image.

- *Use shading in your resume.* Others may advise against this practice because too much shading can be a distraction. However, in discussions with principals and other readers, most seem to agree that if not overdone, shading can make a nice presentation and help the document stand out. Use your own discretion, but you may want to try it and see how it looks.

- *Supply appropriate references.* Avoid the popular "references on request" phrase. Principals do not have time to dig this information out. Provide the name, title, and relationship of at least two references on the resume. **Be sure you include the name of the person who directly supervised and evaluated you.** Do not list relatives, other colleagues, or people who were not in a supervisory position. The one exception to this is your cooperating teacher during student teaching. If you are just entering the profession, the cooperating teacher is a must. Very few principals or superintendents call references unless you are being strongly considered for the position. If there is a problem or delicate situation with someone at a former place of employment, discuss this situation at the interview.

BUILDING THE RESUME ONE SECTION AT A TIME

Now it is time to put this information together and construct a resume that will command attention. It is best to first divide the resume into neat, identifiable sections. This will provide easy reference for those conducting the interview. As with cover letters, entire books are available on the topic of resume writing. There are literally dozens of formats. The suggestions in this chapter reflect those most pertinent to interviews for teaching positions and below are a list of the recommended sections.

Certifications: List any and all certificates you hold. If you do not yet hold a certificate, but have made application, list that certificate by name and provide the date on which you applied. If you hold certificates in other states, they should also be listed. If you have certificates in subject areas or job categories that are not directly applicable to this position, you might list them as well.

Education: It is only required that you list your college credentials. Generally, your high school experience is not relevant unless
you are an alumnus of the school to which you are applying or there
is some other direct connection. Place the college name and city on
the left with your dates of attendance on the right. If you received a
degree from the listed institution, identify it along with your major.
If you graduated with honors, be sure to indicate that next to the
degree. If you have advanced degrees, list the highest degree first
and work down to the lowest.

> Indiana University   1997-1999
> Bloomington, Indiana
> MAT, Elementary Education
>
> Bethany College   1993-1997
> Bethany, WV
> BA, Cum Laude, Early Childhood Education

Educational Experience: This is perhaps the most important section of your resume. Here you will list all relevant teaching experience along with a few important elements of your work while in
each position. This is where you will specifically link your background to the stated needs of the school. Let us assume you know
the school uses block scheduling for some classes and has a pull-out
program for basic skills students. Your resume can clearly reflect
where and how your background matches those aspects of the prospective school. Look at the following sample to see how this relationship is drawn.

> **Forest Hills Elementary School   1997-98**
> **4ᵗʰ Grade Teacher**
>
> - Planned and taught Language Arts and Math in
>   90-minute blocks four days per week. Utilized
>   multi-path lessons and learning centers to maxi-
>   mize student involvement and learning activity.

- Developed individualized learning packets to help pull-out students maintain their standing when classes were missed. Also worked with the BSI teacher to coordinate student schedules and workload.

Notice how each bullet targets an item the school will see as important. Although there were numerous experiences and skills in your background from which to choose, your resume must focus on those that meet the needs of the prospective district. Include a few bullet items for each school you list on your resume. They add power and they *will* receive notice!

In listing your experience, begin with your most recent employment and work backward to the earliest teaching post. Unless you have a great deal of experience, you should list your student teaching. Each listing should include the dates of service, teaching duties, and specific school information. If there are gaps in service, this is not necessarily a negative point. Simply be ready to discuss what you were doing during that time. A good explanation is generally accepted.

Other Pertinent Educational Experience: This section describes any special workshops, in-service training sessions, summer courses, or other relevant training you have completed. **REMEMBER***: Include any and all clubs you advised, sports coaching, or other extra-curricular activities.* Principals are looking for teachers who involve themselves in the full school program. Wherever possible, indicate an interest in activities or programs where the prospective school has a recognized need. Review the many in-service days you attended and select those that complement your new school's agenda. For example, if the school recently conducted a training session on brain-based learning and you once attended a seminar on that topic, highlight the experience.

- *Attended an evening PDK workshop with David Sousa who described his book on Brain-based Patterns of Learning.*

- *Participated in a half-day in-service that taught how one creates instructional activities that improve retention.*

You can see how the second item might not be a perfect fit, but it is close enough to reflect your continuing growth in a relevant field. It is unlikely that everything in your background will be a perfect fit to district's initiatives, but you can include entries if there is a reasonably close match. Use this section of the resume to build that all-important connection between your background and the school's interests. It will pay big dividends!

Do not forget to provide areas where you can help with the coaching or co-curriculum. Look in the newspaper where you saw the original position advertised. Were there also coaching vacancies or other openings listed for which you might be qualified? If so, note them prominently on your resume and get to the front of the interview line!

References: As pointed out earlier in the chapter, it is important to include specific references on your resume. Principals will appreciate your consideration in this matter. Anyone you intend to include as a reference should be alerted in advance that he or she is on your resume. It also makes sense to suggest what specific information you would like him or her to provide if contact is made. Whenever possible, obtain a written reference from the people you list on the resume. Some candidates attach reference letters directly to their resume. If you choose to do this, only include one letter. You can bring the others to the interview and offer them at the proper time.

CONCLUDING THOUGHTS

Your resume and cover letter are the only documents to represent you when applications are first being considered. The extra time you spend to research the district and align your credentials will be well worth the effort. You cannot afford to send a bland cover letter and resume similar to all the others. Follow the directions provided in these last two chapters and you will have first-rate documents that get an employer's attention. Sample resumes follow for your review. The first uses borders and shading while the second is simpler and more traditional.   Use a format that you feel reflects your personal style and interests best. Most of all, write an impact resume that will place you on top of the "Must Interview" pile. Good luck.

RESUME
James T. Hopeful

38 Deerpath Lane   *WORK: (908) 555-1212*
Clearbrooke, NJ 07777   *HOME: (732) 555-8513*

CERTIFICATION

NJ Comprehensive Science Teacher Certificate
NJ Supervisor/Principal Certificate

EDUCATION

INDIANA UNIVERSITY   1998
Bloomington, Indiana
MS Secondary Education

UNIVERSITY OF TENNESSEE   1996
Knoxville, Tennessee
BS Science Education
Magna Cum Laude
Phi Beta Kappa

EDUCATIONAL
EXPERIENCE

SCIENCE TEACHER GRDS 9-12   1998-Present
WILLIAMS HIGH SCHOOL
Farragut, New Jersey

* *Served as team leader for 9th grade learning team*
* *Developed Science Department block schedule for laboratory work*
* *Helped design the on-line science academy for enrichment*
* *Participated in the Homework Hotline*
* *Coached Soccer and Track*
* *Advised Ski Club*

SCIENCE STUDENT TEACHER   1996
GRADE 7
NORRIS MIDDLE SCHOOL
Norris, TX

- *Developed cooperative learning experiences for all classes*
- *Worked with co-operating teacher to plan a thematic unit on "Evidence and Argument."*
- *Co-advisor of school play*

OTHER PERTINENT EXPERIENCE

- *Attended a summer institute on "Writing in Science Class"*
- *Participated in the "New Teacher Workshop: Beyond Madeline Hunter."*
- *Attended seminar with Roland Barth on "Becoming a Lifetime Learner/Leader."*
- *Member of NSTA, PDK and NJEA*
- ***Head girls soccer coach***
- *Assistant volleyball coach*
- ***Adviser to school newspaper***
- *Organized school ski club*
- *Co-advised science club*
- *Teacher representative to PTA*

REFERENCES

Dr. William Summers
Department Supervisor
Williams High School
(999) 555-4957

Dr. Carol Jones
Cooperating Teacher
Norris Middle School
(111)555-1907

RESUME
JANE B. WRIGHT

1095 Lake Front Drive   *WORK: (908) 555-1212*
Bear Lake, TN 07777   *HOME: (732) 555-8513*

CERTIFICATION	Tennesee Elementary Teacher Certificate Teacher of the Handicapped Certificate	
EDUCATION	EAST TENNESSEE STATE UNIVERSITY Johnson City, Tennessee ***MAT Special Education***	1998
	TUSCULUM COLLEGE Greeneville, Tennessee ***BS Science Education*** ***Oliver Gray Scholar***	1996
EDUCATIONAL EXPERIENCE	**RESOURCE TEACHER** **GRADES 9-12** **NORRIS ELEMENTARY SCHOOL** Norris, Tennessee	1998-Present

- *Served as case manager*
- *Member of Child Study Team*
- *Assisted in developing inclusive education program*
- *Chaired the School Resource Team*
- *Assistant Coach for Girls Soccer*
- *Co-advised Student Council*

STUDENT TEACHER   1996
GRADE 3
DOAK SCHOOL
Doak, Tennessee

- *Established Writing Laboratory*
- *Worked with co-operating teacher to plan a thematic unit on "Preserving Our Environment"*
- *Co-advisor of school play*

OTHER
PERTINENT
EXPERIENCE

- *Attended a summer institute on "Writing Workshop"*
- *Participated in the "New Teacher Workshop: Beyond Madeline Hunter."*

- *Member of Tusculum Alumni Relations*
- *Taught 3rd grade Sunday School*
- *Teacher representative to PTA*

REFERENCES

Dr. James Cost
Director Pupil Services
Norris Schools
(999) 555-1010

Mrs. Sally Bible
Cooperating Teacher
Doak School
(999)555-1907

A Teacher's Story

My story has probably happened in most classrooms, but it served to remind me why teaching is worth sticking at, even when things look pretty hopeless.

I had been placed in a very difficult class of 11 -12 year olds who were desperately insecure and thus had no desire to try at anything. The atmosphere in the classroom was depressed, nasty, and tense. Not a good learning environment!

I had been told to do a math unit on statistics and probability. In the pretest, nobody got higher than 11/25, and the majority got about 5/25! I made a huge effort to make the lessons relevant, fun and inclusive, but I was plagued by children whining "I can't do this." "John" in particular just did not believe he could learn at all. I gave out the posttest in fear and trepidation, and after the children had completed it I sat down to grade them. When I got to the final paper I was so astounded that I had to go back and remark the entire class. Every single person in the class had passed, not just passed but most had improved by at least 16 points! They had passed with flying colors, and "John" got 100% - the only child in the class to do so. When I announced the results to the class, and announced that "JOHN" - insecure, low self esteem, pain in the proverbial, "John" had gotten 100%, there was an audible gasp from the class and then a spontaneous burst of applause. "John"! almost cried!

I will never forget the look on his face. From that day onwards "John" and the rest of the class were different people. It was as if the wind had been put into their sails - they had tasted success, and wanted more of it. I know that "John" will remember the time when he was the one person in the class to get 100% for the rest of his life and I am so glad I was there to witness it.

By - Rachael Shamy

4
BUILDING YOUR INTERVIEW PORTFOLIO

WHY BUILD A PORTFOLIO?

The prepared applicant will bring something visual to show the prospective employer. An interview portfolio, if it is well designed, can accomplish this task. The key to success will be in what you include and how your portfolio can enhance your story. A badly constructed portfolio can actually detract from an otherwise good candidate's viability. There are a number of do's and don'ts regarding the construction of your portfolio and we will examine these later in the chapter.

The first thing to recognize is that an *interview portfolio* is different from a *professional portfolio.* Every teacher should build a portfolio that begins with student teaching and continues throughout his or her career. In the professional portfolio you include a wide variety of materials, mementos, artifacts, and documents that provide a moving chronology of your professional vision, work, and achievements. It is meant to be comprehensive and reflective in its construction. An interview portfolio, on the other hand, is smaller and has a definitive focus and purpose. The contents of your interview portfolio are dictated by the goal(s) you want it to achieve.

In building an interview portfolio you must first consider the limited amount of presentation time. Generally, you will present your materials at the end of the interview when there might be other candidates waiting. The principal and committee will want to move onto the next applicant in a timely way, however, they are usually willing to spend a few minutes reviewing the work you have done with children. As a rule of thumb, portfolio reviews should not take more than five minutes. Again, keep in mind that your portfolio is not designed to tell your life story. Its purpose is to enhance your resume and highlight the things in your background most likely to be seen as important by the interview committee. This means your portfolio strategy is dictated by what you know about the district and its values.

With time at a premium, include only items that add high impact to your presentation. The more closely the items match the school's values, the greater the impact. For example, you may think photos of your class experience on a local nature excursion demonstrate your ability to motivate students with a "hands-on" approach. However, if you are interviewing in an urban district with no such facilities and where outside experiences are unsafe, the impact of your photos will be limited. You should consider a different piece to demonstrate the hands-on approach provided students in your class. If district initiatives are underway, photos of work reflecting skills needed to carry on those missions will be well received. For example, if two million dollars was recently invested in technology upgrades, pictures of your class working on an Internet enrichment piece will be more meaningful to the committee. Such matching activities resonate with committee members and can move you toward the top of the committee's "most desirable" list. Most candidates will not do the necessary homework and fail to link their credentials to specific district goals. This oversight provides you the opportunity to tell a more compelling story. Attention to details gives you the advantage!

WHAT KINDS OF ITEMS CAN BE INCLUDED

- *A copy of your teaching certificate:* This can be the original certificate but a copy will serve just as well. When copies are used, they should be clean and crisp. If you have not yet received a certificate at the time of the interview, you can omit this page. For most candidates, the certificate is their lead page.

- *An innovative unit plan:* The plan should be described on a single sheet of paper. Be sure to include your broad objectives, the main activities and timelines, assessment strategy, and any other information you determined the district would see as important. Additional components might include interdisciplinary connections, real world relationships, technology links, enrichment activities, or other design features.

- *Student work samples:* Work samples can effectively highlight the results students can achieve under your direction, but consider a few guidelines when putting this section together. First, always delete any names or identifying information on the work sample. Confidentiality is essential. Select a cross-section of student work. The committee will be interested to see how a variety of students perform in your class. It is important to show that you are proud of all your students, not just the top few. Use a highlighter to bring out elements of the students' work that demonstrate critical learning. Do not underestimate the power of this section; student performance is something every interviewer wants to see. As a principal who has viewed many portfolios, I was always favorably impressed when a candidate showed me work samples from a struggling student who had risen to a higher level. Almost every teacher can produce good results when they have the brightest student, but success with low ability students connotes a higher level of teaching skill.

- *Student surveys:* If you are currently teaching, give the students a teacher survey form and request some honest feedback about their views of the class and your teaching. Include two open-ended questions of the type shown below.

  1. What did you like best about this class?
  2. What did I do that most helped you to be successful?

To focus student thinking on specific teacher actions or classroom events that will help build a strong portfolio, you need to "seed the pot." To accomplish this goal, provide suggestions or ideas that will help students start their thinking.

  "In question #1 you can think about things like the field trips we took, activities we completed, our circle discussions, the computer centers, and so on."

By identifying specific areas, you almost insure students will reflect on some of the things a prospective school might value.

Once you have the surveys, make copies. When constructing the portfolio, select surveys that fit your needs and use a
highlighter to underscore items you want the committee to see. It is
important for the committee to *see* how students enjoyed your class
and were well supported by your teaching stance. Student comments have a very persuasive voice in verifying your teaching expertise.

• **Selected photos:** This section can easily be overdone. Only
  include photographs that specifically exhibit a quality of your
  teaching you feel is important. A dozen well-chosen photographs
  with a purpose are more effective than a potpourri of forty or
  fifty meaningless snapshots. With regard to photographs, there
  is often question about the use of student faces and the need for
  release forms. If you do not plan to show the portfolio in a public
  setting, it is not generally necessary to have signed releases.

  When thoughtfully arranged, photographs can make a powerful statement about your work in the classroom. Pictures of
  interactive bulletin boards, field studies, project fairs, group work,
  and laboratory settings effectively show innovative teaching.
  Think about why a photograph is included and what story you
  will tell about it. A last tip on style is to include people in your
  photos. Bland snapshots of your class or decorations are tedious
  and create scant visual impact. Photographs of happy students
  engaged in learning will be far more effective in stimulating a
  positive discussion with the committee.

• **Copies of parent communications:** If you have sent out parent newsletters or information letters to launch new units and
  involve parents, place samples of those in the portfolio. If students made special presentations to the class and parents were
  invited, such expositions exemplify a commitment to involving
  parents in the education of their children.

• **Copies of evaluations:** Many interviewees like to include copies of good evaluations. These are not the most effective way to
  verify your instructional competence. Most interviewers are
  smart enough to know you will only include puff pieces that say

good things. As a result, the credibility of such documents is limited. This can be improved if you yellow-highlight statements in your evaluation that compliment teaching skills the district values. For example, if the prospective district has a strong interest in innovative assessment and your evaluation identifies assessment as your lesson's strength, highlight those remarks for the reviewer to see. Do not include more than two evaluations, no matter how glowing. Checklist evaluations are superficial and have almost no impact; eliminate them altogether.

- *Letter(s) of reference:* A good letter of reference is somewhat more effective in speaking to your qualities as a candidate. As with evaluations, interviewers know you are likely to only include good letters but when they are from respected members of the school, they serve a useful purpose. If possible, when you ask for a letter of reference, ask the writer to directly address those elements of your professional background you want to underscore at the interview. Again, use a yellow-highlighter to make the pertinent passages stand out. No more than two letters should be included in your portfolio. **TIP:** *Make a number of copies of each reference letter.* Multiple copies will allow you to use one for each portfolio and accent the valued areas for each school. Always keep your original fresh and unmarked.

- *Videotapes:* Classroom teachers should leave videotapes out of their portfolio. Interviewers will not have the time required to view a tape. If you are a music teacher, however, you may be asked to supply a videotape of one of your concerts. You may wish to create well-edited videotape of ten to fifteen minutes' length. This tape will probably be viewed at a separate time and only if you are a candidate under serious consideration.

- *Copies of musical programs:* If you are a music teacher, you should include a copy of two or three typical music programs that you have presented. Principals will definitely want to see examples of your work in this area. The public aspect of concerts makes these documents an important part of your portfolio.

CLOSING THOUGHTS

As you enter the interview, carry the portfolio in your brief-case or in an unobtrusive way. It is best to produce the portfolio only after the committee has indicated their willingness to review the contents with you. When you show the portfolio, provide an oral explanation of pertinent details. Do not just hand over the book and sit back while the committee leafs through the contents – guide the process. To add power to your presentation, plan the key points you will make. Go over each item and make note cards outlining details that need emphasis. Rehearse your presentation a few times, pref-erably with someone who is able to provide constructive feedback. Interviews are stressful times and it is easy to leave important things unsaid. You will be surprised how polished you will become after you have rehearsed your portfolio presentation a few times.

The good portfolio is not a scrapbook or trophy case; it is a testament to the teacher's ability to create a passion for learning in his or her students. With a little effort and planning, the visual images along with a persuasive commentary will be an excellent closing to your interview. It will make a powerful and lasting im-pression the committee will find hard to forget. When the portfolio review is over, your committee will have seen your professional com-mitment to children, enthusiasm for learning, instructional skill, and planning. The portfolio will have demonstrated your ability to relate to children and insure their success. Try these ideas and end your interview with a portfolio that slams the door on the competi-tion!

5
Dressing for a Successful Interview

MAKING A FIRST IMPRESSION

There is a saying: "You only get one opportunity to make a first impression." The moment a candidate walks into the interview, minds begin to make judgments regarding his or her suitability. If you do not present a neat, professional and well-groomed appearance, be sure your chance of success just went down. The visual image, confidence, and demeanor you project will be well noted by each person on the interview committee. You will be measured against the other candidates and any subjective expectations the interviewer has regarding the school image. Keep in mind that dress and grooming affect behavior and self-image. When you look great and have impeccable grooming, your confidence improves and you become a more formidable candidate.

PERSONAL GROOMING

FOR THE GENTLEMEN

Personal grooming directly affects the impression you make. Men should have a recent haircut. Excessively long hair on men is not generally well received. Also, research has shown men with ill-kept beards have a significantly lower chance of being hired. Whereas the ponytail may have been fine in college or at the beach, it is not generally accepted in the professional world. Gentleman, pay attention to your nails! Dirty, uneven or badly cut nails will be seen every time you show your hands and they can undermine your entire appearance; be sure they are cut, filed and clean for your interview. Use a good mouthwash before you leave the house. It is a good idea to carry breath-freshener or mints in the car and take them just prior to entering the interview site, but you should not eat them in the office or during the interview.

It should go without mention that body odor is guaranteed to be less than well received. Controlling this problem is unique to each person. Take whatever steps are necessary to prevent it. Keep in mind that the added pressure and anxiety of an interview can add to this concern unless you have taken precautions.

FOR THE LADIES

For women, much of the above applies to you as well, however, a few other special areas require comment. Your interview is not the time for the ultra-deluxe, fancy, designer nails. You know the ones – inlaid jewels, pictures of kitties, Bill Blass stripes, or other complicated treatments. Have a good manicure with a nice coat of fresh nail polish in a subdued color. Keep in mind that your hands are generally on display for the entire interview and you want to avoid them becoming a focal point. For hair, it is best to spend a little time at the salon and have someone provide a good styling to fit the business image you are going to present. By taking the extra time to present yourself as a professional who understands the importance of his or her image, you are telling your prospective employer you respect his or her time and school. The visual image you leave in the minds of each person on the interview committee can be long lasting.

GENERAL NOTES ON PERSONAL ATTIRE

For both men and women, a conservative look will serve best, but this should not infer plain vanilla. Many fashionable outfits make a positive statement, so it is not necessary to assume you are limited to only the traditional plain blue suit. The most important thing is whatever you select should be neat, well pressed, and well fitted. It is not necessary for either men or women run out and buy the latest in contemporary fashions; just insure that your attire sufficiently reflects current standards.

CREATING A CONSERVATIVE LOOK FOR MEN

Suit or Jacket?

Many authorities strongly suggest men wear a contemporary suit to a first interview. Most experts also recommend a color in the blue or gray family and that is considered safe advice. If you already own a pinstripe or light chalk-stripe suit, this can provide the conservative look you need. If a suit reflects your taste, then by all means go with it. For school interviews, however, a well-chosen sport jacket with neatly pressed slacks is also quite serviceable. Well-dressed teachers often wear sport jackets and they are perfectly acceptable at an interview for a teaching position. Contemporary men's fashions feature many well-designed jackets with a traditional look. When well selected, sport jackets can offer a high quality appearance, but a word of caution is in order. You should maintain a conservative look and avoid the more flamboyant color combinations. Plaids and big bold stripes are too flashy and draw too much attention to your dress. Save those for the country club or casual party. If you choose a sport jacket, make your matching slacks a solid color to compliment the jacket. **WARNING**: *Never ever, ever wear white slacks no matter how warm the weather.* The yacht club is a nice place for these, not a professional interview.

Pay attention to fabric and fit. Although there are many fabrics available, conventional wisdom suggests wool or a wool blend is often your best choice. It maintains its neat, fresh look and makes a nice appearance. The bottom line is to wear something in which you feel comfortable and look good. **WARNING**: *Pay attention to fit!* The sleeves should extend to about two inches above the top of your thumb. If you have a few pounds to hide, make sure the chest size on your jacket is correct. You may have worn a 44-long all your life, but if it is a bit tight when buttoned and the lapels do not lie flat, allow a competent tailor re-measure and refit the garment. The right size will make you look and feel a lot better. Suits that are too small can make you look like a stuffed sausage and we do not want that, do we? The sign at a local, upscale men's store says this best. "Approximately – is not your size." Any questions?

Here are some last minute thoughts to consider before you leave for that important interview. Make sure your interview suit was professionally dry-cleaned and pressed just before the big day. If you are wearing an older suit or jacket, be sure it has *all* the buttons (yes, including those along the cuff), is not frayed and relatively in style. Think ahead about your drive to the interview, how long will it take? I like to hang up my jacket in the back of the car. Sitting on your jacket for a long drive can ruin the freshly tailored look you worked so hard to achieve. When hung in the car, it will be sharp and ready to wear when you arrive. A last thought pertains to wearing a topcoat or raincoat. If the day calls for one, make sure it has been recently cleaned and pressed. The "Colombo" look is not what you want when you first enter the office.

Choosing an Appropriate Shirt and Tie

When selecting a shirt, choose one that compliments your suit or jacket. Many stores now feature dark colors and they are considered "in." Perhaps this is true for some occasions, but not an interview. Avoid the mistake of wearing a dark colored shirt that makes a "big statement." When in doubt, follow the rules given by almost every writer on the subject and take the safe route with a white, off-white, buff, or light blue shirt. Save the "Regis" look for another day when you have your own game show. Also, when wearing a suit, straight collars should be worn. A button-down is fine with a sports jacket ensemble, but the more formal presentation of a suit makes the button-down shirt contradictory.

I suggest a new shirt, but if you have a recently purchased shirt in good condition, that will be fine. If you must use an older shirt, make sure there is no fraying along the collar or cuffs. Check to insure all the buttons are present and in one piece. Look at the collar; does it have some dirt around it that cleaning no longer removes? If so, it is not for this interview. Invest in a new one. Take my word for it, such imperfections *will* be noticed. I prefer to wear a 100% cotton fabric that has been professionally cleaned, pressed and starched. Cotton looks and feels better than a blend or synthetic and, unless you are an ex-marine who really knows how to press a great uniform, spend the dollar and let a professional makeup your shirt. Avoid anything that is "wash and wear." You can be sure, there is no such thing. Finally, a long-sleeve shirt is an absolute must, no matter what the weather. It is the standard in the professional world.

A final thought is to double-check the fit of the shirt you choose. If you have a 16-1/2-inch neck, please do not try to squeeze into a 15 1/2 -inch shirt. It looks positively ghastly to see someone's neck overlapping the collar and straining at the button. And for heaven's sake, do not try to get away with just leaving the top button unbuttoned so you have "a little" breathing room. Likewise, if your arm has a 35-inch length, a 34-35 inch sleeve *will not* do. A 36-37 inch sleeve that extends three inches past the end of your jacket to cover half your hand also provides a very poor image. Proper cuff length extends slightly past the end of your jacket sleeve; see that it does or buy a new shirt.

Men should take care in the selection of their tie. A good tie can make an ordinary suit or sport jacket look very sharp. Conversely, a tie that is too loud or contains clashing colors can ruin an otherwise good appearance. The tie must provide the complement to your suit or jacket. A conservative stripe or print will wear well. If you are unsure, go to a good men's store and seek advice from one of the salesmen (I said the salesman at a *good* men's store, not the kid at Wal-Mart). Avoid the more modern ties with large, bold patterns and nouveau designs. Currently, there is a tie series under the name, "Save the Children." The thought is nice and there are some who might see the gesture as indicative of a child-centered person; nonetheless, unless you know that to be the case, you are better served with a more traditional look. If you are going to wear a tie that has been worn before, check its cleanliness. The knot area tends to collect grease and dirt from your fingers and can become discolored. There is nothing more unsightly than a tie with a soiled knot area. Remember, the neck area is a focal point during the interview and everyone will see this oversight for the entire time. Your best bet is to buy a new tie for your outfit. There are numerous discount men's stores where you can purchase good, name-brand neckwear for around $20.

Don't Forget Your Feet

If you wear a suit, then a matching pair of tie shoes should be considered. Loafers present too casual a look, but with a sports coat loafers are fine. Stick with the brown or black color and, unless you will be attending the track after you fail the interview, avoid two-tone shoes. Another important point is that your shoes must be well shined with good soles and heels. For goodness sakes, do not wear a shoe with a hole in it and think you will just keep that foot on the floor so no one will notice! You may laugh, but I have seen it. In my experience, many candidates have arrived wearing scuffed shoes or worn heels and soles. It made their entire appearance shabby. Do not be misled; your interviewer will look at your footwear at some point during the interview, so make the impression positive.

Completing your Image

Men should be sparing with jewelry and accessories. A nice leather briefcase for your portfolio and other materials is fine. If you bring a briefcase, some additional words are in order; be sure it is organized and not overstuffed. You do not want to release the catch and have it blow open to disgorge its contents all over the principal's conference table. This is considered poor form, indeed.

Let us review other items such as watches, rings, hankies, and cologne. A conservative watch can add to your appearance, but stay away from flashy or fad watches. Even if you are now the proud owner of the original "Clinton Growing Nose" watch, this is probably not the time to show it off. A wedding ring is fine, but be careful of gaudy rings that attract too much attention. (You know, the big horseshoe one with all the zirconium diamonds that you wear to Las Vegas sometimes.) Also, do not wear the fashion hanky in your jacket pocket. They may look fine on game-show hosts, but they say all the wrong things about a professional teaching candidate. A final thought is cologne. Forget it. You are not going on a date and the presence of strong cologne does nothing to enhance your appearance or chance of success.

CREATING A CONSERVATIVE LOOK FOR WOMEN

A Business Suit, Skirt or Slacks?

As with men, women should first consider the primary aim of their attire. A lady requires a professional appearance that compliments her purposeful approach to the school and organization. Your outfit should be conservatively tasteful. This does not mean you have to limit yourself to dull and uninspired attire in drab colors. As more women have entered the work force, fashion designers have added business suits, pants outfits, and skirts for the workingwoman of today. Martin Yate, in <u>Knock 'Em Dead 1999</u>, identifies Sharon McCollick's, Essential Suits as a company that has responded to this market. (Yate, 1999) Many large chains such as Nordstrom, Macy's, and Lord & Taylor have also established excellent areas for the businesswoman to shop.

In selecting your wardrobe, a simple suit is always safe. As with the men, there are attractive jackets with matching skirts that also work well. It is really a matter of taste and what fits your style and personality best. Conservative color selections in the blue and gray families are a wise choice because they coordinate easily and carry the traditional look we seek. Nonetheless, I must admit I have seen very smart outfits in other colors as well. If you should choose a color, take care that is not too loud or bold.

The suit or jacket should suit your shape and style. Comfort is important and you should take care regarding fit. Clothes that are too small strain in all the wrong places when you are seated and can be quite uncomfortable. A poor fit can be distracting and upset your concentration because you are trying to keep that blame skirt in place. By the same token, don't wear oversized clothing that hangs like a potato sack. One certainty in life is that fashions in skirt length change. But no matter what the current style, shorter skirts do not generally serve well at an interview. This suggestion is not intended to limit you to only skirt lengths of which our Puritan forefathers would be proud, but a length that extends just to or below the knee would be more fitting.

Fancy Footwork

A wide range of footwear styles is available to women and this can be a challenging decision. My recommendation is to choose a leather shoe that matches the color of the skirt, either the same color or slightly darker. The closed toe is the style of choice, but I have seen a few conservative open toe shoes that will suit as long as they are carefully chosen. The interview is also not the place for 5-inch stiletto heels. Heels are fine if they are not too high, but flats are also acceptable. If you are already tall, you may be more comfortable in flats and there is no sense in towering over the poor principal. Sneakers are inappropriate at all times – even if you *are* the PE applicant.

Completing the Look with Jewelry, Accessories and Makeup

Accessories are an important part of a woman's presence and should not be overlooked. As with men, I suggest a good leather briefcase where you can keep your portfolio, a pad, pen, and folder with extra copies of documents you are bringing to the interview. (See the warnings provided to men on this subject. The same applies to the ladies.) Leave your purse in the car and just bring the briefcase to the interview. Having both can make you look as if you are coming for the weekend, plus shaking hands can be awkward if all of your hands are full.

Jewelry should be kept uncomplicated. A simple necklace, small earrings, and wedding or engagement rings is sufficient. Avoid gaudy or oversized costume jewelry. Long strands of pearls, multi-band bracelets, or other jewelry can be a distraction and should be avoided. A good rule of thumb is, "When in doubt, leave it out."

My grandmother used to say she could not go somewhere important without "putting on her face." This is wise advice. Makeup is a key part of a lady's preparation and we understand you want to rise above the "Plain Jane look." Still, keep things simple. A light coating of lipstick or gloss is fine, but the bold, high-impact varieties are probably not a good choice. Rouge or heavy eye makeup is also best left for another occasion. If you need a little mascara, fine, but keep it light. If the interviewers are likely to take sharp notice, it is probably too much. Similarly, if you must wear eye shadow, keep it light and subdued. Perfume is not necessary or desirable. Save it for that grand evening at the ballet or opera.

FINAL THOUGHTS

It is critically important that you are well attired and prepared for your interview. Obviously, you are going to spend more time putting this ensemble together than you might for just an ordinary day at the school or office. You want to make a positive and lasting impression on those who will be conducting the interview. I would suggest that you put this outfit together in advance and have someone look at you. This person should be able to be objective and provide constructive criticism (We love Mom and Dad, but they are rarely objective with their beloved crown jewel children – no matter what the "child's" age.).

As a general goal, you want to look professional, but not flashy. Have some fun with this. Everyone likes to shop and select things in which they look good. Try things out and see how you look. I wish you luck and now we are ready to move onto the next phase – THE INTERVIEW!

One is taught by experience to put a premium on those few people who can appreciate you for what you are.

Gail Godwin

6
GENERAL INTERVIEW QUESTIONS

GUIDELINES FOR USING THIS SECTION

The questions included in this section are taken from actual interviews or were given to me by administrators with extensive interview experience. Items from a variety of sources provided a wide base of information. The chapter includes questions that are designed to determine specific attributes of a candidate's background and understanding of the teaching-learning process.

For each question, the discussion describes those elements of a candidate's qualifications and training most commonly sought by interviewers and principals. It is important to understand, however, actual answers at an interview will need to be shaped to each individual's background, experience, and philosophy. One cannot simply memorize the discussion information and recite it at an interview. Look at what each question tries to uncover and then select items from your background that highlight your strength in that area. At the end of each question you will find a set of:

 Keys to Your Response:

These present essential answer components in an abbreviated format. When you are preparing for an interview, these keys will provide quick reference and refreshed thinking.

The primary objective of each chapter is to provide advance opportunities for you to see potential questions and help you pre-think sensible, power-laden answers. Do you remember the adage, *"To be forewarned is to be forearmed."* That works for us.

In shaping your answers, it is helpful if you can shape your answer around critical issues or themes that underpin successful teaching. All of the themes will not be reflected in a single answer, however, each interview question is likely to test your knowledge or background on at least one central theme. Here are those themes:

- ***You are a child-centered teacher and recognize your chief goal as the promotion of individual achievement and growth in students.*** In public education today, you are required to teach children who possess a wide variety of ability levels, degrees of motivation, and educational backgrounds. In a single class there may be gifted students, special needs students, and so-called "regular" students. An important concern shared by every principal is that teachers show a genuine care for *every* student. Most teachers will tell you they entered the field because they love children or enjoy helping children learn. Fine, but that platitude does not count until it reaches the individual level and becomes, "I genuinely care about Fred or Sarah." Principals need to know you have the understanding, skills, and motivation sufficient to reach out and touch every child.

- ***You have clear mastery of content knowledge in the area(s) you intend to teach.*** If you are applying for a science position, there are a variety of subjects subsumed in that discipline. You will need to demonstrate competence in the areas you expect to teach. If you are applying for a language arts position, the committee will want to see strong evidence you understand the most current strategies to teach writing and communication. Knowledge of the content you intend to teach is essential to your success.

- ***You have the instructional skills required to convey a body of knowledge to students of all backgrounds.*** It is one thing to have a child centered approach and another to have the technical teaching skills necessary to insure student learning. Principals want to know you understand the principles of learning necessary for successful teaching. Will you effectively plan instruction? Will you have strong and clear presentation skills? Will you be able to diagnose and remediate learning problems? Will you employ effective assessment strategies? Teaching is an art and a science. You must demonstrate a comprehensive knowledge of both.

- *You possess sufficient classroom management skills to organize curriculum, control student behavior, and manage resources.* You cannot teach anything to a class that is disorganized, off-task, or lacking sufficient materials. There are specific skills teachers employ to maximize their efficiency in these areas. The interview committee will want to know your strategy and approach to each vital management skill. What are your discipline strategies? How do you manage space and time? How do you maintain materials? Can you manage the curriculum? These are all questions you will need to answer.

- *You possess personal and professional characteristics that will enhance the teaching staff.* The interview committee will continuously assess the degree to which you embody the qualities of professional behavior they seek in their teachers. These qualities include, but are not limited to, teamwork, reliability, dedication, integrity, loyalty and pride. You need to clearly demonstrate how you will add to the good chemistry of the school, department, and team on which you will serve. It will be important to identify yourself as someone who is motivated, a self-starter, and a persistent seeker of excellence. You will need to show how your character and skill combine to make you a teacher with the potential to command respect from students, parents, colleagues and administrators.

As you are asked each question, try to identify which of the above theme areas is addressed. You should see opportunities to demonstrate your attributes within most or all of the areas at some point during the interview process. You may even find that more than one theme can be addressed within a single answer. In any event, you will find it easier to organize the response when you know what the committee is seeking.

RESPONSE STRATEGY: *It will be to your advantage to conduct a self-assessment in each area and jot down ideas that establish your qualifications.* This exercise will promote clarity in your phrasing when the interview questions begin to fly. If you have done no preparation and attempt to develop your ideas as the interview proceeds, you will find it a difficult and anxiety ridden experience.

GENERAL ADVICE FOR ANSWERING QUESTIONS

Keep something in mind; the interview committee or principal is interested in you. If you were not a candidate they thought might fit the position, you would not be in the seat you now occupy. As this is so, you now want to clearly and confidently address the issues raised in their questions. **KEY POINT:** *Do not concern yourself that every element of your answer needs to be a solid 10; it does not.* None of the candidates will answer every question to perfection. *Your approach needs to be professional, clearly articulated and designed to highlight strengths and minimize weaknesses.*

By its very nature, the interview is a time when nervousness is common. For that reason, it is also a time when flaws can creep into your responses. Therefore, before we specifically look what you might be asked, lets review some general rules for framing answers to interview questions.

GENERAL RULES TO FRAME ANSWERS:

- *Listen carefully to the question and answer what is asked as precisely as possible.* One of the most common flaws in providing a good answer is what I call question avoidance tactics. The candidate talks and talks but does not address the question asked. A clear example occurs when a principal asks the candidate to identify any recent workshop experience and he or she talks at length about his or her summer reading and college coursework. The conclusion of the principal is there was no workshop experience or the person did not listen well. Either way, the candidate made the wrong impression. If you are not certain what the interviewer asked, then by all means get a clarification.

    "You ask an interesting question, but I want to be sure I understand. Would you be kind enough to explain it again?"

If the question probes an area that is not your strength, one of the worst things to do is "wing it" or dodge the issue. You might simply say something like:

> *"As I was not recently in a position to take advantage of workshop opportunities I haven't any to share at this point. I would like to say, however, I think workshops are a valuable part of every teacher's continuing growth. I would be very interested in attending workshops about technology in the classroom, values education, or diagnostic teaching strategies. Does the district have some specific workshops which they would like me to attend if I am selected for this position?"*

This answer is on target and shows you understand the value of professional development. More importantly, you are clear about a few areas where you want to expand your ability. Strength is added by the last phrase because it opens an avenue for the principal to link his or her priorities to the agenda.

- *Be concise! Direct your answer to the question and make a few powerful points.* Every interviewer's nightmare is the candidate who takes five or six minutes to answer a simple question. Rambling answers that are convoluted and repetitive steal power from your response and diminish your effectiveness. A good rule of thumb is to limit answers to two minutes. If the question is complicated or has multiple parts, you may have to exceed the two-minute time limit, but these questions are not the norm. Also, if you hear yourself repeating information, draw your answer to a close, it generally means you have exhausted the good ideas. **KEY STRATEGY:** *The length of an answer has no relationship to its quality.*

- *Provide specific examples or points to underscore your ideas.* When you give a specific example of how you would apply a principle to a real situation, you add power to your answer. For example, a common interview question asks how one would deal with off-task students. The typical candidate will simply talk about a few strategies he or she "might try." This is not necessarily a poor approach, but it lacks power. A better candidate will provide a specific example from his or her experience and background.

> *"Although this has not happened often, your question does bring one student to mind. In that case I did three things and they proved so successful I have used the strategy several times since."*

Then go on to detail the three steps and their effect. This answer is stronger because it shows how you *applied* the classroom management principles you outlined.

• ***Do not be afraid to reflect and frame your thinking before answering a complicated question.*** Candidates often feel obliged to begin their answer immediately at the end of the question. For more complicated questions, you might need a little time to mentally organize your response. If you have a pad in front of you, you might even wish to jot down a few key words to help you stay on target and cover important points you want to make. Whereas there cannot be a full minute of dead silence, ten to fifteen seconds of organization and thinking is not unreasonable.

SAMPLE QUESTIONS

There are many other pointers and suggestions to discuss as we proceed, but now we are ready to look at a few of the tough questions you may encounter on your interview. These questions are a representative sampling of those a school administrator or committee might ask. I selected items that were most common, difficult, or interesting.

> ***Describe the aspects of your background that best qualify you for this position.***

This question, or a variation of it, is often the lead question in an interview. It is also one of the most commonly mishandled questions! This is the perfect opportunity for you to sell yourself and your skills, but too often a candidate will just review the same information contained in his or her resume. Worse yet, he or she embarks on a long narrative that wanders all over the lot and never addresses the substantive issue posed in the question; "aspects of your background you believe <u>best</u> qualify you for this position."

Target your answer to what you know about the district and its students. Focus the committee on specific teaching skills you use that match the needs of their student body. Tell them about projects you designed that fit their vision, extra-curricular work you have done that will add to the quality of student life, or any other item in your background that matches the district's needs. If you have not researched the district, it will be impossible to match your background to specific school values, so be sure to complete this important step before the interview day. **KEYPOINT:** *The key to a successful interview is the match between your skills and the school's needs.* Keep in mind the school is not looking for just a teacher – it wants an impact player who will be a key contributor in his or her first year. This answer can set that tone, but you must provide enthusiasm and power with sharp, hard-hitting connections.

A good conclusion to your response will outline your commitment to student achievement and personal dedication. You might say,

> *"Finally, one of my most important strengths is a commitment that every child in my class should leave school at the end of the day saying my class was one of the highlights. To that end, I will direct my best efforts all day, every day!"*

KEY POINT: *Put this ending in your own words, but keep in mind that your ending statement is often the most lasting in the memory of the committee.*

Keys to Your Response:

- Be specific and stick to the question. DO NOT WANDER.
- Target the elements of your background that *best fit* what you know the district values.
- Include information about your teaching style, special projects, or ideas that relate to school initiatives.
- End with a statement about your dedication and energy. Let them know you will be an impact teacher from the first day.

 Describe a difficult classroom challenge that confronted you and what you did to address the problem.

This is another common question. Its purpose is to see how you think on your feet and evaluate your problem solving ability. The committee wants to know what approach you will take in dealing with the tough situations that will confront you. Here is a possible approach.

"I first recognize that a difficult problem in my class is __my__ problem, but there are always others who can provide insight and assistance if necessary. I generally use a four-step process to determine my best course of action. One, I identify the specific elements of the problem and who might be involved. Two, I outline some possible steps that might be employed. Three, I discuss those steps with a colleague or administrator to see if they have other insights or suggestions. Four, I take action."

With this approach, the principal knows you do not just take a trial and error approach to difficult problems. You are a deliberate problem solver with a plan. But this does not fully answer the question and, as you know, that is one of the serious flaws we want to eliminate. Now, give an example of a problem and what you did.

This question is common enough to warrant the time you will devote to a pre-thought answer. In the heat of an interview, your mind may not land on a problem that will effectively demonstrate this key skill. The following is a good example given during an interview I held some years ago. It should provide insight as to how you might prepare your own answer.

"When I took over a class as a permanent sub, the class had had five different teachers in two months. There were no classroom routines and student behavior was unruly and hostile. I determined there were two root problems. The first was the lack of a classroom structure and the second was the presence of a group of alienated students. As a class, we decided to suspend all academics for two days. We used the first day to identify problems and some possible solutions. The students developed three classroom rules we would all follow and posters were made for placement around the room. The second day, we examined the curriculum and I listed the things we could study that fit into our curriculum. We decided which of the areas to pursue. We began our work with an improved, although not perfect, level of participation and energy. Although it took over a month to establish a good routine and mutual respect, the cooperative approach to decision making was a sound strategy that we all made work."

This answer was a perfect practical example of the described strategy! We hired this teacher. Think about what you will say and similar results may well follow.

 ### Keys to Your Response:

- Begin with a specific problem-solving design.
- Provide a specific story or example of how that design worked in a difficult situation.

> **Outline how you assess student performance and how you address the differences in student backgrounds and abilities.**

This is a double-barreled assessment question and one you may well encounter in your interview. Begin by identifying the components of the question. The first part wants to know how you determine student progress while the second wants modifications you will make for students with unique problems or abilities.

Assessment has become more complex over the last ten years and encompasses a variety practices. You will have to choose those that best fit your style and the school's philosophy. If you know a school is involved in authentic tasks, problem-based learning, or some other initiative, then by all means learn about it and be ready to use that information in your response. To prepare yourself for questions in this area, you might want to read articles by Grant Wiggins. He is a recognized expert in assessment and provides sound thinking for use in an interview.

To approach the first portion of the question, how you assess student performance, begin with a statement of how you recognize the different roles assessment can fulfill. Discuss the ways you see assessment as having changed over the years.

> *"When I was in school, the only use of assessment was for the teacher to figure out your grade at the end of the marking period. Teachers gave us quizzes and tests, added in our homework, and gave us a grade. Now, we know there are many ways to use the assessment process."*

Go on to describe the numerous roles assessment would have in your class. Specifically talk about how you might use assessment to make teaching decisions and guide student learning. Describe the distinction you make between diagnostic assessment and grading practice. If you use self and/or peer assessment strategies in your class, be sure to describe them.

From this foundation, move to the second portion of the question and state how you will account for different educational backgrounds and abilities. Describe the way you alter your grading practices to meet individual differences. The principal will want to know if you use differentiated testing practices, multi-level homework, extra-credit, self-selected projects, peer tutors, cooperative learning, technology, or other techniques to insure the success of struggling students while still presenting challenge to the brighter students. Which strategies you choose are not particularly important. ***What is important is that you have specific plans to use a variety of assessment practices and a sound rationale for their employment.***

This is one of the more important questions and the committee wants to know how you will use your knowledge of assessment to promote student success. Are you a teacher who knows how to reward the exceptional student and maintain his or her challenge? Do you have the flexibility and strategies that will insure strugglers, poor readers and below average students have an opportunity to succeed if they put forth a fair effort? Most administrators fear they will hire an inflexible, dogmatic teacher who has such a narrow grading philosophy that it promotes a setting where the strong survive and the weak are left to fail.

 Keys to Your Response:

- Do your homework on the district to identify any information they have on their assessment practice. Select assessment strategies in your style that match the district philosophy.
- Identify a few purposes of assessment and describe how you will use them to design instruction and to help students learn.
- Outline how you might vary your assessment patterns to meet the challenge represented by students with different abilities.
- Tell the committee about your grading practices, but be sure to let them know you understand both the need for individual

grade success as well as your responsibility to help students *attain* the required goals of the course.

> **Tell us what qualities you believe are essential to being a good teacher. Of those qualities, which is your strongest?**

This is an excellent question for you to separate yourself from the pack! It is an open invitation to talk about your knowledge of teaching and underscore your strengths. Look at how this might be done. First, just what are the essential qualities of a good teacher? Qualities you need to include are the ability of the teacher to relate to students and inspire their learning; to possess the instructional skills necessary for inspired teaching; to understand class management skills; and to manifest a high sense of professional behavior. When you suggest any strengths you have, provide a practical example to add power to this part of the answer. The question further asks which dimension you feel represents *your* greatest strength. A good approach to this answer might combine two areas.   For example:

"One of my strongest qualities is an ability to relate instruction to the world of children and design activities that interest and motivate their involvement."

KEY POINT: *Whatever qualities you identify as strengths, they should be supported with short anecdotes.* It is from this connection the answer draws its strength. A good answer to this question sets a positive tone to the entire interview.

 Keys to Your Response:

- Describe the qualities that are essential to being a good teacher.
- Use practical examples showing that you possess those qualities.

- In describing your personal strengths, try to use an anecdote to tell your story.
- This question is asked often enough to make it worthwhile to pre-think an answer. If you have not prepared, your examples are likely to be less effective.

> **If we were to speak with your students, what would they tell us about the educational experience they had with you?**

This question can be phrased in different ways. Sometimes you will be asked what your supervisor would say, or your department head, or principal. Each question asks the same thing: how do others perceive your work? Even if there have been some problems in your background, it is in your interest to remain positive and focus only on the good things that might be said.

If you are currently teaching and can conduct a student survey, do this and include a question that asks students to write what they like about your teaching. From their responses, select a few comments to share in an interview. Even if there has been criticism about a few elements of your class or teaching, focus on the qualities students said they liked. Do not forget to select a few student response forms to include in your interview portfolio.

If you have never conducted such a survey, it is acceptable to relate things a student may have told you. You may also talk about the things you did in class that students responded to best. Your goal is to convey the fact that students liked your class and responded well to your teaching efforts.

Be aware that the committee may offer a follow-up question that asks, "Was there anything your students disliked?" **WARNING:** *This is a loaded gun waiting to go off.* There is no need to bare your soul and convey every complaint. On the other hand, telling the committee it was all peaches and cream and there was nothing students did not like will not play well either. There are many things students can dislike about a class that do not reflect poorly on the teacher. Examples include weekend homework, resubmitting papers that were not up to standard, too many tests, and so on. You know your classes and what students may have found less enjoyable. Select something you feel will meet the needs of this question. If you have an ability to add a humorous tone to this area, it can be very effective. If not, just be honest and open. The committee will respect the candor.

 Keys to Your Response:

- If you are now teaching, do a student survey. Select a few responses that highlight your better qualities and have them ready.
- Select student comments from your classes that indicate a positive relationship existed and have those ready to share.
- Leave the committee with the knowledge that students liked your class and responded positively to your work.
- Be ready for the reverse question, "what didn't your students like?"

 Motivating students of today is a difficult task. What do you do to inspire your students to actively learn in your classes?

There is almost always a question to identify what you know about student motivation. Students do not thrive in boring, uninspired classes. Moreover, those classes are exactly where discipline problems and public relations nightmares go to spawn. **TIP:** *I do not wish to raise your anxiety, but you <u>must</u> do well on this question.* Let us begin by examining some of the key variables that influence motivation. Each of the items listed below has a proven influence on student motivation. Once mastered, these variables can be woven into a good response.

VARIABLES OF MOTIVATION

- *Classroom atmosphere*: Is the class a warm, safe place for children to learn?
- Level of *active student involvement*: Is this a class where there are lots of activities and engaged student experiences?
- *Pace* of class: Do you have a variety of daily activities and events that move the class swiftly towards the learning objectives?
- *Interest*: Are the teachings and designed activities stimulating and connected to the real world of students?
- *Personal success*: Do students feel as if they are learning and attaining good grades? Do they enjoy a sense of accomplishment?
- *Recognition/reward*: Do you recognize students for good work and effort? Do the rewards have both intrinsic and extrinsic value for the student?
- *Level of concern*: Are students held accountable? Do students have to meet reasonable expectations on a consistent basis?
- *Engagement in purposeful, worthwhile experiences*: Do students see a reason for what they are studying? Is the effort they are putting forth seen to be worth it?

This is not the all-inclusive list of items and you can find other variables discussed in the literature. In your answer, select two or three of these variables and describe how you utilized or manipulated them to achieve positive results. Feel free to tick off the entire list at the beginning, but you only have time to expand on a couple. Again, supply practical examples wherever possible. This answer can be made even more powerful if you cite an instance where you had a poorly motivated group and used your knowledge of these variables to reverse the situation. Under-motivated classes are a common problem and the committee or principal will be favorably impressed to know you can deal with those issues when they arise.

Keys to Your Response:

- Learn the keys to motivation before the interview.
- Begin your response by providing a list of variables that affect motivation.
- Select two or three variables and provide a more in depth discussion of how they were used in your teaching.
- Provide classroom anecdotes to strengthen your points.
- If you can provide an example of a poorly motivated class and what you did to turn that situation around, your answer will be complete.

> *You are likely to have special needs students as part of your class. How will you alter your instruction to meet the needs of this group?*

Schools want to be confident that you know how to handle special education students who may be placed in your class. If you plan a career in public education, it is a near certainty you will encounter students with special needs. If questions are permitted, you might want to ask if the district has an inclusive education policy and how the policy is implemented in the school where you would be working. The interviewer will often give you valuable information regarding his or her expectations and the school model. You can use this when crafting your answer.

There are a few important points to make when giving your answer. First and foremost, all special education students have an Individualized Educational Plan (IEP) and this will be the controlling document in designing any aspect of the student's program. Describe the ways in which you try to individualize assignments, class-work, tests, and other class activities to meet the specific needs of students. It is wise to add that you do this for any child who might be struggling and not just identified students. Discuss your reliance on the case manager who can provide valuable direction and assistance. Additionally, there is usually a support class for identified students. Describe how you might work with the support class teacher to mutually guide the student through your class and towards successful learning.

When you have concluded this answer, you want the committee to recognize you as a teacher who will be responsive to individual needs and ready to use a range of professional services on behalf of students. Flexibility in both your teaching practice and assessment is an important quality to demonstrate because it lies at the heart of your ability to respond to the needs of special education students.

 Keys to Your Response:

- Ask the principal to describe the program for mainstream students in his or her school. Use this information to frame your response.
- Explain your knowledge of the IEP process and how it will be used to shape student programs in your class.
- Describe program or class modifications you have made for students and where you felt such individualization was appropriate.
- Convey your willingness to assume a collegial approach and use the case manager, support teacher, and other professionals to craft student programs.
- Illustrate your ability to be flexible and adapt your teaching to the special needs of students.

 What is the role of homework in your teaching and how do you organize it to support the learning process?

Homework has many purposes. With this question, the interviewer wants to know how you design and use homework in your class. Begin by asking if there is a school or grade-level homework policy already in place. If there is, ask for a description and use this information in your answer.

Your answer needs to begin with how you will use homework. **TIP:** *The current research identifies a variety of homework purposes. Include this variety in your answer.*

USES OF HOMEWORK

- The application of learning outside the class.
- The enhancement of speed and proficiency on new learning.
- The reinforcement of the degree of original learning.
- Preparation for new learning.
- The development of a home and school connection.

Use these ideas to frame the opening of your answer and illustrate the variety of ways you have used homework. For each use, give a practical example that clearly demonstrates your point.

It is important to outline the homework routines you commonly employ. Information such as the frequency of homework and typical length of an evening's assignment should be provided. The committee will have other questions. How does homework fit into the overall assessment pattern? How do you handle late assignments? Is there a role for parents in the homework process? These are important aspects of a teacher's homework practice the school needs to know.

Keep your answer upbeat and convey the idea that homework is a vehicle you use to promote student success and measure their understanding. **TIP:** *Most candidates will describe how they assign and grade homework. The better candidate will talk about how student performances on homework can help shape his or her decisions on future instruction.*

 Keys to Your Response:

- Ask if there is a homework policy in place and, if so, use its key points to shape portions of your answer.
- Cite several ways you use homework. Where possible, supply examples.

- Describe the homework policies and practices you use.
- Describe to the committee how you use homework to promote student achievement and shape future instruction.

> ### *Describe what relationship you would establish with parents.*

If there is one skill where principals want to be sure of a teacher's competence, it is in how he or she deals with the parents and community. In my review of hundreds of interviews, a majority had at least one question concerning parent relations. It is critical you prepare yourself to address the important goal of keeping parents informed and involved. Describe specific steps you will take to reach that goal and your answer will resonate well with the committee.

Communicate specific steps you have taken in the past to promote productive parent involvement. Do you send out newsletters or notices at the beginning of units? Do you call student homes to provide positive reports rather than just call when there is a problem? Are parents invited to special events in your class? Do you provide parent guides to help students succeed? If you have any well-received parent newsletters or other communications, you may wish to include an example in your interview portfolio.

Many textbook publishers have now included entire programs in their Teacher Manuals to promote home involvement. You can paint a picture for the committee of just how important enlisting parent involvement will be in designing the unit introduction and ongoing instruction. At the end of the day, the committee must see you as a person who invites parent participation.

 ### Keys to Your Response:

- Inform the committee that your key goal is to keep parents informed of the progress of their children and aware of any major events that will take place in your class.

- List specific strategies you have or intend to use to open lines of communication.
- Describe how you use materials provided by the publishers of textbooks and their <u>Teacher's Manual</u> to introduce units and design communication.
- Do not forget to put sample copies of any newsletters, information flyers, or other forms of parent communication in your portfolio.

> **How do you approach parent conferences?**

Parent conferences, when they do not go well, often end up in the principal's office as an even bigger problem. Successful conferences result in a parent's increased confidence in both the teacher *and* the school. Answer this question in a way that shows your understanding of this reality and your intention to take sufficient steps to maximize the probability of successful parent conferences.

The first question a professional teacher must address is who initiated the conference and why. In framing your answer, cite the necessity of good planning. You might use the following phrasing:

> *"I want to establish a purpose for the meeting, identify goals we want to achieve, and think of a means by which we can cooperatively work towards the attainment of those goals."*

Also, let the committee know you are a good listener who uses conferences to open dialog and promote communication. Show that you recognize parents as the ultimate consumers of your services and state how you would want to do everything possible to insure their satisfaction.

A key to a successful conference is the ability of the teacher to enter the meeting with an open mind and willingness to hear what *the parent* is saying. **TIP:** *Too often, teachers are more inter-*

ested in letting parents know why the teacher is right. That may be a teacher's goal, but I can assure you it is not the parent's goal. If you let the committee know you are aware of this problem, you have taken a large step forward.

Consider ending with this idea: What parents really want to know is that whatever they perceive the problem to be, you are willing to work with them to improve the situation and make the class better for their student. Sometimes this means both sides must do things differently, but if everyone is willing to work together, great results can be achieved. *With this approach you will be right and will have taken a long step in the direction of a new position!*

 Keys to Your Response:

- Begin by exhibiting your understanding of the importance of successful parent conferences.
- Describe how you will plan for a conference and determine the conference goals.
- Be sure the committee sees you as a good listener and cooperative problem-solver.
- Convey the understanding that you are willing to work with the family to make adjustments on both sides that will improve their child's experience.

> **Each year we give all students a norm referenced test called the Iowa Test of Basic Skills. How would you use the results of this test and what are its limitations?**

In years long past, this question might not have been asked. However, in today's world of increased accountability, standards testing, public scrutiny, and media attention, normed test results are a larger concern for schools. They want to know they are hiring teachers who can produce student results on achievement tests.

To answer this question, you might begin by describing how the results of achievement tests can be productively used and follow with a few of their limitations. Some general information to consider for your answer is listed below.

PRODUCTIVE INFORMATION ACHIEVEMENT TESTS CAN PROVIDE

- Individual achievement results and itemized inventories can be used to design specifically needed instruction the following year.
- Norm-referenced results will allow parents to see how their student's achievement compares to that of other students in their age group.
- A group analysis allows teachers to identify strengths and weaknesses in specific content areas for an entire class.
- A general report to the district and public regarding the general achievement patterns of students will be available.

LIMITATIONS ACHIEVEMENT TEST REPORTS MIGHT HAVE

- Because the tested group has moved to the next grade level, it is risky to use these results in making curriculum changes for next year's class. The new students may not share identical learning characteristics.
- Individual results, good or bad, are subject to more variables than just curriculum and teaching. In other words, the test may not tell the entire story behind student achievement.

When crafting your answer, describe how you approach the task of data analysis and what you would do to put those findings to work. If you have served on school-wide committees charged with the responsibility to analyze achievement test data, this is the place to include that information. As long as you convey a clear strategy to analyze and use achievement test results, you will be further ahead than many other candidates.

Keys to Your Response:

- Describe the productive information norm-referenced tests provide.
- Give some limitations of the test results and specify areas where teachers must take care in their analysis.
- Explain how you go about data analysis and where the gathered information is put to use.
- If you have past experience in this area, be sure to describe it.

> *This position calls for a results oriented person. Describe a project or school initiative in which you were involved and its most significant contribution.*

This is another question where a pre-thought answer will serve best. It is asked often enough that the small amount of time spent thinking this through could pay large dividends in the end. Even if this exact question is not asked, you may find an opportunity to weave in portions of the prepared answer somewhere else during the interview. In answering the question, some candidates like to begin with the following:

> *"I am certain my most significant project work and contributions are in front of me, however, there is one important initiative I can describe now."*

You need to know this opening is somewhat overused and the interview committee will have heard it at least once. Nonetheless, it is a sound introduction to your answer and may provide some improvement to your standing if only because it exudes self-confidence.

Take the time to decide on a good committee and project. Your example should include a basic description of the reasons your project was undertaken, the short list of steps and actions taken, and any useful outcomes achieved. What was your involvement? Be careful not to take too long with your answer. If you have worked on a committee or project similar to an initiative or program in the prospective school, that is the work to describe. If you can illustrate elements of your background that match what the district has underway, you add impact to your response.

Before you draw your answer to a close, be sure you have addressed the last part of the question that specifically asks how your work made a "contribution." This account does not have to be lengthy. Provide two or three outcomes or benefits that came from the project and draw your answer to a close. In this discussion, link the project's benefits to student interests wherever possible. Be careful, this is an answer that can easily wander off track if you are not watchful. Good luck.

 ### Keys to Your Response:

- Pre-think this answer and decide on a committee or project that had some significant contribution or merit.
- Select a project that is close to initiatives or values held by the prospective school.
- Give the reason the committee or project was undertaken along with a brief list of activities and your role.
- End with a statement about how this work was important to the students and benefited the school.

> *Tell us about the most significant professional article or book you have read in the last year. What was its impact on your approach to teaching?*

WOW! *What a question!!* I have seen this one stump some of the best applicants. It has literally stricken fear into the unwary simply because they never anticipated it would be asked. Fortunately, you will have read this book and will be ready to sparkle with a sharp, well thought answer.

One of the important professional qualities a school seeks in their candidate is a current understanding of pedagogy. They want to know he or she is a learner who constantly seeks improvement. This question helps identify that quality, yet it often strikes with such surprise the candidate cannot even offer an answer. Although not generally a knock out question, do not let a question like this take *you* by surprise. Begin now to read some of the journals and books that are available. As the question allows you to choose a book or an article, you may be best served by a current article. Look at people like Grant Wiggins, Roland Barth, Madeline Hunter, Jon Saphier, J. Howard Johnson or others in your field. Journals like the <u>Kappan</u> or <u>Educational Leadership</u> have many articles and are available in most libraries.

Remember to answer the second part of this question, " . . . how did it affect your teaching?" If you have an actual example of how you have read and used an article in your teaching, then by all means use it now and go to the head of the class! Application is the most important element of this question because it tells the committee you are a teacher who can put ideas to work.

A last thought is, there are interviewers who only ask for *books* you have read; articles are not an option. To avoid a problem, read a book as well. Two good choices would be, <u>The Passionate Teacher</u>, by Fried and <u>Awakening Genius in the Classroom</u>, by Armstrong. Both are just great books with lots of classroom ideas you can use. I assure you that if you can speak intelligently on either of these books, your committee will be most impressed!

 Keys to Your Response:

- Read some books and articles!
- Decide how the ideas presented by the author could be used in your class.
- **BEWARE:** You cannot bluff this answer, so use candor if you have not done the reading. Honesty will be far superior to a shallow answer that will not stand up to inspection.

> **Describe the ways you would include technology in your classroom to make the teaching/learning process more effective.**

Many districts have invested substantial sums of money in upgrading their technology. They will want to know the teacher they plan to hire recognizes the significance of technology and can put these tools to good use. It is the second half of this question, however, that embodies the essence of what the committee really seeks. Did you see it? It asks how you, ". . . make the teaching/ learning process more effective." The interview committee is not interested in your course background, familiarity with Microsoft Office, or other personal skills *unless* you can draw a direct link between those skills and the teaching of students.

Before you attempt an answer, you might want to ask the interviewer what kinds of technology are commonly available to classroom teachers and if specific district initiatives are in progress. This will do two things; provide an opportunity for the principal to trumpet some good things he or she has to offer and further identify the kinds of technology he or she wants to see used. With this information, you can outline how you might use the Internet, computer assisted learning programs, laser disc resources, test preparation programs, or other software designed for classroom use. Bear in mind that many classrooms have only one or two computers. If this is the case with your prospective school, you might describe how you could use these computers to create learning centers. Go on to explain how such centers can extend learning or provide remedial lessons. If you can talk about how you have already designed lessons to include technology, the power of your answer is dramatically increased. **WARNING***: Do not talk about a technology unless you are able to discuss it in at least some depth.* There is often a follow-up question based on your response and you would not want to get caught name-dropping. This is a good question for you to display your creativity and resourcefulness. Go for it and let the principal know you are the kind of teacher who is ready for the new century.

Keys to Your Response:

- Ask what technology is available and if there is a specific training program you will be expected to complete.
- Provide information on the technology you have already used in class. To add power, use specific examples to show where it was used to inspire children.
- If you have used learning centers, include information on how they were designed.
- If you are familiar with specific "learning-centered" software, describe it and tell how it was used.

> *Every school wants teachers who are great team players. Tell us about the personal qualities you have that make you a good team player.*

There are two goals you want your answer to achieve. First, you want to establish the fact you have sufficient human relation skills to work in a variety of collaborative settings with a diversity of groups – fellow teachers, administrators and parents. Second, you want to show you are the kind of professional who has the energy, dedication and drive to serve on a variety of committees and school initiatives. You are someone who will help the school move towards its vision.

Some of the characteristics that make a person a good team player include personal initiative, problem-solving, listening skill, leadership, persistence, task orientation and communication skills. Describe your qualities in these areas. Relate specific anecdotes or examples where possible. Make these points and you will have answered the question well.

 Keys to Your Response:

- Begin with a personal commitment to the collaborative process.

- List a few important qualities of a team player and describe how you embody those characteristics.
- Discuss a practical example of your collegial approach or team leadership. (If you have anything in your evaluations that compliment this skill, highlight it during the portfolio review at the end of the interview.)

> **If you are the person we hire, tell us what extracurricular activities you would be willing and able to advise or coach.**

This question is becoming much more common. Anyone who believes the role of a teacher is defined by just what he or she teaches in a classroom knows little about professional teachers or the needs of today's schools. A good school cannot run unless teachers are willing to involve themselves in the daily life of students and school programs.

This question provides a golden opportunity for you to demonstrate your utility and increase your value. All things being equal amongst the candidates, if you can coach, advise clubs, mentor the after-school homework group, or run the yearbook, your value rises significantly above those who offer only limited involvement. Make a point to ask the principal what kinds of activities are in need of help. Even if you have never been involved with some of the activities he or she lists, you can indicate your willingness to try. If the principal does not identify areas where help is needed, be sure to let him or her know of your interest in specific co-curricular programs in the event he or she should need an advisor in the future. **TIP:** *If this question is not asked, then provide this information at the end of the interview.* Do not leave the room without letting everyone know you are willing to help with after-school activities.

 ### Keys to Your Response:

- Begin with a brief statement that demonstrates you understand the wider range of responsibilities today's teacher must be prepared to undertake.

- Be ready to share a list of extra-curricular activities and areas where you have advised or coached.
- List areas where you have an interest but not yet had an opportunity to participate.
- Do not limit your answer to student-oriented activities. Building level committees, district initiatives, teacher workshops, enrichment teaching for parents, or anything that benefits the school or community can be included.

 As a new teacher, what kinds of support would you need from the administration and teaching staff to help you adjust to the new position?

Here is the **WRONG ANSWER**. *"Oh, I'm very self reliant and won't need much assistance at all."* Unfortunately, it is an answer too often given by the uninformed candidate. Quality teachers are not loners, so suggesting you need only "minimal" assistance generally fails to win points or enhance your standing.

This question affords you the perfect opening to introduce your interest in working with other teachers or building leaders and to find out more regarding specific expectations and department routines. Use it! Tell the committee you want to learn more about district initiatives and how you can involve yourself in workshops or other in-service activities. Talk about things you did to adjust to your last teaching or student-teaching position. Don't forget the students. You want help to learn more about the students in your class. Guidance will be an important resource. You may want to speak with the library staff or computer teacher.

You do not want to come across as a high maintenance pest with a question for every situation, but you need to appear enthusiastic and interested. Choose a few areas where you feel help would be legitimately welcomed, speak to those, and move on. If you have done your homework and know of a few district initiatives or workshops, now is the time to indicate your interest in learning more in those areas. Let this committee know you are interested in professional development and anxious to work with others in the school.

Keys to Your Response:

- DO NOT portray yourself as a loner in need of no assistance.
- Identify support members of the school who will be able to help you be a more effective teacher.
- Describe how you will look for staff development opportunities in the district and where you may want to spend time improving your craft.

> *It has been stated that good classroom management is an outgrowth of good teaching. What does that mean to you and how do you intend to put that maxim to work in your teaching?*

The district wants to know you understand the relationship that exists between well planned and successfully delivered lessons and the management of student behavior. Use this opportunity to describe how you plan lessons that command the attention and involvement of students. There are numerous classroom strategies relevant to this goal and you will have to select those best fitted to your philosophy and practice. A few ideas you might consider include: multi-activity lessons, use of real-world relationships to involve students, innovative use of technology, discovery lessons, novel learning activities, multiple assessments during the period, or other strategies that lead to high student involvement.

An important variable that helps maintain strong student participation and low off-task behavior is the principle of momentum. When kids are interested and busy, there is little time for management problems to present themselves. Similarly, poorly designed lessons lacking vitality and activity will invariably invite off-task behavior. The key is to engage students as quickly as possible and maintain that interest through the lesson. Once we get students started on an interesting activity, we need to recognize that it only has a certain life span. Eventually, children will tire of the work and become restless. Momentum is maintained by skillfully shifting students through a variety of activities AND having something worthwhile to do should they complete their task early.

If you describe your awareness of how class activities must move and how you plan for these transitions, you are a light-year ahead of most candidates. The pace of the lesson is maintained because the teacher reads the feedback signs from the class and makes continuous decisions regarding when and where to shift gears. Illustrate how you will do this in your class and see if there is not a higher level of interest on the part of your committee. Use your knowledge of good teaching to convince the interview committee you can create great lessons and go right to the head of the class!

 Keys to Your Response:

- Convince the committee you will be well planned and have a variety of activities each day.
- Give examples of innovative and engaging teaching practices. Use an anecdote to add meaning to your discussion.
- Illustrate ways you maintain class momentum, use transitions between activities, and pace the instruction so that interest is maximized.

 We will be interviewing a number of candidates. Why do you feel we should hire you as opposed to one of the others?

This is one possible end question for your interview. It is also another question where a lesser candidate might drop the ball with a weak, self-deprecating response.

> *"Gee, I don't know the other candidates and I wouldn't want to say I'm the best. I'm sure I could do a good job, etc., etc., pap and blather."*

Poppycock!!! We go for it right now! And your answer will be concise and hard-hitting. Avoid a reprise of the entire interview; everyone will go to sleep. Go right back to what you know the district values and tick off a few skills you have already shared that meet those needs.

"I know this school only wants competent professionals who can motivate students and competently deliver instruction. I have described my training in this area and outlined a number of strategies I know will make my classes a place students look forward to each day. We're going to learn and have fun doing it!"

Use a targeted approach and deliver short, powerful points to <u>underscore your</u> <u>match</u> to this job. Convince the committee right now that you are a child-centered, team player with instructional competence and high motivation. You have already given complete, powerful answers to each of the committee's questions, so you need only a few well-chosen refreshers at this point.

A good conclusion to your answer might describe your dedication and work ethic.

"Without knowing anything about the other candidates, I can only promise that you will not interview anyone who is going to work harder or be more concerned with the success of <u>every</u> child than I. I know I am the right teacher for this job."

Why is this, or something like it, an important last statement? What you say last is the one thing that *will* last. Last statements, if carefully crafted, linger in the air well after you have left the room. This committee must know and remember they <u>will not</u> meet a more dedicated or enthusiastic candidate than YOU!

 Keys to Your Response:

- Your goal is to ensure the committee recognizes you as a child-centered, instructionally competent, motivated team player.
- Provide short powerful statements on each of the above qualities.
- Remember to <u>match your answer to what you know are district needs</u> wherever possible.
- End with a strong message that will be remembered.

> **Is there anything you would like to say that we haven't already discussed? Do you have any questions for us?**

This is the other possible last question. Candidates often take a pass on this and say "no." **THAT IS A MISTAKE!!!** *You have a last chance to make an impression, use it.* If you did not have an opportunity to talk about your extra-curricular work during the question portion of the interview, describe it now. If you did not see a place to use the closing outlined in the preceding question, this is a great place to include that statement. Use the last moments of an interview to make lasting and memorable statements. Leave thoughts in the minds of committee members that will help you stand out when discussions begin regarding which candidates impressed them most. Make that candidate you!

Note how the phrasing of this question provides an opportunity for you to ask questions. If you choose to ask a question, take care that you do not fall into an open manhole and ask one that might diminish the good impression you have worked so hard to create. Here a few questions you should avoid at all cost.

- *Could you tell me how much sick time I am allowed each year?*
- *If I have to stay past the contract, will I get paid?*
- *What is the district's position on non-tenured teachers becoming a part of the Association?*

There are many other questions that convey the wrong impression, but I think you can see the point we are attempting make. **WARNING:** *Avoid asking any question that may suggest you are as interested in the contractual requirements of the teaching position as you are in the teaching of students.* Questions regarding your contract are best left until an offer is made. Inquiries about the district benefit package and salary are expected. Principals will not mind providing this information. In many cases, if you are to be strongly considered, the committee may discuss these topics without prompting. A last caution is to limit your questions to one or two. Choose what you feel you need to know now and save the other questions until an offer is tendered.

With the end of your answer to this question, the interview is over and you are ready to close the sale! This is the time to invite the committee to take a few minutes to review your portfolio. Be sure to tell them you will only take a few minutes and stick to that limit.

7
THE ELEMENTARY SCHOOL INTERVIEW

GENERAL INFORMATION

Interviewing for an elementary school position is different from middle and high school. Beyond the age difference, elementary school teachers are usually required to teach multiple subjects and manage the core curriculum in a self-contained setting. This carries a wider requirement for him or her to display subject area competence. In addition, class management, momentum and subject transitions become more complex issues and the committee will want to explore these in depth.

Within the academic curriculum, interviewers tend to focus on mathematics, reading and language arts more than science and social studies. The reason is twofold. First, these are the essential process skills that underlie the academic success of each student. Second, they are the areas most commonly assessed by state and national achievement tests. Those scores are often used as a barometer to gauge the effectiveness of the school and teacher. You should prepare yourself to answer in-depth questions in these important areas.

The area of classroom management likewise draws a great deal of interview attention. There is a little publicized fact you should consider. **FACT:** *More teachers lose their position due to poor classroom management than sub-standard teaching.* Of course the two areas are greatly interrelated. Good teaching materially reduces management problems and management difficulties interfere with good teaching. Prepare for questions about your classroom procedures, discipline, and student rules. Identify a few of your better strategies before the interview and have your ideas ready to share with your committee. When questions come rapidly from several directions, it is difficult to do your best thinking and craft high quality answers.

Elementary school teachers tend to be more involved with parents and community matters than do teachers at other levels. The interview committee will want to explore your feelings about parental involvement and how you might handle various situations. This is a subject on which you should gather a few articles and read the advice of others. Sound thoughts or strategies on this topic can go a long way to placing you at the top of the candidate pool.

Now that you understand a few areas where school committees or interviewers might focus their attention, take a look at some possible questions and how they can be approached.

SAMPLE QUESTIONS

> *There has been significant controversy regarding the whole language versus phonics approach to teaching reading. Which of these do you support and why?*

If you know the prospective school has already adopted and made a large investment in the whole language approach, you must be prepared to speak on the strategies and advantages of whole language. Conversely, if you know the school uses a basal, phonics, or literature-based approach, you need to speak about these programs with clarity and confidence. Before attending your interview, it will be wise to refresh your mind on the philosophies and instructional approaches of contemporary reading strategies along with their reputed strengths and weaknesses.

If you are not certain of a school's specific position regarding reading instruction, it might be best to take the high ground and provide an answer that incorporates more than one school of thought. You might also just ask the principal about the school's preferred approach before you begin your answer. Someone on the committee will probably give you useful information. Your question might sound like this.

*"In approaching reading, I know every child is differ-
ent and has a learning style that may be benefited by one or
both of these teaching approaches. I like using the whole
language approach in some instances because of its . . . (list
two or three strengths) but I also know how a strong understanding of phonics has been shown to help students with
essential decoding/encoding skills. Is there a preferred
approach here at this school?"*

After the committee has provided additional information on their
program, you are ready to fashion your answer around the teaching
approaches they identify.

Make no mistake, this is an important question and you need
to demonstrate your knowledge about current reading approaches.
You can expect one or two follow-up questions to explore elements of
your answer in depth. Do not be thrown off by such questions, it is
a good sign and generally indicates interest in your answer.

 Keys to Your Response:

- Investigate your prospective school and learn whether it is
  using a whole-language, phonics or blended approach. If you
  cannot get this information, begin by asking a question that
  identifies the school's practice.
- Discuss the relative strengths and weaknesses of each reading approach to demonstrate your understanding.
- Answer the question. Tell the committee which reading approach you support and give two or three reasons. If you
  have specific student performance or research information
  to share, this will add power to your answer.

> *If you were teaching the second grade, how would you prepare your room for the first day of school?*

This is a class management question. An important objective for your answer is that it underscores the invitational atmosphere you want to create in your classroom. You want to capitalize on the initial enthusiasm of students when they first return to school. There are numerous ways to decorate and organize a room and I am sure you have some wonderful ideas of your own to share on the topic. Below are just a few first day issues you can consider in designing your approach.

FIRST DAY OF SCHOOL CLASSROOM CONSIDERATIONS

✓ Student name tags and desk tags
✓ Welcome bulletin boards
✓ Posters with classroom guidelines
✓ Attractive subject area displays
✓ Textbook and materials arrangements
✓ Safety concerns
✓ Daily schedules
✓ Designated areas for handouts, homework, etc.

One caveat is worth mention. This is a question where most teachers can speak for some length of time. Resist this temptation. You want everyone to know you will make the room warm, inviting and organized. If you have previous experience opening school and have photographs, these might be placed in your portfolio to show at the end. Be upbeat and enthusiastic. Provide specific examples to punctuate the features you include, but take care not to make this a marathon answer.

Keys to Your Response:

- Let the committee know of your goal to create an invitational atmosphere and a room organization that works for instruction.
- List six or seven things you will do to your room to reach those goals.
- If you have prepared a room for the opening of school and have pictures, include a few in your interview portfolio.
- Watch your time.

> *Students at the elementary level are occasionally removed from class for a special subject or other worthwhile concern. How do you handle such "pull-outs" so the student is not left behind in his or her class-work?*

"Pull-outs" are an ongoing challenge in many schools. They create concern for all parties – students, teachers, parents, and administrators. Nonetheless, they are a fact of life and, if this question is asked, you can be fairly certain they are a part of this school. With this question, the committee wants to insure themselves of two things. First, that you are flexible and understand both the value and necessity of pull-out classes. Second, you will take appropriate steps to provide comparable makeup work and assist students who miss your class.

One approach to addressing the problem of pull-outs is to focus your strategy around the idea that each part of your lesson has a specific and observable learning component. As such, a handout or compatible assignment can be provided to help a student master the necessary objectives and receive full credit. You will also need a procedure to check student learning and identify where material may not have been fully understood. Your direct involvement will be needed in those areas.

Be sure you have answered both elements of the question before you conclude your response. It is very easy to simply launch into what you would do to help students make up the work. Your support of the other curriculum areas and a willingness to cooperate with other teachers is an important message and will clearly identify you as a team player.

 Keys to Your Response:

- Open by telling the committee that you understand the necessity and importance of pull-out programs.
- Outline the way your lessons will center on specific learning goals so compatible assignments or tutorials can be used to address each goal.
- Underscore how the creative use of time can occasionally free you up to directly work with a student who missed a class.
- Describe how you can work with pull-out teachers to minimize the impact of a student's missed class-time.

> ### *If you were given freedom to choose, how would you approach the teaching of spelling?*

There are many approaches to this important skill and you can be certain your school has something already in place. The goal of this question is to see how you prioritize and approach this curriculum issue.

There are two fairly common approaches to the teaching of spelling that you may want to address. The first approach is a curriculum defined by an established list of spelling words. These words may be part of a published curriculum, taken from a set of commonly misspelled words, or the school may have developed its own spelling list for each grade. In this case, you will need to identify ways you would teach these words and reinforce their use. Avoid the archaic "provide the list and test on Friday" format if you can. It is antiquated and been shown ineffective. The consistent use of words in student writing is accepted as a more effective way for students to "own" the spelling words they have learned.

The second philosophy or approach is to develop spelling through observation of student writing. In this case practitioners recommend that students and teachers identify words students misspell in their writing and prepare lists of required words for each student. Other methods identify words from student literature selections, self-selected words, or curriculum-specific terms. However the word selection is made, consistent attention to this competence will raise each student's awareness of the need for accurate spelling. The net result is better student spelling.

In your approach to this answer, make the committee aware of your emphasis on word usage as opposed to recitation. Students do not own the word until they can properly use it in their writing. Many teachers will highlight student misspellings in yellow (red is strongly discouraged, so pick some other color) and require students to fix their mistakes before a final paper is submitted and a grade given. Other methods can also be used to identify and fix a student's spelling errors, but a good answer will include specific ideas and details wherever possible.

 Keys to Your Response:

- Begin with a discussion of the current philosophies regarding the teaching of spelling.
- Choose a variety of strategies you advocate and explain how they would be employed in your class.
- Emphasize the necessity that students use correct spelling in their writing and explain a few ways you will promote that goal.

What literature do you recommend to third and fourth grade students?

If you hear this question, keep something in mind; the school does not plan to change its curriculum based upon your answer. All they want to establish is your familiarity with the good literature and authors available at your intended grade level. This is a fairly common question and it will be to your advantage to consider an answer before going to the interview.

You might wish to begin your research by reviewing the suggested reading lists available at local libraries and schools. If you can obtain a copy of your school's required or recommended reading list before the interview, you will see books and authors the school currently suggests. However, do not recite the school's list back to the interviewers. Use that information to frame your thinking on the subject. Select those authors and books you believe to be first quality. **WARNING:** *Be prepared to tell the interviewers **why** you like a particular author or selection.* I almost always asked that question and it was surprising how often the candidate was caught off-guard or stumbled for an answer. In some cases, the person merely knew the name or title and had never done anything beyond read the material. This mistake can be a costly oversight and may even remove you as a finalist. Do not allow yourself to be caught name-dropping authors or titles.

 Keys to Your Response:

- Pre-think your answer to this question. It is commonly asked and important.
- If possible, research the district and determine the kinds of reading they currently endorse.
- Be prepared to cite reasons for your choices of books and authors along with their benefits to children.
- DO NOT NAME BOOKS OR AUTHORS WITH WHICH YOU ARE NOT FULLY CONVERSANT.

> *Describe how you would teach a lesson on adjectives to a third grade class.*

You can substitute any curriculum area you like in this question. The committee wants to hear what a lesson will look like in your class. How do you determine your objectives? Do you have innovative ways to present information? How do your activities support what you want children to learn? Do you differentiate instruction within your class? Will there be learning stations? Do you use cooperative learning or groups? Will you use technology? How do you check for understanding? What do you do to monitor class/individual progress? This list can go on for some time, but I think you get the idea.

This is another question you can expect to encounter at an interview. Pick a solid lesson you have taught and look at the teacher actions that made the class successful. Keep in mind, the lesson referred to by the question pertains to teaching adjectives. How will you introduce this topic? What activities will you use to teach the necessary information? How will you check for student understanding? What re-teaching strategies will you have? It might be a good idea to have more than one approach to this lesson. Do not forget technology. If you know of websites, writing workshops, or other items, you can work them into your daily plan or learning stations.

You may not be able to fully pre-think an answer to a specific question such as this, but if you have a wide range of teaching strategies and activities available you will be able to make an excellent account of yourself. This is a great question on which to shine so let those creative juices flow!

 Keys to Your Response:

- Know the elements of good teaching and be sure to incorporate several strategies in your response.
- Identify more than one lesson design and describe occasions when each might be used. This variety will win bonus points.

- The question asks about adjectives. Tailor your response accordingly.
- Have a good sample lesson in your portfolio for review.

> ### How would you teach writing to second grade students?

This is an open-ended question and is so complex that entire books have been written on the subject. Recognize that the committee is interested in learning about *your* strategies to teach writing. What writing skills will you prioritize and how often will you include writing exercises in your curriculum? What essential skills must a second grade student master?

Begin your answer with a brief description of the writing process. **NOTE:** *Writing Process is a specific strategy and, if you are not aware of its steps, you need to acquaint yourself with those before the interview.* If you are familiar with writing process, tell the committee how you use this method in your teaching. Talk about the conferencing and editing strategies you employ. Describe the use of writing folders. Explain any efforts you consistently make to integrate other areas of the curriculum into student writing. Provide a description of how and where student writing will be displayed.

Writing rubrics are essential to the editing and assessment process. If you do not currently have a few rubrics for use in your class, you should get a copy of the holistic scoring rubric from your state. It will be an excellent reference. Most teachers employ a simplified rubric for everyday use. Remember that writing is a developmental skill and grade-level considerations need to be taken into account. This question asks about the second grade and you should keep your description of the instruction geared to beginning writers. Show the committee you have a measurable and objective means by which you and your students will assess writing performance and growth

Writing is a subject that often evokes follow-up questions. As in the other cases, follow-up questions are a sign of interest and another opportunity for you to showcase a depth of understanding. Stay calm and provide concise responses to the new areas the committee wants to explore.

 Keys to Your Response:

- Begin with background information on your knowledge of the writing process.
- Describe specific teaching strategies you intend to employ and say that writing will be included in your day-to-day instructional pattern.
- Describe your writing rubric for this grade level and describe how ongoing assessment will be used to determine learning and design instruction.
- Take time to speak about home communications and tell how parents might be included in the teaching of this process skill.

> ***Describe a difficult classroom management situation you have encountered and what you did to resolve the problem.***

There are two elements of your background the committee is reviewing with this question; 1) your judgment and 2) the diversity of classroom management strategies you employ. Although classroom management questions often refer to behavior, they can also refer to curriculum planning, class organization, or the management of materials. For this question, the majority of candidates will offer a description of a disruptive or defiant student who needed correction. In those cases, the solutions tended to reprise the traditional isolate, correct and reinforce strategy that has been given so often it has become redundant. It will be satisfactory, but such answers are predictable and fail to distinguish one's problem solving skill.

As this is an open-ended question and you are free to provide any response you choose, I would suggest you offer a more innovative scenario. Choose something that will demonstrate multiple dimensions of your professional ability. For example, have you had an experience with an unmotivated special education student where you worked collaboratively with the Child Study Team to find a solution? Did you encounter a highly gifted child who may have been frequently off-task due to boredom? Have you been involved with a "gang related" predicament? Look into your background for a problem that can demonstrate your child-centered approach and how you may have worked with others to resolve a situation. By offering something unique, you will stand out from the group and provide a more memorable response.

 Keys to Your Response:

- Choose an uncommon problem that allows you to showcase more than one dimension of your classroom management skill.
- Demonstrate your ability to work with others on difficult situations.

 If you were preparing an agenda for a meeting of the first grade team, what items would you include for discussion?

Principals and interviewers will want to examine the kinds of issues you feel need planning by your team and how you will approach the team process. They will want to determine if your management style will work and fit with other teachers at your grade.

In listening to answers that have been provided to this question in the past, many candidates tended to focus on the contents of the agenda. This is a sound place to begin. Consider opening with curriculum issues because these are always a worthwhile part of team planning. Within the area of curriculum you can include topics such as writing process skills, team math problems, targeted spelling words, or other issues you feel a grade level team should address. Additional agenda items would include the construction of a calendar of events, newsletters, or home communications. Special events need to be cooperatively planned. Based on your experience, you can add to this list, but you now have a good idea of what needs to be planned.

The committee will also be interested to know how you plan to work with other members of your team. This is an invitation to do what other candidates might fail to do. Move directly to how you will work collaboratively with the other teachers on your team. For example, describe how team members will have an opportunity to place their items on the agenda. Will you provide a form or visit people individually? Will you distribute copies of a "tentative agenda" in advance of the meeting? It is important for you to give ample demonstration of a cooperative approach to the process. Show the committee how you will make others an integral part of the decision-making that must go on each day. This information will take your answer to a higher level than the average candidate.

 Keys to Your Response:

- Discuss the need to include your colleagues in forming the agenda and how that will be done.
- Provide a list of the kinds of items that might be included.
- Describe your use of a tentative or advance agenda.

 What experience have you had with learning centers? Describe one or two you might recommend for a second grade class.

You can adjust the grade level indicated in the question to whichever grade you intend to teach as it will not change the nature of the question. The first part of the question is simple and a brief, direct answer will suffice. You have either had experience with learning centers or you have not. If you have not been directly involved with the concept, you should make that clear and then go on to describe what you have read or know about these centers. Even if you have not had direct experience, the second part of the question provides an opportunity to recover lost ground.

There are many fine articles on the topic of learning centers and it is not necessary to cram volumes of information in one answer. When you frame your response, begin with the purposes for which your centers might be designed. For example, your center might be designed to supplement instruction, provide remedial assistance, allow for enrichment activities, or target an area of student interest. Describe what the centers will ask students to do. Will it be an Internet exploration, question-answer program, a packaged software program, or some other activity? Tell the committee specifically what students will learn and how such knowledge is useful. Here is how a simple answer might be phrased.

> *"A great learning center for a fourth grade class deals with the issue of preserving animals that are considered endangered species. <u>An enrichment center</u> could focus on five or six different animals on the endangered species list such as manatees, California condors, wolves, or some other high interest animal. A student visitor to the center would choose an animal, review its profile card, visit a website, and complete a brief response form. Conservation efforts and clubs can extend the center's work to the real world. The student might even revisit the same station and learn about all six animals if there is sufficient interest and time."*

Before you conclude your example, be sure to identify one or two objectives you will want the student to master. You can also highlight any enrichment benefits, how the student work is related to the regular curriculum, and any other value you see for the student who visits this learning center. Have fun with this question. It is a great opportunity to showcase innovative ideas.

Keys to Your Response:

- Tell the committee of your previous experience or, if you have none, provide your knowledge of this teaching device.
- Give an example of a center you would use and include the learning goal, student activities, and assessments.
- Demonstrate the ability of your learning center to create value-added learning experiences for your students.

> ***How would you teach fractions to a class of fourth grade students?***

You can expect at least one question to explore your instructional ability on math concepts. Mathematics is one of the test areas every state uses to identify student progress and achievement. Principals are anxious to know a teacher candidate is well founded in his or her content understanding and instructional skill in this important area. In this question, we focus on fractions because it is a concept that so often presents difficulty to children. In analyzing student performance on norm-referenced tests, fractions are frequently listed as a weakness in the group cluster scores. Whatever math concept your question might address, let the committee know you are aware of the test history for students in that particular area of math.

Questions that ask you how you would teach a complicated concept are best attacked through the use of what is called a task analysis. A task analysis identifies all the key information and skills a student would need to successfully accomplish the new concept. For example, in order to divide fractions, students would need to understand multiplication, reciprocals and a few basic division rules. In your response to this question, open with a description of your task analysis for the specific fraction skill and list a few sub-skills you see as essential to student mastery. This question is complicated and you might ask the committee for a little time to organize your thoughts. Use your pad to jot down a few sub-skills and refer to them during your answer.

Once you have outlined your task analysis, provide an overview of how you would organize the instruction. Identify the critical concepts that require direct instruction, visual models, guided practice, and designed activities that will promote the all-important initial understanding. Tell the committee how you plan to use classwork and homework to advance proficiency and build retention.

The principal will take a keen interest in how you plan to check for student understanding. How often will you diagnose student mastery? What will you do to assist students that may be slow to grasp the concept? How will you extend learning and see that students recognize the use of fractions in their daily lives? Your approach to these questions will provide the foundation of an excellent answer. However, other candidates will also provide responses that satisfy the basic question. So, how can you furnish an answer that will stand out from the other candidates? Our goal is to provide a response that contains an element others might overlook. With this question we can accomplish our goal by speaking to every principal's concern – student test scores.

As you draw your answer to a close, tell the committee that you recognize how important it is that *students retain this important math skill* through the statewide assessment and into future years. Explain that once you determine the skill has been mastered, students will need consistent distributed light practice to maintain their speed and accuracy. Whereas practice would not be a nightly necessity, a problem or two would be routinely provided every week to ten days. When possible, fractions would be included as part of other problems so the concept would not always be seen in isolation. Most candidates will only talk about the initial teaching of this topic. It is rare for them to describe how they will maintain understanding and proficiency. By including this short discussion in the last part of your answer, you will show an added dimension and become more memorable. The more complete discussion of your short and long term strategies will have the committee's attention and endorsement.

Keys to Your Response:

- Identify one or two of the challenges you see to the teaching of fractions.
- Choose a specific skill involving fractions and describe your task analysis and sub-learning components.
- Illustrate how you would teach one or two components.
- Identify how you will insure that students are learning each essential skill.
- Propose a system of distributed practices and periodic test questions to maintain student understanding and test preparedness.

> *It has been said a teacher has 25 press releases at the end of each school day – one from each student he or she teaches. If true, what would those press releases say about your class?*

What will students really think about you and your class? Keep in mind that parents' perceptions of the school are a direct function of the messages children bring home regarding your class. If your class is dull, full of routine work, and uninteresting, this is what will be described at the dinner table each night. If, on the other hand, your class is full of interesting activities, lively discussions and warmth, this will also be communicated. With your answer, you want to describe an image of your class that will last in the committee's mind. There are many strategies and teacher dimensions that lead to classes kids love. Listed below are some suggestions around which you might arrange your answer.

I create a caring, warm and safe environment

Describe how you go about making each student feel special. Tell what you will do to make the child understand you truly care about his or her success in your class – not only academic but personal and social as well. Talk to ways you will build personal connections to each student so they will see you as a trusted mentor and support person. Provide a description of the physical environment that will promote warmth and student identity.

I use instructional strategies that promote interest and meaning

The committee wants to hear how you will make your instruction exciting for children, so give it to them with clarity and conviction. Talk about some of the novel ways you have presented past lessons or any unique teaching approaches. Describe something you consistently do to add interest and excitement into your daily teaching. Identify ways you link classroom experiences to the world around children. Explain your use of vivid hands-on activities to enhance performance and interest. A key to this question is a clear demonstration that you are a teacher who will use innovative and stimulating strategies in your class. Think about this answer. Even if this specific question is not posed, elements of your pre-thought answer can be included at other times or during your summary at the end of the interview.

As a way to make your answer stand out from others, you might identify a few ways you try to differentiate lessons for students with special needs. Students who find the class too easy or well beyond their understanding can become bored and have less than a first-rate experience. The material and activities for the day must be arranged in a way that is within their grasp. The short time you spend on this matter will tell the interviewers you consider all children in your planning and are willing to take the extra steps required to insure each child's welfare. What a great message! It is one many candidates will miss, so take advantage of the opportunity.

 Keys to Your Response:

- Describe your personal qualities and the elements of your teaching style that will create a warm, caring, child-centered classroom.

- Underscore the ways in which you will produce meaningful, high-interest lessons that promote student involvement.
- List a variety of ways you will differentiate instructional patterns and expectations to meet the needs of children with varied abilities.

> **How will you help students see the real world connections that relate to the concepts and skills you are teaching?**

This is an extension of the last question, but it often appears as a separate item. Everyone finds more meaning in new learning when he or she sees how the information relates to his or her own world. For that reason, you want the committee to know how you will make this connection come to life in your class. Field trips, outside speakers, real-life simulations, and technology can be powerful tools to link the daily learning experiences in your class to the everyday lives of children. Home projects and cooperative adventures can also add dimension to the teaching. Let your creative thinking flow and give the committee a real insight on how you will capitalize on this vital area of concern.

If you are just finishing student teaching, you may have already designed a sparkling unit that has lots of bells and whistles. Do not be afraid to refer to this and use it if you believe it highlights the dimensions we have listed. If you have had only limited classroom experience, think back to exciting units or lessons where you were a student and choose a few good examples. The provision of a practical example for each suggested method of connecting your lesson to the real world is a commanding way to make your point.

This is an important question and you should introduce as much enthusiasm into your answer as possible. Although the concrete suggestions you provide in your answer are important, the excitement you generate in your delivery can also help carry the day. Even the best teaching, if it is described in a lackluster manner, will be flat and unlikely to inspire the listeners. If it is upbeat and full of vitality, it can enliven the listeners. Excitement is contagious and your energy and enthusiasm will transfer to the committee.

 Keys to Your Response:

- Specify how you will connect the outside world to your daily teaching.
- Tell the committee you will use application-problems and provide a description of each lesson's purpose.
- Give a brief description of a high-impact lesson or unit you have taught.
- BE ENTHUSIASTIC AND UPBEAT IN YOUR DELIVERY.

CONCLUDING THOUGHTS

The topic areas an elementary teacher will be asked to address can cover a broad range of subjects and skills. This chapter has provided good examples of questions you may encounter and offered insight on the professional qualities a principal might want to explore. A thought to keep at the forefront of your thinking is this: **KEY POINT:** *the outstanding elementary school teacher is a highly child-centered, instructionally skilled and motivated individual.* If by the end of this interview, you have been able to convey a clear sense of these qualities to the interview committee, you will be one of those receiving final consideration for the post. Good luck in your search!

8
THE MIDDLE SCHOOL INTERVIEW

GENERAL INFORMATION

Middle schools have a different setting and mission from elementary or high schools. The student population is comprised of students who are going through puberty, sociologic conflict and a myriad of other transitional dilemmas related to the move from childhood to adulthood. As a result, every teacher interviewing for a middle school position must be aware of these issues and the means by which he or she can help students through this difficult time. In your interview there will be a variety of questions designed to test your knowledge of student-related issues, unique middle school programs, and instructional strategies appropriate to the age group.

Some states offer certificates for middle level teaching and their teacher training institutions offer degree programs tailored to the middle school teacher. Colleges and universities in other states, have insufficient course work to offer even a minor in the middle school area. If you seek a middle school teaching position, you will do well to undertake college coursework that focuses on the specific education of middle school students. If you live in a state that offers middle level certification, obtaining the formal certificate is even better. If no certificate for the middle school is offered in your state, check with your county or state offices to determine what grade levels your certificate covers.

Regardless of the amount of formal training and coursework in middle level education, you will be able to present a strong middle school candidacy once you have reviewed and mastered the information provided in this chapter. Two of the more important factors to your interview success will be your enthusiasm to teach at the middle school and the confidence with which you answer a few basic questions. Let's look at questions you might be asked at a middle school interview.

SAMPLE QUESTIONS

> ### *What do you consider the mission of a middle school?*

This question can be tricky because there seems to be differences of opinion among schools as to how their specific mission is described. You can help yourself by conducting advance research on your school. If the prospective school has a handbook for parents, it will generally contain a mission statement and information on that school's specific goals for students. Although those statements are not the *real* answer to this question, they can help identify things the school sees as important.

The following list contains a number of central tenets that contemporary middle schools generally find important. You should use these ideas to help organize your thoughts and prepare persuasive answers to the questions you will be asked.

CENTRAL THEMES OF TODAY'S MIDDLE SCHOOLS

- Students must receive a strong foundation of core knowledge.
- Students must be proficient in process skills such as reading, mathematics, writing, and problem solving.
- Students need help to cope with the social and emotional changes that occur during this time of life.
- Middle schools must help cultivate the growth of strong character and ethical values
- Students must be exposed to a wide variety of learning experiences and content areas
- Students must see and experience connections between what they are learning in school and the real world around them.

This is not intended to be an all-inclusive list of items middle schools might identify in their mission, but rather a selection of points around which there seems to be consensus. There is one other point on which most middle school principals agree and you should be aware; *the primary role of the middle school is not to "prepare students for high school."* If a middle school is effective in carrying out its mission, students *will be* prepared for high school, but middle school goals encompass a much wider vision.

As you shape your answer, open with a short discussion of some of the above listed central themes. Add an illustration supporting each point you make to help clarify your meaning. For example:

> *"There are a number of areas a middle school mission might address. One of the first items would be a school initiative that attends to the social and emotional development of adolescents. Advisory programs are a good example of this kind of program. Developing teenagers can derive significant benefit from an ongoing mentorship with a responsible adult in the school."*

This statement immediately places you on target with a central issue and establishes your knowledge of an important middle school program. Before concluding your answer, add a statement on the necessity of taking the specific nature and characteristics of students into account before settling on a final mission statement. Let the committee know that after you know the children better, you will be able to expand on these initial thoughts.

The committee wants to know if you understand what makes a middle school setting unique. Whether you are able to frame the quintessential mission statement is not the important matter. Show that you know a few central issues and link them with specific ideas or programs. Do this and you will more than satisfy the committee. **CAUTION:** *This is another question that can elicit a long answer.* For that reason, I suggest you carefully time yourself and avoid rambling. If you discuss two or three recommended items, you will have convinced everyone of your middle school knowledge. That is your goal.

 Keys to Your Response:

- Conduct advance research on your school and review parent or student handbooks for key information.
- Review the central themes listed in this section along with others you find and open with a brief discussion of a few well-supported ideas.
- Link specific practices or programs that relate to each central theme you offer. This will help establish your familiarity with the middle school mission.
- End with a statement of your commitment to work with the total child and not just subject matter.

> *The literature on middle schools frequently talks about the importance of "character and values" education for students at the middle school level. If you had to choose one over the other, which do you feel is more important – teaching academics or teaching values and character?*

Oh brother, this is a loaded question! Interestingly, it was one of the first questions asked of me at an interview for a principal's position in New Jersey. This may initially appear to be one of those mousetrap questions where whichever component you choose, you run the risk of being in error. The quandary created by this concern has caused a number of candidates to get tangled in their logic by trying to divine what the committee wanted to hear. Attempting to discern what the committee wants to hear is almost always the wrong approach and likely to lead down the slippery path of destruction. **KEY STRATEGY:** *In all cases and for all questions, it is best to* *provide your best, <u>most honest</u> response and let the chips fall where they may.* Even if a committee member should disagree, you will be respected for your candor and the courage of your convictions.

How then do we approach *this* question? The important thing to remember is that you are applying to a middle school. Therefore, you can be certain the issue of character and values is seen as critically important. The reason for such emphasis is an assumption that people make important life decisions based on their system of values and in keeping with their character. During the middle school years, a significant portion of a person's character and values matures. Failure to provide proper priority to these important areas can lead to calamitous results. I once had a candidate take an interesting approach in responding to this question by turning it around and asking the following question of the committee.

"You ask an interesting question, but what would we prefer? Would we rather a student who knows the significance of the Stamp Act but develops into a sociopath or would we prefer a well valued, interested student who missed the significance of the Stamp Act and had to learn it later?"

This response was clearly oversimplified, but it made a very effective point and had a number of committee members nodding in agreement.

In your answer it might be best to lead with the importance of values and character with the addition of a strong statement in support of a solid academic program as the other main ingredient in a first class education. No school worth its certification can ignore its central responsibility to provide a sound, visionary academic program, but a school would be remiss if it provided an academic background without sufficient attention to the other issues of developing adolescents.

Unless stated as an either/or question, this approach allows you to have your cake and eat it too. The trick is to emphasize your understanding of the importance of both dimensions. If, as is the case here, the question is posed as an either/or situation, then you must choose the dimension you feel most represents your philosophy. The point can be successfully argued either way. Many principals might suggest that the values and character side of the issue is often safer at a middle school interview. It is extremely important that sound values, healthy habits of mind, and honest character are reinforced during the adolescent years. Ideals such as perseverance, tolerance, promptness, responsibility and patriotism are all recognized as worthwhile values for young children to cultivate. You can conclude by returning to a statement on the difficulty of the question because both issues are so important.

 Keys to Your Response:

- Begin with a short discussion of how and why you see each issue as critically important.
- Be sure to emphasize the role values and character play in the decision-making processes of developing adolescents.
- Select the dimension that best fits your philosophy and expand on why it would have central significance in your teaching.
- Conclude by returning to your view that middle school children have both an academic and values-rich education.

> **What important qualities should new teachers have to effectively work on a teaching team?**

In other words, will your personality and teaching style fit the other personalities on the team where we intend to place you? This is an important issue and, in some cases, can even be a knock out question. The school must hire someone they are confident will be a good fit to the personalities, work styles, and educational philosophies of the other teachers on the team. Even if you convince everyone you are a good candidate, if someone suspects you will not be a good team member, it is unlikely you will get the position.

Below are a few qualities that lead to solid professional relationships and around which you might frame a good answer. You will need to reflect on your own personality, philosophy, and working style to identify how you personify these characteristics.

BUILDING PROFESSIONAL RELATIONSHIPS

- **Flexibility**. Can you adjust your thinking to the wide variety of ideas, plans and positions sure to arise from other team members?
- **Chemistry**. This is the element of a personality that is concerned with one's ability to get along with others. Do you have the "people skills" required to make everyone feel at ease in your company? Can opposing ideas surface and be discussed without tension? This is one of the more important dimensions because poor chemistry can undermine your effectiveness in other areas.
- **Perseverance**. When there is a project or team initiative in progress, will you have the endurance to see the project through to its full conclusion?
- **Problem solving**. Teams need someone with good, fresh thinking who can formulate multiple solutions to problems and discern a sound course of action.
- **Listening and communication**. These skills are listed together because listening is an important *part of* communication. One must communicate clear and concise thoughts, but he or she must also be a good listener when the ideas of others are presented.
- **Reliability**. If you are supposed to be at a team duty or meeting, will you be there on time and ready? If you have something to do, will it be well done and ready? The team needs to feel confident they can depend on you.

There are other qualities and you may wish to add a few of your own. Choose several qualities for your answer and provide an in depth discussion of how they apply to you. Where possible, a personal anecdote or story can add depth to your response. If you have had experience working on a team, you can talk about the positive elements of that work. If you can tie specific experiences to one or more dimensions on the list, you will improve the impact of your statement.

End with a more general discussion of your commitment to the team effort. Your dedication and energy can make a good team even better and you will give 110% to achieving that goal. If you can convince the committee members you are someone who works well with others and everyone will be happy to have you on their team, you have answered the question well.

 Keys to Your Response:

- Begin by mentioning four of five of the personal qualities required for good team participation.
- Choose qualities where you are strongest and provide a short discussion of each. If you can describe a practical example, do so.
- End with a statement about your commitment to the success of the team and the diligence you will use to make that success a reality.

> *What do you see as critical issues a good team of teachers must consider during their common planning period?*

The principal wants to determine what you know about the function of a team and the team planning process. Many schools already have specific planning formats for the team meeting period and you may want to ask if this is the case at your school. You might also ask how often and how long teams meet each week. The answers to these questions can dramatically influence your answer.

COMMON THINGS A GOOD TEAM MUST PLAN

- Curriculum placement for academic units.
- Interdisciplinary concerns or integrated teaching
- Field trips and related outside experiences
- Advisory activities
- Homework
- Class test schedules
- State-test preparation
- Monthly calendars
- Parent communications
- Student related problems
- Social events

You can begin with an overview of as many of these items as you can remember. If in the past you planned additional issues you felt were important, include those as well. There is no minimum or maximum number the committee needs to hear. Once you have provided the comprehensive list, select one or two items and describe how the planning would be approached. For example, illustrate your approach to planning an interdisciplinary unit. Identify activities you would place on your calendar and how they would advance the unit goals. Discuss how guiding questions would be developed. You should provide sufficient detail for the committee to see you are someone who thinks things through, but do not go on so long that snoring begins in the gallery.

End with a statement that you understand how the team is in charge of the entire educational program for all its students. Trust that the committee will ask follow-up questions on any areas they consider important or where they want more information about your answer. Try to relax – if you have reviewed our discussion of this question, you will give an excellent answer.

Keys to Your Response:

- Start by providing a list of items the team should attend to in the planning process.
- Select a few items from your initial list and add an in-depth discussion of how the planning should take place.
- Provide examples of your work on teams in the past.
- End with a general statement on the necessity of good planning and the team's responsibility to plan the entire program for students in its charge.

> ***What do you know about advisory programs and their importance to the success of a middle school mission?***

Advisory programs are most often designed to meet the need for adult mentorship in the lives of adolescent students. The original advisory concept assigned small groups of students to a single adult who would meet with them on a regular basis to provide assistance in both their academic and social lives. J. Howard Johnson of the University of South Florida speaks with compelling logic about the need for adult mentors to developing adolescents.

Many middle schools now have advisory programs and it was one of the strong recommendations made by the Carnegie report on middle schools in the book, <u>Turning Points</u>. **NOTE:** *If you have not read <u>Turning Points</u>, I would recommend it to you now.* It is full of good information that can be used in any middle school interview. More importantly, some candidates will not have read this important work and your possession of such knowledge will significantly advance your standing.

The school's handbook or brochure will generally tell you if the school currently has an advisory program. Use this information in your answer and move your standing up another notch. Such an answer might sound like this:

"I saw from your parent handout you already have an advisory period here at the school. I am excited about that prospect because I will be able to use this time to . . (whatever you will do). . . for students."

If you are unaware of the presence of an advisory program, you will have to speak in more general terms.

"I realize that an adult guide or mentor is essential to the sound growth of adolescents. If I were to have a group, there are several things I would like to do with my students. First, I would set aside a time each day to check student organization and readiness. Second, we would hold discussions on issues that affect student life. Third, I would facilitate guided activities to help my advisees shape those all-important adult values and character."

As you can see, this answer chose three or four of the items from our list and simply described a possible teacher action. You need not have a shopping cart of ideas included in your answer. Three or four well-chosen, supported activities will be more than sufficient. Below are a few activities with which advisory teams have traditionally been involved. Look them over and select those most familiar or important to you. Whatever you choose, you should be prepared to speak on that item in a little depth.

ADVISORY PROGRAM TOPICS

- ✓ Academic planning and assistance.
- ✓ Social problem solving.
- ✓ Values clarification discussions.
- ✓ Test preparation.
- ✓ Goal setting.
- ✓ Self-esteem builders.
- ✓ Organization skills
- ✓ Team building
- ✓ Leadership

There are many more activities to consider. Books have been written on the topic. The principal and committee simply want to know if you understand how the advisory time can be effectively used. If you have already worked as an advisor in your school, by all means, underscore this experience and describe the work you did. Practical experience will go a long way towards a solid answer on this question.

Now – let's take another step to set you apart from the pack. An excellent way to end your answer is with a declaration of how you intend to be an advisor in each of your classes and all during the school day! There are always opportunities in the class, hallway, cafeteria or after-school where you can be a good role model, teach courtesy, help a student solve a problem, or conduct some other advisory function. Point out how it will be your goal to work with students in an advisory capacity at all times, not just in the period set aside for that purpose. Unless you are interviewing with the five pillars of granite, you can sit back and watch smiles come to the faces of those around the table. Add all this up and you have a solid answer!

 Keys to Your Response:

- Begin with an overview of your knowledge on the subject of advisory programs.
- Describe a variety of items that might be included and then focus on two or three about which you have specific knowledge or experience.
- If you have already been a part of an advisory program, cite one or two positive experiences.
- End by describing how you will act as an advisor to students at all times.

How familiar are you with interdisciplinary units and how would you plan to include these learning experiences in your class?

Integrated instruction or interdisciplinary units have become more common in the pedagogy of middle schools over recent years. The concept refers to units of study where two or more disciplines are combined in way where the concepts learned in one discipline are similar enough to enhance those taught in the others. For example, the English class might study, <u>To Kill a Mockingbird</u> while students learn the rules of evidence and argument in their Social Studies class. The concepts of evidence and argument are then employed to analyze the legal case presented in the novel. Students see how their work in Social Studies can be applied to a new situation in a different subject area; thus both disciplines receive benefit.

Note, however, the question also asks you to discus how you would *plan* interdisciplinary teaching in your class. Many candidates will talk about the formal team planning process that takes place. Below are a few actions you might list for the committee.

PLANNING CONSIDERATIONS FOR INTERDISCIPLINARY UNITS

- Describe how you will use the team-planning period to develop curriculum maps or teaching calendars.
- Find places where the curriculum overlaps and integration makes sense.
- If necessary the time frames for units can be adjusted to facilitate an interdisciplinary unit.
- Develop guiding questions and group activities that will direct the student learning and unit goals.
- Describe what assessment will take place at the conclusion of the unit and how you will introduce quality control into the teaching process.

These planning steps constitute a good answer and one a knowledgeable candidate will offer. The better candidate, however, will add ways he or she integrates learning from other subject areas into his or her *daily* teaching routines. If you are to be on a teaching team, you are likely to have weekly discussions about the topics being taught in other classes. Let the committee know how this will allow you to use this information to draw connections from other classes to your subject area. This response might sound something like the following:

> *"The large interdisciplinary units are excellent and I am eager to see what my team has planned in that area. I should add, however, that I like to integrate other subjects with my own on a regular basis. For example, when I am teaching students about conservation, I often ask them to research some of the literature and history of this movement to reinforce the real-world purpose of what we are studying. This involves both social studies and literature so students can see how different subjects can work hand in hand."*

If you can provide an example such as this you will receive maximum bonus points and place your answer ahead of many others. If you think about it, I am sure there are things you have already done to integrate different subjects in your previous teaching. Add those strategies to our other ideas and move to the top of the candidate list.

NOTE: *If you have a well-planned interdisciplinary unit already completed, include a one-page summary in your interview portfolio.*

 Keys to Your Response:

- Open your answer with a description of what you know on the subject of integrated or interdisciplinary instruction.
- Provide an example of a unit you have already taught.
- Describe the planning that is necessary to create a new unit.

- End by demonstrating how you independently integrate instruction in your regular class.
- DO NOT FORGET TO ADD A SAMPLE TO YOUR INTERVIEW PORTFOLIO.

> **Research has suggested that the climate of a room significantly affects student learning. What do you do to have your room tell every student this is a place where learning takes place?**

This question actually has two parts and most candidates only address one. First, there is the physical aspect of your room. Second, there is an emotional climate that you create through day-to-day interactions with students. Both are important in promoting a positive feeling tone in your class and should be addressed by this answer. Take care to address both elements of the issue.

It is easier to attack this question by addressing the physical aspects first. You undoubtedly have numerous ways you like to arrange your room and everyone is somewhat different in this regard. This is fine because the "what" of how you organize your room is not as important to the committee as the "why" behind those decisions. You can open your answer with an overview of how you intend to use bulletin boards and what they will do to enhance the feeling tone of your class. Are you familiar with "interactive" bulletin boards? If not, there is a wonderful book entitled, <u>Interactive Bulletin Boards as Teaching Tools</u>, by Joan Dungey. It is a part of the Analysis and Action series by NEA and I recommend it to your attention. Describing an example of an interactive bulletin board will, as TV's Chef Emeril might say, "kick your answer up to heights unknown."

There are other considerations you must take into account such as topical displays, posting of student work, posters, class management guidelines, and so forth. Add other ideas on how you support the academic and social goals you have planned. If you have read the chapter on how to construct an interview portfolio, you will remember we advised you to include pictures of your room.   The physical aspects of your room will supply a sound foundation to the photographic part of your portfolio presentation. An important element of this response is to clarify the logic behind any actions you take to create an invitational, high-energy atmosphere for your room.

The second element of this answer should address the emotional climate you intend to create in your class. The best approach is to use short, powerful ideas that lead to a student-centered environment. You might discuss how you will maintain student dignity, self-worth, and fairness in your teaching. Underscore how you will model a sense of inquiry and vitality in your work. Let the committee know you understand that students must feel cared for, safe, and respected if they are to function at their best level. Armstrong's, <u>Awakening Genius in the Class</u> is an outstanding discourse on this topic and will fill you with marvelous ideas to share. Whether or not this question is asked, you should read Armstrong's book because it will make you a better teacher. As you underscore these big ideas, provide one or two strategies you will employ to build strong student relationships. The specifics of your teaching practice are of keen interest to the committee. Provide what we have outlined and you can be assured of a winning answer to this important question!

 ### Keys to Your Response:

- It is best to start with the physical aspects of your room. Be sure to include the "why" for what you plan to do. It will create impact.
- Move directly to the second portion of the question, the emotional atmosphere. Talk about your methods to create student warmth.
- If possible, conclude with one or two of Armstrong's dimensions for creating the joy of learning in the class.

> *What role, if any, would parents have in the education of their student in your class and what would you do to produce and nourish this relationship?*

Experience and research suggests that as children move through the grades, parent participation in the school tends to decline. Middle school is traditionally a time when parent involvement begins to diminish. Parents stay fairly close to the child's school experience through about sixth grade, but in grades seven and eight you may experience reduced parent participation. Some parent detachment is acceptable because students at this age begin to seek more independence, but too little parent involvement is not good. This question requires you to address specific ways you plan to increase parent communication and involvement. Most teachers already have a few strategies in this area, but here are other ideas to consider.

TEACHER ACTIONS LEADING TO INCREASED PARENT INVOLVEMENT

- *Class letters* are mailed at the beginning of units to provide information on upcoming lessons and what parents can expect at home.
- *Phone calls* are made to alert parents to positive class behavior or results. Parents like to receive "good news" phone calls. These can take under a minute, but their effect is most encouraging.
- *Parents are invited to special class presentations or luncheons* that the students organize. If students are to make special presentations of projects to the class, parents can be invited for the day.
- *Special evening programs.* Cooperative programs that involve both parents and students such as "Math Counts" or "Science Night." can be organized. One teacher had the parents come in for a *Chef's Training* class that the *students taught!* The stomach is a wonderful tool for winning friends – just ask me.

- ***Student letters to parents.*** The students write a short letter about the exciting things they are doing in class and mail it home. If e-mail is available, this can be another avenue.
- ***Great Work Postcards.*** The teacher keeps a pack of post cards handy and when a student contributes something special or completes exemplary work, the card is filled out and mailed. The students can make out two or three self-addressed cards that you keep. This reduces clerical problems.

I think you can see how this might work. Show the committee you have some ideas and ingenuity of your own to increase parent involvement. Let the committee know that you recognize the role of the parent in promoting the success of the student in your class. Tell them you plan an active role for the home to promote their student's success. You need parents to stay on top of homework, communicate noteworthy issues taking place in the child's life, serve as a class parent or chaperone, offer positive reinforcement to student performance, and keep education high on the priority list of household concerns. Such goals are easy to recite, but do you have positive ideas to offer that promote these kinds of relationships? It is the presence of a specific plan with well-formulated ideas that will move you ahead of other candidates who only just "talk the talk."

At this point there is a lot of information to consider so look at how an answer might be phrased. This will help you shape an answer of your own should the time come when you are faced with a question on this topic.

"I realize these things are sometimes easier said than done, however, I do have some strategies in mind that will promote my effort to involve parents. First, I want to establish a pattern of positive communications to put the parent at ease in my company and with our contacts. For that reason, I call each parent at least once a quarter with a positive report regarding his or her child. Second, I always have a few special classroom events where students do presentations and parents are invited to attend. Additionally,

I involve myself in the PTO and try to work with parents where they see me in a different role.

As with many of the suggested answers, a short and succinct method of listing two or three clear points is employed. The ideas are practical and designed to maximize the affect on your audience. Your answer might well employ different parental-involvement strategies and you should only include those you have already used or intend to use in the future. The important thing is to let everyone know you are attentive to the teacher's role in this effort. Your concluding statement need only restate your commitment to a strong home and school bond. Leave the committee with the understanding that you will take specific steps and work with all parties to help every student succeed.

 Keys to Your Response:

- Begin with your recognition of the trend for parent involvement to decrease as students get older.
- List the kinds of activities you and your team might collectively take to maintain parent support and participation.
- Identify ways you will establish a positive pattern of communication with each home.
- Conclude with a restatement of your understanding of the important contributions parents can make in the success of their student.

> *Research has indicated that many disaffected students were "turned off" to education during their middle school years. What will you do to prevent this from happening in your class?*

Should you uncover the definitive answer to this question, please e-mail me immediately so we can co-author a book and make a great deal of money. The complexity of the issue notwithstanding, this question is one that principals like to ask. H. L. Mencken once wisely said, *"To every complex problem, there are a host of simple solutions – all of which are wrong,"* and so it is with this question. Nonetheless, it is on the table, and we must deal with it by presenting ways to keep our class interesting and motivating for everyone.

Through the work of Hunter, Saphier, Gardner and others, numerous strategies have been identified that increase student interest, participation, and purposeful learning. This question presents an opportunity for us to stand on the shoulders of these giants in education and use their ideas to describe how we will create the kind of classes students want to see. Because there is so much information on this topic, candidates may be tempted to offer an extensive list of ideas. Try to resist this temptation and instead employ a more focused, thoughtful approach to your answer. The last thing you need is a marathon answer that wanders all over the lot and leaves everyone with the question, "What was that all about?" **KEY STRATEGY:** *In most cases, consider ways to make your point with precision as opposed to volume.* A good answer can have both brevity and power if you speak in specific terms. To accomplish this, phrase an answer that contains three or four central ideas around which specific activities can be designed. It might sound like the following:

> *"I realize middle schools have a special responsibility to maintain student involvement. In my view, some of the things most responsible for student detachment from their education include, 1) a sense that school has nothing worthwhile for them, 2) dull and boring classes, and 3) a continuing series of negative experiences or failure in past classes."*

This approach breaks the question into three very important, manageable pieces. You should go on to address each piece and offer a strategy to limit the identified problem. *An exhaustive number of strategies for each issue is not warranted.* One or two will convince everyone you are on the right track.

> *"We can address the boring, uninspired lessons about which students continuously complain. I try to overcome*

such teaching by breaking my lessons into several different parts with hands-on activities that keep students moving and involved. I use this variety to maintain teaching momentum. Beyond that, novelty, humor and high-interest instructional episodes are used to focus their minds on the joy of learning.

Use what you know from your experience, methods courses, or workshops to bring out your best thinking and spice the answer with specific teaching examples whenever possible. **TIP:** *When you show your portfolio, come back to answers like this and use one of your unit designs to place an exclamation point to the end of the presentation.*

Many applicants will focus all their attention on the instructional side of this issue. They miss the all-important affective dimension of this problem. We can do better. **Students do not become disaffected** *only* **because of uninspired teaching**. Very often, there is also a history of school failures, a lack of school involvement, a sense of isolation, and a perception that teachers do not care that alienates students from their school. This problem was the third element mentioned in our introductory statement. Be prepared to talk about how you understand the importance of these affective variables and identify a few concrete teacher actions you will undertake to minimize their negative effects. For example:

"We all know how consistent patterns of failing grades can de-motivate students and shut down their enthusiasm to learn. My goal is to consistently promote and reward the legitimate success for every student. I not only attend to this in the area of course grades but in the student's self image as well. We will use success as a springboard to higher motivation."

You may feel other dimensions more accurately describe your philosophy and approach, but these few sentences have such a powerful message you will leave the committee with a good feeling about your keen insight on this issue. In any middle school interview, you are well served with that result!

Keys to Your Response:

- Begin the response by defining a few central *causes* of disaffected youth in school.
- Provide two or three solid, *consistent strategies* you will use in your classes to minimize the ability of those causes to present themselves.
- Close your answer by describing specific ways you intend to *address the <u>affective issues</u>* that underlie disaffected behavior.

> ***How much homework should middle school students receive and what are your practices in this area?***

In this question, the committee wants to see how your views on homework align with theirs. A prime issue raised by the question is how you will use homework to promote the learning process. Since almost every school has a position on this subject, it is wise to ask if a homework policy is currently in place for the school or team. If the answer is yes, ask the committee to describe its components. Perhaps your advance research will have provided information on the school's approach to homework. Whatever the source of information, try to align your answer to practices that fit the prospective school's system.

If there is no existing policy or your question to the committee fails to bring out useful information, you can begin with an explanation of homework practices you have used in your prior experience. Include such things as how often you provide homework and the kinds of assignments you make. It will be important to let the committee know you have used homework for a variety of purposes. There are numerous ways homework can be used which include:

USES OF HOMEWORK

- The provision of practice and extension of learning
- The refreshment of past learning
- The preparation of students for new learning
- The application of learning to the real world
- The reinforcement of newly learned concepts.

In addition, be sure to describe how you will work with the other members of your team to plan a student homework schedule that is reasonable and worthwhile. The committee needs to see how you are a candidate who recognizes the value of a team process. This is an excellent place to showcase that part of your teaching style.

Now look at how we can make your response stand out from the other candidates. Add the dual themes of home projects and differentiated assignments. Student projects are appropriate to this discussion because, in most cases, the bulk of work is done at home. As a parent, I can tell you the home-project is the bane of almost every household. Those Saturday crises trips to the library, craft store, rag shop, and other places you hardly knew existed represent one of true "joys" of parenting. Nonetheless, outside projects can be a wonderful addition to your curriculum and provide golden opportunities for students to excel who may not be particularly strong with tests and quizzes. You should come to the interview with a successful project already in mind. If so, use it now. In your discussion of projects, there are a few important concerns to clarify.

TEACHING CONSIDERATIONS FOR HOME PROJECTS

- You must space projects so they do not over-burden the student or home.
- You must plan all large assignments in consort with your team to insure students are not faced with multiple projects at the same time.
- You must take steps to insure that work is designed at the correct level of difficulty.

- You must provide clear project designs and ample time in class to personally guide the work of students and benchmark their progress.
- Include design strategies that will promote student success.

Some teachers like to add a presentation of the project to the class or at a full team gathering. If the school has a strong technology program, you might integrate the project presentation with computer education and have students construct a "power-point" lesson. Consider whether you will invite parents to a showcase of the good student work. Before leaving this topic, make a strong statement as to how you make *all* projects relevant to the curriculum and worthwhile pursuits. **TIP**: *If you have an outstanding project that was already used, describe its key details on a single sheet of paper and put it in your interview portfolio.* Even if this question is not asked, you will have a chance to present the work at the end of the interview.

A second strategy that will add dimension to your answer has been around since Horace Mann, yet it is amazing how infrequently candidates suggest its use. That strategy is the "differentiated assignment plan." Think about how you can design assignments to include varying levels of difficulty and length so as to meet the individual abilities of students. This pattern does not need to be used for every assignment, but during each unit you can provide a few times when *tailored assignments target the specific learning levels of students* in your room. Perhaps you will want to grade some of these assignments as a take-home quiz. You can allot more points to the difficult assignment and somewhat fewer points to the easier tasks. Nonetheless, every child has an opportunity to add points to his or her grade. This is an excellent way to adapt your program to special education students or others who are just "strugglers."

   Keys to Your Response:

IMPORTANT: *Do not underestimate the significance of this question. Homework is a critical element in the learning experience!*

- Find out if the school has an established homework policy.
- Discuss the different purposes homework has in your class.
- Describe key elements of your homework practice and indicate how homework is related to the curriculum.
- Provide an overview of how, where, and when you use projects. Give an example of a high impact project you have used or planned.
- Discuss the use of differentiated assignments to meet individual needs.

> **Bullying is a very common problem in middle schools. To students who are on the receiving end of abuse, it is educationally debilitating. What role do teachers play in minimizing this behavior in students?**

This problem has reached epidemic proportion. Schools are highly focused on the issue and a question in this area can be expected. Open your answer by firmly stating **RULE #1: *The role of the teacher is central to the solution of this problem.*** The teacher must take the initiative to prevent and defuse unkindness in the classroom. *Bullies are present in every school and rely on the failure of adults to intervene.* Explain how you will exercise a policy of zero-tolerance to unkind behavior. You will put a stop to put-downs, insults or other cruel remarks. Courtesy and supportive behavior will be modeled, required and expected from everyone. Tell the principal you intend to be at your door between classes to watch hallway activity (a favorite place for bullies to harass others) and put a fast stop to any questionable behavior.

Go on to talk about the values and character issues you would like to address during homeroom, advisory or activity periods. Most middle schools have time when teachers and teams can work on social issues. Discuss how your team can work to teach students the important values of tolerance, kindness and mutual support. There are many commonly accepted values to employ and you can be sure the committee will be interested in hearing about those that interest you. A proactive approach to prevention as opposed to just a reactive response will work well in this answer.

Close with a statement about your concern for the disastrous consequences that can arise when harassment and bullying are left un-addressed. The newspapers have chronicled a number of tragic school incidents in the last few years. The single common element in those students who perpetrated these tragedies was a profile of disaffected behavior at school. These students had themselves been harassed and/or ignored. Illustrate your knowledge of this fact and provide assurance this will not be the case in your class.

 Keys to Your Response:

- Begin with a statement of your awareness regarding the issues driving the problem and tell how the teacher must play a key role in their prevention.
- List specific steps you plan to take in your class to promote an atmosphere of respect and safety.
- State your recognition of harassment as a central element in the recently reported school tragedies. Add your intent to reduce this problem in your class.
- Provide assurance that you will be anxious to assist in any school-wide or team efforts to reduce student harassment or unkindness.

> **Describe how your grading practices can be adapted to make adjustments for students with special needs.**

Begin by deciding what this question asks and what it does not ask. It asks about your grading policy for "special needs students." It does not ask you to describe your entire grading policy. The committee wants to determine how flexible you are regarding special needs students and the variety of grading strategies you have at your command.

First assure everyone you recognize the multiple factors that must be considered before selecting an assessment strategy for a special-needs student. You need to speak with the case manager about the student's Individualized Educational Plan (I.E.P.), level of expectations, specific goals that have been set, and the kinds of assessment practices used in the past. It is best to develop a mutual strategy with the case manager so he or she can reinforce your efforts.

From this point you can catalog the evaluation strategies you use. For example, there may be authentic tasks, conferences, drawings, small group projects, open-book and open-notebook questions, or other options that allow the student to demonstrate his or her proficiency. Suggest that in some cases a student goal may be fulfilled by his or her mere participation.

The important message to convey is how grading will be completed with expertise and compassion. Each student will be viewed individually and progress will be measured in a realistic manner.

 Keys to Your Response:

- *Focus* your answer on flexible, wide ranging grading practices for special needs students.
- Outline how you and the case manager will determine when and where modifications to grade practice are in the interest of the student.
- List a variety of grade strategies you employ and how you design an assessment plan in consort with the student's case manager.
- End with a commitment to view each student as an individual and utilize a compassionate and realistic approach to determine his or her grade.

CONCLUDING THOUGHTS

This chapter has a great deal of information. It is impractical to attempt full recall. Once you have read the information, go back to the **Keys to Your Response** segments and revisit those ideas. If you are unclear of specific points, you can reexamine the more complete discussion in the text. If you have a computer, you may wish to select a variety of questions and enter them with the main elements of your answer. These can be printed out later to provide a study sheet.

Middle schools are exciting places with high-energy students and innovative programs. When you interview, understand the committee is looking for a person who is committed to the middle school and the young adolescent student. If your heart is really at the high school or elementary school, you should focus your attention on interviewing for those jobs. Some candidates apply for middle school positions because they need a job and a middle school teaching position was listed in the newspaper. Since their certificate covers the middle school, an application was sent. For those who follow this strategy, there is **BAD NEWS**: *A person's true feelings and lack of commitment to middle school education will always come across during an interview and one is not likely to do well if that happens.* On the other hand, if middle school is just what you want, make sure the committee is aware of this preference. Enthusiasm coupled with a few good answers can make all the difference. So, you now have the skills – *Get that Interview and Get Hired!*

9
THE HIGH SCHOOL INTERVIEW

SECONDARY SCHOOLS

This chapter provides questions commonly found in interviews for a high school position. Please note that the issues or qualities addressed by these questions are not exclusive to the high school, but are ordinarily of slightly higher interest to committees at the secondary level. The items included in this chapter came from several sources. Many are questions I used when I was an assistant principal for curriculum and instruction. Interview sheets supplied by high school principals also added material used in designing the sample questions. In selecting questions I focused on those most frequently asked or likely to be part of an actual interview. I have also included a few more difficult questions to help you prepare for the possibility of an in-depth interview.

When interviewing for positions at the secondary level, one must recognize the relative isolation of teachers in the high schools of today. High school teachers are organized into departments of specific teaching disciplines. Teaching teams are rarely used and opportunities to engage in mutual instructional activities such as common planning time, integrated instruction, and collegial work sessions are uncommon. When teachers do work together, it is generally an informal arrangement between colleagues rather than a regularly scheduled meeting time. The relevance of such isolation for the interviewee is that he or she must demonstrate a willingness to reach out and establish fertile lines of communication with other professionals. School officials will note your spirit of team involvement.

High schools have a higher interest in identifying your subject matter knowledge and instructional skills. You are likely to encounter somewhat fewer child-centered questions than were present in the elementary and middle school interviews. This statement should not be construed to mean that high schools are *disinterested* in student-centered teaching. In the elementary and middle school chapters, many extremely compelling answers in the affective domain of teaching were offered. You will almost certainly find these ideas useful in high school interviews because every principal wants teachers who genuinely care about students. Simply realize that high school questions are more often focused on content and instruction.

SAMPLE QUESTIONS

> **Seniors who have already been accepted by colleges often believe it is no longer necessary to put forth their best efforts. What steps would you take to prevent this letdown?**

This is a common problem in today's high schools and the wise candidate is ready for questions on motivation. A brush up on variables that affect the area of motivation can be found in the works of Madeline Hunter, Carol Cummings or Jon Saphier. A number of their ideas will be presented later in this discussion. An excellent way to address questions on high school motivation is to illustrate specific strategies and class activities that will promote student engagement in your course.

You might consider opening with a description of a class discussion on the differences between extrinsic rewards such as college acceptance and intrinsic rewards such as personal understanding and process skills. This introductory discussion can be used to set up a teaching episode where you will raise student awareness of how process skills learned now will transfer directly to success in both college and later life.

Place the committee on notice that you see the problem presented by the question as an outgrowth of weak motivation rather than student complacency. By recasting the question in this way, you will have seized control of a more manageable response strategy. **KEY STRATEGY:** *In cases where an answer offers a variety of good steps one can take, offer the plan in a series of hard-hitting, concise statements.* Below are a number of variables that improve student motivation. Choose two or three you feel fit your philosophy and style, then construct a response with this compact, hard-hitting plan of action: identify the strategy, give a brief discussion of its importance and provide a practical example – one, two, three, and move on. We will look at how this might sound in a moment, but below are some variables affecting motivation that you can use when you shape your answer.

<u>VARIABLES THAT AFFECT MOTIVATION</u>

- ✓ High interest lessons or activities
- ✓ Strong purpose or real-life connections
- ✓ Atmosphere of encouragement
- ✓ Reward
- ✓ Feelings of Success
- ✓ Accountability
- ✓ Choice

Now we can look at how a sharp response is shaped around the variable you chose.

"To keep students involved toward the end of the year, I like to motivate them through the use of choice. This is a strong motivator because seniors seem to like the idea they are directing their lives and have control. I accomplish this in two ways. First, as a group we look through the last units of the book and select the ones that seem most profitable to study and prepare for college. Second, I supply a number ways students can study the information and a few activities from which they can choose. Through having control, students are required to act in a more "college-like" way and assume more personal responsibility. That's the goal!"

Did you see it? One, two, three, and move on. Look at the answer again, and you will be able to identify the three-step tactic described. Its strength comes from the concise manner of presentation and its focus on the issue presented by the question. Keep in mind the committee asked about college bound students. Extra effort was taken to relate the answer directly to that group.

Think through some of the outlined suggestions and you will see how the variables of motivation can be manipulated to work together like a toolbox of different but complementary teaching devices. You may wish to conclude by noting how no single strategy works in every case or with every student and, as you come to know your students more fully, you will be in a better position to select those practices most likely to match their profile and needs.

 Keys to Your Response:

- Note the differences between extrinsic and intrinsic rewards and state your intention to increase student awareness of the importance of amplifying skills that transfer to college work.
- Review a variety of motivation variables and select two or three you feel offer the most impact. Use our 1, 2, 3 delivery strategy.
- End with a statement of your need to know the students and select variables that fit the characteristics of those individuals.

 Describe your grading practices and how you determine a student's marking period grade.

This seems like a straightforward and easy question, but watch out! **WARNING:** *This is a potential knockout question and, if answered wrong, can seriously damage your chances of securing the position.* Why? Controversy over student grades is an issue that can cause public relations problems faster than almost anything else you can name. Grades determine class rank, sports eligibility, graduation, summer school, and possible college acceptance. Grades are a very serious business at the high school level. An administrator wants to be assured you are not an inflexible, die-by-the-test monolith that will have his or her phone ringing with irate parents at the end of every marking period. Candidates should prethink an answer to this question and avoid the possibility of a shallow response. A question on this topic has a high probability of appearing on your interview.

When you reply, it is best to provide the broad variety of assessment measures you plan to use in your classes. Talk about the need to focus on achievement and positive reinforcement. Speak of the specific ways you might modify grades for included special education students. Describe how you will provide additional time or assistance to struggling students and list steps you will take to help students succeed. It is always a good idea to articulate the idea that when students are unsuccessful, you share in that lack of success. For this reason, every step possible will be taken to prevent student failure. The key to this answer will lie in the energy you place in making students successful. You must demonstrate sufficient flexibility to meet individual student needs at all academic levels. A student-centered approach to grading is essential to a successful response.

 ### Keys to Your Response:

- Avoid taking this question too lightly. It can be a knockout if answered incorrectly.
- Include a very wide variety of assessment measures so students of all ability levels have a chance to succeed.
- Discuss how you will use flexibility in your practice when dealing with special needs students.
- Let the committee know you take student failure personally and intend to do everything possible to help each person succeed.

> *If we examined your class grade distribution in your last school, what would we find?*

Here is a variation of the last question, but it is interesting enough to include. Many an interviewee assumes the real question being asked is "how many failing grades were given in his or her classes?" **AVOID THE TRAP!** *Do not focus your answer on the low end of the grade spectrum. Balance your response so that you address both ends of the grade curve.* Of course, the committee will be concerned if you tell them there was a ten or fifteen percent failure rate. In fact, such an answer might even knock you out of the race. But as we noted in the last question, high school grades affect many things and strong student performance is a central expectation of principals. *The more astute candidate will focus on the <u>upper end</u> of the grade scale and speak to how students not only pass, but also prosper in his or her class.*

The answer to this question need not be long. In fact, precision will help maximize the power of your response. There is nothing like a long-winded philosophy speech on academic rigor to put the committee into its own state of rigor — rigor mortis. Long-winded philosophy speeches are generally considered the private domain of superintendents on the opening days of school. You need only demonstrate concern for student success and mastery. Commitment to the pursuit of a strong academic program *and* student mastery is a central goal of this answer.

A good place to start any answer on grade distribution is to draw a distinction between the traditional bell-curve model of grading and the approach you will take in your class. When the goal is student mastery, there is an expectation that students *will* learn what we teach. In successful teaching, a grade distribution curve will have a sharp skew to the right because of the high success rate. Look how you might phrase this concept:

"In education we have for many years accepted the bell shaped curve as the norm for grade distributions. In my class, the classic normal curve is not appropriate. First, a perfect bell shaped distribution often describes the results of random activity. My teaching and student success is certainly not a random activity. Second, I take the necessary steps to insure that the majority of my students are learning enough to be at the B or A end of the grade spectrum. Moreover, I am unhappy if anyone attains only a D or F level of proficiency and diligently try to keep those numbers at zero."

In these half dozen sentences, you have answered the central issue posed in the question. The principal sees a teacher with a sound philosophy and commitment to student achievement. But we are not quite done.

Now move to the second phase of this answer and provide practical measures to meet this goal. A teacher can take numerous steps to promote successful learning. Select a few from your background and provide one or two anecdotes that show how you have maintained high student performance in the past. That statement can sound like this:

"Each quarter I included an outside assignment that was directly linked to material we had learned in class. The projects were divided into two levels of difficulty and students could choose one that met their needs. So students knew exactly what was expected and how to achieve an "A," I supplied rubrics, anchor papers and models to demonstrate precisely what I wanted. As projects went forward, I held conferences and provided specific feedback to help each student remain on track. The conferences also let me know who needed more help. By using this approach, I have consistently been able to help students attain a legitimate high level of success."

This answer draws power from its compact nature. The projects allow students to use and demonstrate proficiency with relevant new learning. The statement provides *five* separate student success builders of the project in one short statement. To form your own answer, you must think about what you have already done and identify teaching strategies that have been successful. Specifically, what have you done to help students succeed? Some possibilities include before or after-school help sessions, peer tutoring, outside credit, retakes on work that was below a B, alternative assessment strategies, take home quizzes, or the inclusion of other grade boosters. Any of these can be woven into a response for this section.

Close your answer by returning to the underlying concern of the question, student grade-success. Provide assurance that you will do everything possible to ensure that students will meet high standards of performance and you look forward to their success. This puts the final touch on a good answer.

 Keys to Your Response:

- Begin by describing how the normal bell-shaped curve will look different in your class because of the high success rate of students.
- Offer one or two descriptions of things you do to ensure student mastery and grade performance.
- End with a statement of commitment to student success.

 How would you modify your teaching if you were told the school intended to adopt "block scheduling" the following year?

Some high schools use block scheduling and you should be prepared to address how you would teach in that design. You should be able to find out if this is the case in your school by conducting research on the district prior to your visit. If you are not conversant on the topic of block schedules, by all means get to the library and review the literature. Before you begin your answer, ask what kind of block schedule the school has in mind. For example, the school may have you meet ninety minutes every day for a half-year, or you may meet every other day for two periods, or perhaps another design is in place. You will need to know the timeframes under which you will be expected to teach. They each have their strengths and weaknesses.

How you craft instruction will depend on the length of the block, but you can assume the time to be approximately double that of a standard class period. In a ninety-minute class, you will have to alter the amount of lecture time you provide and space a wider variety of activities. The expanded timeframe allows you to increase the number of student activities you undertake and increase the amount of time students will devote to each. Students might also engage in more complicated, hands-on problems. In science, complete laboratory experiments and post-lab discussions can be accomplished in one session. Students will now have time for both guided and independent research. Students will be able to keep reflective journals. You will have time for individual student conferencing. Depending on the subject you teach, you can decide how to include real-world learning activities. When phrasing your answer, give the committee a snapshot of what *might* be done in a given class session.

> *"For example, with this longer time I might have several specific learning objectives and organize the time into two or three sub-blocks. Each block would contain some information, guided instruction and a hands-on activity. We would conclude each learning segment with a short check for understanding so I will know if the material has been mastered or needs an additional attention."*

This answer design provides the committee a general framework that will be easily understood. Add a general statement that catalogs a variety of activities from which you will select those most congruent to the objective you have for the day.

"When I plan for a longer class, I would select activities based on what students need to learn. In the past I have used, ... to build student understanding."

This question affords you a chance to showcase a variety of teaching ideas and describe exciting projects you have in mind. Your enthusiasm and creative ideas are what count. Even if your understanding of block schedules is somewhat imperfect, you can more than compensate with a great set of classroom teaching ideas. Make the most of this opportunity and go for it!

 Keys to Your Response:

- Begin by asking what kind of block schedule is under consideration.
- Discuss how a block format will impact your teaching decisions.
- Give a sample lesson design to be used in your class.
- Catalog a set of classroom strategies from which you will choose those that best fit the objectives.

 Let us suppose you have a student who has been frequently off-task throughout the year, rarely prepared and often treats others with disrespect. Today, when you ask the class to work in small groups, this student leaves his seat and seems to be disturbing another group. When you ask him to please return to his own table and begin the assignment, he blows up and tells you, "If you ever assigned anything worthwhile, maybe I would work. You just want to get on my case and I'm sick of it. My group doesn't want me and can do it without me!!" What do you do?

This is an example of a "situational question" and represents a type that is becoming more popular with interviewers today. Such questions are gaining in popularity because they test a candidate's ability to deal with difficult, real-life circumstances. There are now interviews where *all* the questions are situational. As a high school applicant, you should be prepared for one or two questions in this format.

In this question, the committee wants to know what you're going to do when "the shooting" starts in your class – and it always does. Begin your answer by stating how you *will not* engage the student in a power struggle or high-tension dialogue. This statement may sound similar to the following example.

*"Before giving my response on what I will do, perhaps I should tell you what **I would not** do. These kinds of confrontations sometimes arise and we all wish they wouldn't. I have an entire class that will be watching and I am not going to add any energy to this argument by trying to publicly debate the student. My first actions will be to remove energy and diminish the obvious anger."*

There is a very important phrase in the wording of this question: *". . . frequently off task throughout the year."* Do not let this phrase pass without answer. Principals hope no teacher would allow the situation described in this question to go on **all year.** You certainly would not and you should make that clear. You would have been working with this student on his off-task behavior, consulting with the home, and involving other building professionals long before the situation reached this level.

Confronted with this explosive predicament, the committee wants to know what you will do *now*. Unless you are planning for a short interview and early lunch, sending him to the principal's office is not an option. A first step you might offer would be to separate this young man from the group while you provide the remainder of the class a "do now" assignment or some other independent work. You must limit your first discussion with the student because you still have a class to teach, but the first order of business must be to *restore order* and *defuse the situation*. Let the committee know you will approach this volatile confrontation with a calm and deliberate voice. Since working with his study group was one of the student's problems, you should offer a few thoughts as to what might effect a better situation. Changing the student's location, using a learning center or briefly working together with the entire group to get the student re-started can do this. Let the committee see how you will act as a problem solver. You will need additional time later for a longer discussion to address courtesy, behavior expectations, and the deeper problems presented by this outburst.

Later in the day, when there is more time, you might involve the parents, a counselor, or a social worker. There are two issues around which additional work is required: 1) the relevance of the assignment and 2) his feelings of alienation from the group. Whether this student felt the assignment was interesting should not be an issue for negotiation. Students do not get to choose whether they will work based on their level of interest. Certainly, you can review the kinds of work required and look for ways to add interest, but that is not the issue with this student. The real issue is acceptable class behavior and mutual respect. Stay focused on those points.

With regard to the student's feelings of alienation from the group, you can interview the other students and obtain valuable insights. Use this information along with the services of other professionals to deal with the human-relationships problem that appears to exist. Given this question's information, the student's group alienation may be a long-term issue in need of counseling. Immediate steps you might consider include changing his group, changing the location of the group, or increasing the amount of supervision you provide.

This question allows you to display your ability to manage student behavior in a difficult circumstance. The committee wants to know you will not lose your composure and you have the insight required to handle real problems. It is a great opportunity for you to shine, so make the most of it.

Keys to Your Response:

- Begin by focusing your initial effort on defusing the situation and avoiding a power struggle.
- Make sure the principal knows you would not have let this situation get so far out of hand before you took proactive action.
- Identify your strategies to restore order and stabilize the situation.
- Discuss your intention to involve others in creating an appropriate long-term solution.
- Close with your approach to improving the class environment that contributed to the outburst.

> *One of your female students tells you that boys have been making fun of her and, in low tones so that you couldn't hear, made suggestive comments. They also write filthy things on the desks. She is not exactly sure which boys, but it is coming from the back. What are you going to do?*

This is a real doozey! It is another of those popular situational questions to explore how you might handle a potentially explosive situation. With sexual harassment suits at an all time high and getting higher, school districts are increasingly concerned with teachers and how they handle such problems. Take care in giving your response as this is another case where a wrong step can damage your candidacy.

KEY STRATEGY: *In all situational questions, take at least a few seconds to diagnose one or two important underlying issues and then design a strategy to address each one.* In this scenario we have a complaint of sexual harassment from a female student. Let the principal know you will take action immediately. Indicate your intention to first review board policies or school guidelines for any required actions. There are likely to be board policies but they may be very general, nonetheless, you must first follow any practice the school district has in place.

Unless district policies provide specific direction, you should take a few immediate steps. **KEY STRATEGY:** *Situational questions are often best answered with a set of decisive and concise steps.* Principals will be impressed if you can offer a few concrete actions you plan to take. For example, look at the following:

> *"After I review existing policies I would implement a three step plan of action. **First,** I will assure the young lady that I take her comments very seriously and will get this behavior stopped. This means I must investigate the young girl's statements as completely as possible <u>that day</u>. Further action will depend on what I find and if I can identify any parties who may be involved. **Second,** I will place any parties to this behavior on notice that their actions will not be accepted and I must discuss appropriate consequences with the principal. **Third,** I will document the incident with my findings and actions, place them on file and notify the principal so he or she is aware of the incident."*

You may feel inclined to offer a different set of actions that suit you better, but I think you now see how to phrase the approach. Be advised that this particular answer lends itself to an important follow-up question; what will you do if you are unable to identify specific individuals in your investigation? This circumstance will require you to take additional steps. You will need to provide a clear and firm restatement to your classes regarding your stand on the harassment of others. Second, you will need consistent vigilance and watch this situation closely over the coming weeks. In fact added vigilance will be required in either event.

It is essential that you let the committee know of your intention to make the principal aware and keep him or her fully informed. Tell everyone that you are willing to participate in any additional steps regarding home notification. In my experience, I like teachers to call the parents, let them know of the complaint, and assure them that action is being taken. **BEFORE** a teacher makes any home contact on a matter like this, he or she must speak with the principal and allow him or her to offer advice. You can also speak with the nurse or school social worker to set up at least one session of counseling.

The committee needs assurance that you understand the gravity of sexual harassment complaints and will act in a way that protects the student, the school, and the teacher. A good answer to this question will secure confidence that you are a person of good judgment. Judgment is an important teacher quality and it is not one often taught in college.

 Keys to Your Response:

- Establish your understanding of the gravity of such allegations and your intention to take action.
- Review any board or school policies to identify required action.
- Tell the principal exactly what steps you will take immediately to protect all parties.
- Assure the principal of your willingness to participate in follow-up activities with both the home and any recommended counseling services.

CONCLUDING THOUGHTS

During the chapter introduction, it was suggested that high school teachers should expect more questions on content area expertise. Yet, this chapter contained no questions that directly quizzed subject competence. You will find these questions in the coming chapters that relate to specific subject areas. You should carefully read and consider these chapters, they are important to your preparation.

High school positions carry unique burdens because the age group is older and more socially advanced than elementary and middle school students. Generally, high school students are not as easily motivated as the younger students and require a higher level of sophistication in teaching material. On the other hand, good teaching is good teaching – at any level. If you can offer a sound command of the principles of learning, content area knowledge, and good classroom management, you will be an excellent candidate. The trick is to make the committee understand that *you have* these skills. Armed with the information in this and the following chapters, you will be more than ready to do just that, so take charge and let them know who you are!

10
LANGUAGE ARTS/ENGLISH QUESTIONS

GENERAL INFORMATION

At the secondary level, Language Arts classes have significant importance to principals and interviewers for two important reasons. First, such courses deal with communication and literacy skills essential to successful living. Second, the content of subjects in this area strongly transfers to the SAT and other normed tests. Student performance on these tests is frequently used as a measure of how well schools serve their community. Interviewees can count on a thorough set of questions to explore their philosophies and classroom strategies. Test preparation is another important concern and questions in this area can be expected as well.

Almost all states require students in public schools to take four years of coursework in English. Therefore, be prepared to answer questions about your ability to teach students at all ability levels. It is not uncommon for student skills in reading or writing to range from two years below to two years above grade level. Your capacity to diagnose and deal with both skill deficiencies and enrichment teaching will establish you as someone who can teach a wide range of abilities. It is important that you convince the committee or your ability to educate students at all levels.

A fundamental theme that should be consistently expressed through your answers is that of literacy development. Emphasize the aspects of your teaching that deepen and strengthen student ability to interpret the world and communicate in an intelligent, competent manner. Literacy is a process skill that is essential to a well-formulated educational program.

SAMPLE QUESTIONS

> **What do you know about our state standards in Language Arts and how would you ensure that your students reach these standards?**

Nearly every state has established written standards in language arts. It is considered essential that students develop necessary literacy skills to promote a successful adult life. General goals might include proficiency in written communication, critical reading, analysis, speaking, and listening. One of the New Jersey standards provides the following direction:

> *Students need opportunities to help them discover the inner joy and self-awareness that evolves from reading great literature and communicating at high levels in speech and writing.*

I offer the phrasing of this particular standard because it represents an excellent way for you to begin an answer to this question. In one sentence, you have addressed several main goals of a literacy program as well as the affective domain of learning.

If possible, get a copy of whatever state document is in place for your state. If you are not sure where to find them, go online and log onto www.taskstream.com and go to the "Standards Wizard." (Appendix B) Every state is listed, and there is pertinent information of every variety. Familiarize yourself with each requirement and any specific performance indicators attendant to student mastery. For example New Jersey has five separate standards with a set of specific proficiency indicators for each standard. To support teachers, there is an accompanying *Frameworks* document that outlines suggested teaching strategies and assessment plans. Many states have similar support materials and, if you plan to teach language arts, it is essential you be aware of the requirements students must meet – *particularly if they are part of a state assessment test!*

KEY STRATEGY: *To answer any question on standards a three-step formula will serve you well.* **First,** give a broad overview of your knowledge of the standards' requirements. **Second,** choose one standard and outline specific teaching strategies that will promote initial student understanding. **Third,** describe ways to deepen initial student proficiency and maintain his or her retention through a regimen of distributed practice.

The question specifically asks about your approach to mastery teaching – *"how would you insure your students reach these standards?"* Be sure to respond to this matter carefully. The basics of mastery teaching include how you diagnose the degree to which students understand, how you deal with students who are below the mastery level, and any plans you have to reinforce student skills after they are learned. **NOTE:** *Chapter 11, which deals with mathematics questions, has additional information on how to address the elements of mastery teaching and you should review that information as well.*

 Keys to Your Response:

- Give an overview of your knowledge on the standards for your state.
- Choose one standard and outline a concise set of steps to teach and reinforce the related proficiencies.
- Show the committee your approach to mastery teaching through the use of consistent assessment/diagnosis/remediation strategies.

 What strategies do you use to identify and deal with students who are reading significantly below grade level?

The question has two main parts. The first part is concerned with your *identification* of students who may have pronounced reading difficulties. The second part asks about your ideas on *how to deal* with students who are below grade level. An approach employed by many candidates is to center their opening on the use of classroom diagnostics to identify the student reading levels in their class. This approach is acceptable, however there is a far faster and more accurate manner of making this decision, **check the most recent standardized test results!** Tell the committee how you would review the portion of the *School Report* that provides standardized reading results by student. This is a standard report and usually available on request. With this report, you can see in a matter of minutes exactly who of your students is reading below grade level. Not only is this faster, it is likely to be more accurate. You can always add your class observations to the evaluation process, but standardized results will quickly and accurately point you in the right direction. **KEY STRATEGY:** *The use of standardized test score analysis can be employed in any question where a diagnosis of student ability is required.*

The second component of the question is directed toward how you plan to work with below-level readers when you design instruction. This calls for you to identify teacher actions that will help address the variety of ability levels in your class. You will need to explain how you will differentiate your expectations for reading responses, homework, questions, and class assignments. Discuss how you might use cooperative learning, literature circles or other student learning arrangements to minimize student limitations. Focus your committee on the promise such ideas offer for enriched student understanding. Your phrasing for this portion of the response might sound like the following:

> *"I never let students struggle from behind with no assistance from me. Unfortunately, I am only one person and there may be a number of students who need support. To address this need I like to structure a variety of support opportunities to help everyone stay abreast of the instruction. Some of the strategies I employ include: . . . ."*

From this introduction, go on to describe a teaching plan that sustains the learning process of slower students. A concise, direct answer will be appreciated because it provides the committee members only the information they need to hear.

To this point in the answer you have focused on general methodologies. A strong conclusion will add specific ways to directly work with *individual* students and improve each one's reading ability. This differs from full-class remediation in that it outlines a plan for each student's personal improvement in his or her reading skills. You can now link your opening statements on the importance of test analysis and how you will use the *Individual Student Report.* The insight you gain from the test analysis regarding each student's specific skill deficiencies now allows you to provide targeted support in the precise areas where data suggests he or she is struggling. The information on this report can also be used to arrange supplemental instruction for small groups composed of those who share a common deficiency. This well-directed review of how you use test data to improve student performance will place you above most candidates.

 Keys to Your Response:

- Tell the committee how you will use standardized test data to make initial diagnostic evaluations of your students.
- Describe a variety of in-class support strategies for students who may be struggling with the work.
- Identify a strategic plan to improve every student's personal reading ability.

> *Speech is a fundamental element of good communication. What will you do to enhance the ability of students to speak formally and informally?*

This is a process skill about which much is said and little is "taught" in today's schools. By teaching, I mean the teacher has clearly identified a set of essential sub-tasks, planned the content to be taught, and categorized any process skills required for mastery of this competence. It is fair for you to ask the committee if a specific public speaking curriculum is already in place. Expect answers to range from sketchy overviews through very specific curricula and performance expectations. For purposes of our discussion, we will assume very little is laid out beyond recognition of public speaking as an important skill that needs your attention.

A good place to begin your answer is with a review of three or four solid objectives that underlie mastery of this skill. For example, you might feel students need to learn the necessary skills required to speak before an audience. Perhaps they should have instruction to help them master the art of argument and debate. As part of the informal speaking requirements, students must also learn to speak extemporaneously. There are other forms of speaking as well and you can choose those you feel most important. Crafting a few concrete ideas regarding how you will teach students to speak in a variety of settings might sound like the following:

> *"To approach public speaking, I like to break the teaching into a few component skills. The areas I see as important include a student's ability to address an audience, present sound arguments in a debate, and speak extemporaneously. Let me talk about some things I do to teach students about these important elements of public speaking."*

In your response, try to limit the discussion to two or three items as more can make your answer too long. The committee wants to establish your general level of understanding and hear of methods you may employ to teach the identified skill.

Once you outline the content to be taught, illustrate specific ways you plan to teach those concepts. Provide a sample lesson along with ways to deepen and extend initial understanding through the use of distributed practice over the year. For example, explain how you would teach the elements of debate in a short series of lessons. Address the issue of distributed practice by underscoring your use of debate and point-counterpoint discussions throughout the year. Because speech is essential to daily communication, you will have many opportunities to reinforce these skills during the year. Be sure the committee knows you recognize such opportunities and will consistently reinforce everyone's public speaking skills.

One last suggestion that will help vault you over other candidates is the use of assessment rubrics. **KEY STRATEGY:** *When you are working with a frequently used process skill, use rubrics to help students conduct peer and self-assessment.* A rubric is a chart that identifies the critical elements required for mastery of the skill. Essential sub-skills are listed along the left side column and each item is in a separate cell. To the right of each identified skill are four or five numbered cells. Each cell lists the requirements and identifying characteristics that describe that level of proficiency. The lower numbers describe weak proficiency and the higher numbers more advanced proficiency. If you do not know how rubrics are constructed or look, many publishers have included examples in their teacher editions of textbooks (Appendix A). You can also check with your library, ASCD or the Internet. There are entire books devoted to the subject of assessment and rubrics are usually included. It is an important tool and you can use it in a variety of ways. Any time spent to learn more on this topic will be time well spent.

 Keys to Your Response:

- Open with a description of sub-skill areas critical to the mastery of public speaking.
- Choose a sub-skill area and outline a teaching plan to help students master that skill.
- Catalog a variety of speaking requirements and opportunities you will use throughout the year so students will deepen their proficiency.
- Explain how you use rubrics to help students understand critical public speaking elements and conduct self or peer assessment.

> **Writing is a complex process skill that every educated person must master. What is your approach to the teaching of writing?**

Writing is now a very hot topic in education. Student mastery of this skill is constantly measured and used as an indicator of a school's quality. This is true in all fifty states and you can be certain of a question that explores your abilities and knowledge of writing instruction. When answering this question for a high school position, you can sometimes assume certain skill levels to be already in place. In these instances, do not start with writing fundamentals. Performance expectations for high school students are more advanced. If you are to teach remedial classes, ask for more information about the entry-level skills you can expect.

A sound place to begin your answer is how you teach students to add power to their writing style. Cite the need for a powerful vocabulary, strategies to develop rich textual composition, and the use of writing tactics such as alliteration, simile, metaphor and so forth. Books on power writing offer numerous suggestions and I recommend them to your attention. Catalog the variety of writing purposes you will include in your teaching. Some essential purposes might include job applications, business letters, memoranda, research reports, college application essays, letters to the editor, or other writing students must master. Tailor your response to grade level expectations, but show your ability to introduce rigor and stretch to writing exercises.

Teachers must address research papers in this answer. There is a range of disciplines where high school students might be expected to write a research paper and the required skills to accomplish this task are very important. Your approach should be generic and address ways you will teach students to identify and use data sources, construct convincing arguments, synthesize ideas, and develop logical lines of thought. There are also technical aspects of research such as footnotes, tables of contents, references cited, and style. Be prepared to review the various research styles such as APA or Chicago. Explain how you will work with content area teachers to maximize the benefit of the learning experience in your class.

As with other process skills, rubrics can be an extremely effective way to help students understand a project's essential elements and conduct self-assessment. Your response need only highlight a few rubric criteria along with concrete examples of the benchmarks that will define exemplary performance. A nice addition will describe how "anchor papers" or models might be employed to provide examples to which students can refer.

KEY STRATEGY: *Good answers will always end on a strong point.* A wonderful way to conclude this discussion is with your use of writing portfolios to maintain an ongoing record of student performance.   List the kinds of writing a good portfolio will contain, outline how students will identify papers for inclusion and the frequency of portfolio reviews. **TIP:** *If you are familiar with electronic portfolios, this is a perfect place to use that information!* The addition of this exciting technology will jump you over other candidates who will not think of this useful tool. In over 75 interviews of language arts candidates, only one candidate included a discussion of electronic portfolios. Why shouldn't you be that *one* in this interview group?

As you can see, there is a lot to cover with this answer. Therefore your response might take little longer than it will with other answers. As long as you are not repeating yourself or wandering, you will maintain the attention of the committee. A more complete response will leave an excellent impression on the minds of the committee, so organize your thinking and go for it.

 Keys to Your Response:

- Focus your answer on the more advanced writing skills unless you are otherwise directed.
- Highlight skills essential to power writing and provide an example of how you would teach one of these skills.

- Catalog the variety of writing purposes to which you will teach.
- Talk about how research or project papers will be used to add sophistication to student writing.
- Describe where and how writing rubrics, anchor papers, and support information will help students self edit and improve their writing skills.
- Close with a discussion of writing portfolios and their use in your class.

> *Our curriculum requires students to read and interpret good literature. If you were asked to choose a book for a 10th grade class, which one would you select and why? How would you design the instruction for studying this work?*

If you are an English teacher, you can expect this question at any grade level from elementary through high school. This question or a similar item was included on many sample interviews for high school positions. The question has universal appeal because of its ability to provide insight into a candidate's knowledge of literature and how this knowledge transfers to his or her instructional approach. The answer exposes what literature candidates view as important, identifies their familiarity with authors, and provides information regarding teaching methodologies.

First, understand there is no specific reading selection that represents the "right" answer. There is a wide variety of works and authors from which to choose and you should decide on something from your own repertoire. Once your selection is made, speak directly to the characteristics of the author and his or her work that make it a superior teaching example for tenth grade students. Remember too, a book's popularity or interest is insufficient reason to select it as a core reading. Be sure your choice represents a superior example of a literary genre or demonstrates a style of writing that is unique or noteworthy. Add ideas on how your selection will provide a vehicle for smooth transition to the writing process. The more versatility of use a selection can show, the stronger your answer will be. Feel free to add information about what makes this author a noteworthy model of the writing profession. If you choose a well-known author, he or she needs less explanation than someone who is less well recognized.

The final element of your answer must take your book selection and craft a solid teaching design. This must done by you and specific advice cannot be offered. When you describe your teaching approach, you might wish to underscore a set of activities that will require students to analyze and appreciate the literature piece you selected. Showcase strategies such as small group book talks, written reflections, webbing, analysis designs, evaluation responses, journals, debates, discussion techniques, and so forth. It is important to convince the committee you can select and use good literature in an innovative and unique manner to capture its essence.

 Keys to Your Response:

- Select a book with which you are familiar that offers a variety of literary elements.
- Describe how your author is a significant writer and what he or she offers to students who study his or her works.
- Provide a concise outline of the teaching design and how students will analyze this work.

 Is preparation for the Scholastic Aptitude Test (SAT) something that should concern teachers of language arts? If so, what specific steps would you take to prepare students for this test?

The first element of this question is the easiest – of course SAT- preparation is a legitimate interest of language arts teachers. It is a matter of concern for all academic area teachers. As the verbal section of the test will directly measure student skills learned in your teaching area, an added burden rests on your shoulders. This added responsibility is a logical place to begin your response, however, you must make one key distinction; *the SAT is not the curriculum.* Therefore, you need to identify where and how you will teach the skills students need in order to maximize their readiness.

Identify instructional areas you believe will transfer directly to SAT readiness. An example might be how you teach students the various types of analogy bridges and their identifying characteristics. You might cover segments of grammar and usage students must know. Critical analysis of a variety of reading selections is a useful skill. There are many areas appropriate for direct instruction and you should provide one or two good examples.

Describe one or two process skills related to SAT competence that you might address as ongoing objectives. Obviously, critical thinking and analysis are central to strong SAT performance. Provide ideas on how you will provide opportunities for students to develop divergent thinking skill. As the SAT includes a wide variety of literature genre, outline how your curriculum will acquaint students with this diversity. An important message in this segment is your commitment to a long-term strategy for student readiness.

One word of caution concerns the numerous SAT readiness programs on the market. There are computer programs, preparation manuals, and stand-alone courses that purport to help students prepare for the SAT. These materials provide good examples and strategies you might want to include in your instruction. For example, a good computer program would make an excellent learning center in the back of your room. **TIP:** *I would not suggest you propose packaged SAT programs as stand-alone units of study.* The committee will be more impressed with your long-term goals than quick-hit solutions.

 Keys to Your Response:

- Yes, of course SAT preparation is an important concern; but make the distinction that the SAT cannot dictate the entire curriculum.

- Identify specific areas of your curriculum where drawing a connection to the SAT would make sense.
- Describe one or two long-term process skills taught in your class that measurably add to a student's SAT readiness.
- Explain where use of learning centers or stand-alone curricula can extend instruction and reinforce specific skill areas.

> *If we allow you to attend any workshop you like in your field, what would you choose to attend and why?*

The key words in this question are, "in your field." School principals are interested to know where you would focus future professional development activities. The specific workshop you choose is not as important as your explanation of why the area was chosen. For example, if you tell the committee you want to attend a workshop on writing strategies, you should be able to explain what you intend to gain and where you will use these new strategies. If you are applying to a school in New Jersey, workshops on the Frameworks for the Content Standards might be a safe choice. In other states, workshops that deal with their standards are usually available and would be worthwhile attending.

Highlight a strong commitment to professional growth and personal development. The enthusiasm of your answer will be strongly noted by the committee. Principals want professionals who will constantly seek opportunities to improve their teaching skills. Use this question to demonstrate your intention to be a life-long learner.

 Keys to Your Response:

- Choose an area of your interest and explain what knowledge you will gain as well as how that knowledge will be translated into classroom actions.

- Make a strong statement of commitment to personal development and the concept of continuing education for teachers.

> **Experts have identified a skill called "active listening." What does this term mean to you and how would you teach this skill to your students?**

This is a difficult question to answer when it comes out of the blue in an interview. However, as listening has become more recognized as an essential skill to the process of communication, it is worth mentioning in this chapter. A point you will want to make is that active listening is more than just attentiveness. It refers to a person's ability to recognize the meaning behind sounds and then make interpretations based on what they hear. At the secondary level, an active listener is able to do such things as identify various speaking styles and purposes, determine speaker credibility, evaluate media messages, and deal with a variety of presentation purposes. The "active listener" is able to *respond* to what he or she has heard.

With this broader definition of "active listening," you might want to choose one of the above-mentioned skills and propose a compatible lesson. If you choose to do this, it will be important to identify a few specific teaching strategies you will use to check for student understanding. Because listening is largely a covert activity , it is more difficult to assess – but it can be done. Look at the following example to see how such a diagnosis might be phrased.

> *I need to know when students understand the concept of credibility. This requires strong active listening from the student. To insure that students have this knowledge, I like to use an activity that students will find useful. After listening to three commercials, I have the students identify which speaker was the most credible and what techniques he or she used to convey his or her message more effectively?*

This requires students to "demonstrate" their listening *and* evaluative skills. It gives the teacher a clear reflection of what the student has both heard and learned about the analysis process. **KEY STRATEGY:** *When you are describing an instructional segment or something you need students to learn, it always wise to also provide the committee insight into your diagnostic strategy.* If you fail to establish the means by which you will observe and evaluate student concept mastery, you will have missed the opportunity to establish a key element of your teaching skill.

As you develop this response, consider the many places where listening is an important part of daily student activity. Suggest one or two places along with a good lesson design to reinforce a listening skill. It might sound something like the following.

> *A regular part of my class is the inclusion of oral presentations by students. When a lesson contains an oral presentation component, we go over the importance of listening and develop a rubric for students to use when they provide feedback to the presenter. This rubric along with the specific information students must provide a presenter promotes a good pattern of active listening.*

As you can see, this information tells the committee you are someone who recognizes precise ways the skill of active listening can be taught as an integrated part of the curriculum. It will also show how you understand the principle of active participation and its ability to secure on-task behavior in students. There are many places where listening is important and you should choose those that fit your teaching style. The specific area is not as important as the explanation of how it will be taught and measured.

 Keys to Your Response:

- Begin your answer with a concise definition of the term "active listening."

- List several of the sub-skills contained in active listening, then choose one and describe how you will know students are using this skill.
- Choose an instructional design you commonly employ and show how you can incorporate the development of listening skills inside that plan.

> *The consumption of good fiction is an important component of reading literacy, but there are other literary genres. What advanced reading tactics and skills would you teach to students reading fiction and other literary genre?*

As pointed out earlier in this chapter, high school students must master higher levels of literacy competence. For this reason, your answer must address the more advanced reading skills. An example of a more advanced skill you might address is how you will teach students about the techniques writers use to manipulate the reader's emotions or frame of mind.

> *"It is important that students in my class understand some of the more advanced skills required to critically examine a piece of fiction. An area I like to explore with my classes is the devices an author uses to manipulate the reader's emotional state."*

Your answer will gain strength if you provide a specific author and title. You should add ideas on how you would help students identify the devices that a particular author uses to manipulate emotion so the committee will see how you provide depth to your instruction. There are other areas to consider as well. For example, you might address how students will study the relationships between literature and literary criticism. What are the characteristics of key literary movements? Think about other ways literacy skills have been developed in your classes.

Note that the question asked about other literary genre. This is an important element of a complete response and you will now be ready for it. List three or four different genre your class will address and why each is important. The beginning of your answer will sound something like the following.

> *"It is critical that students study a variety of good literature. For example, students should experience poetry, yet poetry normally evokes little enthusiasm. I like to begin the instruction of poetry by having students read such classic works as Shakespeare and Keats. From this foundation we move to more contemporary poets such as Frost and Sandburg. We then look at poetry in music. Lyrics by Johnny Mercer are terrific examples of poetry. Finally students look at artists of their own choosing and analyze their poetic elements."*

As you can see, this outlines a design to teach an important genre. It is not necessary to present every bell and whistle for the unit. The committee will be pleased if you identify a few literary forms and a meaningful way to teach them.

When you are ready to conclude your answer, consider ending with a question. You can insure your answer will hit the right target when you ask the committee if there is a specific genre they were interested in hearing you discuss.

> *"Before I conclude my response to this question, is there a specific area of literature you wanted me to discuss and I missed. If so, I would be happy to give my thoughts on that as well."*

This ending can be used at any time when you may feel the committee still has questions. The only caveat is to use it only once or twice. More than that will become redundant and sound too rehearsed.

Keys to Your Response:

- Begin with a few advanced literary elements you intend to teach.
- Provide one or two examples of key analytic skills and describe how they might be taught.
- List a variety of genres you feel are important. Identify one genre to expand and demonstrate your teaching approach.
- If you are not certain you included all the points in which the committee had interest, end with a question that allows for further exploration.

CONCLUDING THOUGHTS

Language Arts is a cornerstone discipline in every school, therefore there are important interview goals for you to achieve. Be sure the committee knows you have an in-depth understanding of the required writing skills for high school students. You should convey an ability to organize innovative lessons. The committee should see you as an educator who is flexible and dynamic. It is suggested you read this section through a few times and familiarize yourself with the issues that are discussed.

For all questions, your answers must reflect your own experience and teaching style. Be proactive and organize your thinking on the pertinent issues before you attend the interview. The exact questions a committee is likely to ask will be different than those in this chapter, however many of the central issues described in this chapter will be present. If you know how to approach those key issues, you will be ready! Good luck.

11
MATHEMATICS QUESTIONS

GENERAL INFORMATION

Mathematics is another discipline area that is traditionally part of district and state test programs. In most states, districts are required to administer a norm-referenced achievement test in mathematics and report those results to the public. The public and media use these reports as barometers of school and student effectiveness. Because of this reporting, mathematics teachers carry higher levels of accountability. In addition, teachers who will be teaching college preparatory courses must also consider the Scholastic Aptitude Test (SAT). No matter how the course load is to be structured, mathematics candidates can count on a very thorough set of questions to uncover their philosophy and strategy for student test preparation.

Another interest of principals and supervisors is the candidate's ability to work with students who have difficulty with math. Even if you teach Algebra, Geometry or Trigonometry, you can expect some students who struggle just to keep up while others breeze effortlessly through the material. Examiners will explore your plan to work with these diverse populations.

A fundamental interview goal is to establish your credentials as a strong practitioner with an array of instructional strategies that meet the needs of all students. Let the committee know you recognize how important it is to reach *every* student and maintain his or her competence into and through the spring achievement tests. Now examine the general mathematics themes and interview questions that may be asked.

SAMPLE QUESTIONS

> **What do you know about our state's requirements in Mathematics and how would you ensure your students meet these requirements?**

For almost all states there are student competencies in mathematics children must master. Where a state administers a competency test on those requirements, an applicant can almost count on hearing this question. Look for your state standards and initiatives in the area of mathematics and identify how the state determines student achievement. If you are not sure where to find them, go online and log onto www.taskstream.com and go to the "Standards Wizard." (Appendix B) Every state is listed and there is a wealth of information. The principal and committee will assume you are aware of these requirements and ask questions that deal with this knowledge. Such questions are often asked early in the interview and they are important. To prepare, you should get a complete copy of the K-12 Core Standards or whatever documents are in place for your state. Familiarize yourself with each standard and any specific performance indicators required for students to demonstrate mastery. In New Jersey 16 separate standards are tested in fourth, eighth, and eleventh grades. There may also be a curriculum guide or *Frameworks* that provides suggestions on teaching methodologies and assessment. These guides are excellent and, if you can review a copy before your interview, endeavor to become an expert on at least one proficiency area. This advance study will prove useful on your interview day. It will help you identify the specific examples and practical information necessary to infuse power in your answer.

Look at the question the committee posed in this case. There are two significant parts. 1) What do you know about the standards and 2) how will you insure student mastery? **TIP:** *When organizing a response that has multiple parts, go from the general to the specific.* In this instance, begin with a brief overview of your general knowledge on state mathematics standards and how they might apply to the grade level(s) you will teach. Add a specific example of at least one standard and its required competencies. Once the standard and proficiencies are explained, move quickly to provide an illustration of how you might teach to that proficiency in your class. Here is a simple example of how this approach sounds.

> *"One of the standards requires students to solve real-world problems. As problem solving is an essential process skill in math, I have students engage in solving a variety of real world problems throughout every chapter. A key skill required in problem solving is measuring. As an activity, I make every student pretend he or she is a parcel post person who must determine the least amount of wrapping that can be used on an oddly shaped package. This is an authentic task that requires math reasoning and measurement skills."*

Lets review the approach once more. Identify the standard, specify the required proficiencies, and give a practical example. It is crisp and effective. Before you conclude your response, provide a description of the observable and measurable indicators you will use to determine student mastery on the competency you chose.

NOTE: *The question uses the phrase, "all students."* That is an important element and can be easily lost on a less astute candidate. The complete answer needs to discuss plans to help slower students reach a mastery level. Here is phrasing to help you formulate your own approach.

> *"In my experience, not all students master the concepts of measurement right away. This is especially true for the metric measurements. To help those students, I would create two learning centers in my room with computers and CAI (Computer Assisted Instruction) programs on measurement. I give diagnostic quizzes all along the instructional path and students who need a little more time or information can either use the learning centers or get 1-on-1 assistance. To provide the 1-on-1 assistance, I use faster stu-*

dents who have already mastered the concept as tutors. Student tutors receive extra credit when their teaching bears fruit. As soon as their student demonstrates mastery on the proficiency quiz, the tutor receives bonus points on his or her grade. Through the use of these two strategies, I have found student achievement can reach 100%."

To close this question, add a comment on your concern that students maintain their knowledge into *and through* the spring test season. Some candidates only worry about insuring student mastery up to the test. This should not be good enough for you. Make a point of telling the committee you want this learning to be *owned* by the students. Using whichever math concept you spoke to in your answer, illustrate a program of distributed practice on those newly mastered skills that will help keep the learning fresh and proficient into the future.

   Keys to Your Response:

- Be sure you have done your homework and fully understand the standards required by your state.
- Open with an overview of your knowledge of state standards.
- Select one standard and outline its importance along with a teaching strategy. Be sure to include a way to assess student mastery.
- Discuss your plan to provide for those who display difficulty with the concept so all students can attain mastery.
- Close with a discussion of how you will use distributed practice and periodic refreshers to maintain student mastery into and through the spring test.

> **What strategies do you use to monitor student learning and how do you adjust your teaching based on those findings?**

When you hear the terms "monitor and adjust" in the same sentence, it is safe to assume the interviewer is familiar with the work of Madeline Hunter. Perhaps the district has even conducted staff development in this model. If you are familiar with the Madeline Hunter instructional approach, you can include Hunter terminology in your answer and feel safe that it will be congruent to the district's instructional philosophies. If you have not had Madeline Hunter training, do not be concerned, you can still provide a great answer.

This question asks how you "diagnose" student learning and what instructional adaptations you employ as a result of that diagnosis. There are many ways to determine what students have learned and understand. You have probably studied a number of them in your methods classes and used diagnostic questions in your teaching. Use your background and describe a comprehensive plan that contains two goals. First, describe strategies that will determine what individual students have learned. Second, describe strategies that will identify what the group has learned. Here is a sample of this approach.

When I check understanding, I not only need to know if one or two students understand, I need to know if the group is still with me. To do this I use diagnostic samplings to verify <u>individual</u> student knowledge. I ask questions with different levels of difficulty to specific students around the room. This helps me to understand what those students know. I might also ask the <u>group</u> for signals or choral responses to gauge the more general class understanding. As I feel more confident of class mastery, I might ask everyone to write responses to a question while I circulate through the room checking results. This routine tells me about both individual and group mastery."

Observe the two parts outlined by this response strategy. We first used sample questions of individuals, followed with signaled or choral answers from the group, and moving finally to an independent group exercise. The first diagnostic steps provided information about individuals while the second and third techniques addressed group learning. If possible, try to present a wide variety of sampling strategies and help the committee appreciate your assessment versatility. Consider using such ideas as monitored seatwork, homework, journal writing, board work, and recitation to provide immediate diagnostic feedback. Along with signals and choral answers, cooperative assignments can also let you know how groups of students grasp a concept. Would you like to add a power finish to this portion of the answer? **TIP:** *Tell the committee you plan periodic checks of understanding <u>all through each teaching segment</u> because assessment is the only way to quality control teaching.*

Now you must address the second part of the question by detailing how you will alter the teaching based on your diagnostic findings. When one adjusts teaching, there are only four actions he or she must consider:

POSSIBLE TEACHER ACTIONS BASED ON
LEARNING DIAGNOSIS

- If the students and class demonstrate satisfactory understanding, you can **continue the lesson as planned.**
- If the class exhibits minor misunderstandings, you may need to **clarify or reinforce weak understanding.**
- If the class has serious gaps or misunderstanding, you need to **re-teach using a different instructional strategy.**
- If there are such serious misunderstandings that the entire lesson must go back to the planning board, your best option is to **abandon ship and think anew about how to teach the concept.**

This set of teacher actions is straight from Madeline Hunter and it has served many teachers well for over twenty-five years. Use it.

An excellent conclusion to this answer suggests how you will proceed when class understanding is satisfactory but just one or two students may have failed to master the content. This occurs fairly often and you can move ahead of other candidates if you address this common problem in your answer. Almost all candidates omit this important distinction for one big reason – they have not given it much thought. As of now, you are no longer in that category. Believe me, there are excellent teacher actions you can take when the general instruction is complete and only a few students are below proficiency. Here is a response you might consider to address that concern.

"If there are just a few students who do not understand, I will move the remainder of the class to guided and independent practice to build their proficiency. I can then form a small group of students for special instruction or additional guided practice. If the class is not yet ready to work independently, I might employy a few <u>Look Again</u> handouts that contain detailed explanations for students to take home. The "Check Now" questions at the end of the chapter also let me see how these students are doing. If after a few of these steps a student is still confused, I can utilize student tutors for individual help."

After looking at the sample, you may have even more ideas of your own. By all means share these thoughts with the committee. This conclusion is quite strong and likely to leave a positive feeling with every interviewer!

 Keys to Your Response:

- Provide a clinical approach to your answer and break it into the component parts of individual and then group understanding.
- Add a few specific examples of how you check for individual and then group understanding.
- Identify the four teacher actions you use to respond to diagnostic feedback and the learning threshold required to trigger each action.
- Close with your strategy for those times when you have only one or two struggling students and the class is ready to move forward.

> *Mathematics is a subject area some students fear. They may have had negative classroom experiences or perhaps harbor a poor self-image regarding their ability. What will you do to raise their comfort level and lead them to become more confident learners?*

Educational leaders want teachers who are able to create classrooms and lessons that lead to consistent student participation and positive learning experiences. This question comes to the heart of how you will connect with your students and how you intend to infuse vitality to the teaching/learning process. The question centers on the larger themes of motivation and student perceptions. It wants to know how you will foster confident learners with healthy self-esteem. This is a complex issue and there are entire books devoted to the subject. *Your* answer, however, need only focus on what can realistically be accomplished in the span of a daily 45-minute period – insufficient time to warrant a review of an entire book.

The committee's question can be approached more easily if it is rephrased to ask, "What will take place in your class to raise student comfort levels?" To that end, you might begin by detailing how you will organize instruction and class management so students will feel safe and successful. Students can become anxious if the material is beyond their ability to understand and/or if there is a tense atmosphere in the room. In order to design lessons at the right level of difficulty with well-organized teaching approaches, you need a clear task analysis. A task analysis will reveal the key sub-skills or concepts students must master before they can accomplish the final goal. Once these sub-skills are identified, you can conduct a preliminary assessment of student readiness *before* the lesson is delivered. This diagnostic step will keep you from launching teaching lessons when students are not yet ready.

You should also address the issue of student anxiety. The presence of remedial materials, student tutors, differentiated homework and/or re-takes on important tests or assignments can materially reduce the pressure on struggling students. Emphasis on multiple assessment strategies can also reduce grade tension. These are just a few ways you can organize the class for successful learning and raise student comfort level. With these few ideas in mind, look back at your own classes and training. Reflect on things you have done to support students and identify a few of your personal classroom strategies. Once you have gathered a set of successful ideas, you are ready to answer this part of the question.

The second component of this question is how you will produce "more confident learners." Use the "success for all students" message contained in the first part of your answer to set the table for this part of the response. Students often lack confidence when they have experienced multiple failures or frustration. Conversely, their confidence increases when the number of successful experiences rises. In mathematics, you can increase the probability of success if you increase the frequency of assessments and reduce the amount of material to be mastered. If students do not demonstrate mastery on the quizzes or short tests, you can add opportunities for those students to identify their mistake(s) and retake only the portions where they were unsuccessful. The goal is to provide every possible means for students to demonstrate genuine mastery of the material and receive *full* credit for their effort. Reward the additional effort and avoid grade reduction because it took a little longer. There are some who claim such added opportunity and time for selected students is unfair to others who were successful on the first attempt. I respectfully disagree. The goal is the learning, not the time. The real unfairness is treating all students alike when there are such obvious differences in background and ability.

Self-esteem problems can increase when individuals do not learn as fast as the other students. The wise teacher should try to render this a moot issue. The important goal is for students to master the concepts. Why should there be a penalty for someone who learned the material over a longer period of time? To prepare for this question, give serious thought to mastery teaching and identify ways to accomplish this within your teaching style. Whatever you decide, keep in mind that consistent, legitimate *success* is the *only* real avenue toward increased self-esteem and math confidence.

Keys to Your Response:

- Start your discussion by stating your understanding of the problem.
- Identify ways you will organize the curriculum and manage instruction so as to teach at the right levels of difficulty for students.
- Highlight a variety of means by which you will provide strong support to every student.
- Catalog the ways you will build successful mathematics experiences for each student.

> **Do you think some students are "naturally" good in math while others are just not very good in math? How does your point of view on this influence your instruction?**

CAUTION: *This is a trick question and it has appeared on several sample interviews.* The politically correct answer is, "All students have relatively equal abilities and are very capable of learning math concepts." I council *against* the politically correct approach and suggest you take the path dictated by both common sense and collective experience. If you provide a tepid response that whitewashes what everyone with five minutes of classroom experience has seen, you will appear disingenuous and potentially damage your relative standing. You will be more respected and credible if you provide the real answer. **KEY POINT:** *In mathematics, as well as every other discipline, students learn at different rates.* Some students genuinely grasp the material faster and with more ease than do others. Whether this is due to genetics and a "natural" ability is not the point. Students exhibit varying levels of comfort with new learning – period. *Now,* you can go on to make a more important case. You firmly believe that all students are *capable* of learning math *if provided the right resources, sound teaching, and sufficient* *time.* That, my friends, is what the committee really wants to know – *you believe all students are <u>capable</u> of learning math!*

With these points made, you should move on to explain how your belief that all children are capable of learning math influences your instructional patterns. Provide a concise discussion of how you provide adjustments to the key learning factors of time, resources, and instructional formats in order to maximize the probability of success for everyone.

> *"Although all students in my class will be expected to learn and master the material, I know that the same instructional design will not fit the needs of all students. I may have to allow more time for some students or establish learning centers to help students master the key but difficult concepts. I believe achievement will come if I use some creativity and patience."*

This response is realistic and memorable. Your candor and practical approach to individual differences will present a strong case for your candidacy.

 Keys to Your Response:

- Avoid an attempt to be politically correct. Be real instead.
- Underscore your philosophy that students are <u>capable</u> of learning the required concepts if given the right time, instruction and support.
- Provide a detailed example of how your belief that students are capable of learning math affects your approach to student achievement.

> *One of the most common complaints a teacher hears from students is, "Math class is boring!" What will you do to change this perception and make your class an interesting, exciting place to learn?*

Be assured that mathematics has not cornered the market on the problem of student boredom. You can insert the name of any discipline and the statement remains accurate. Whereas it is unlikely you can make every minute of every class "interesting and exciting" to every student, there *are* things you can do to extend the vigor and vitality of each lesson design. Everyone has experienced the math teacher who begins each class with a review of the homework, has students go to the board with their solutions, discusses errors, spends a five or ten minutes on new material and gives the next assignment. Good heavens, we *have* to be better than that!

This question asks for specifics on how you will provide innovative instructional lessons and novel approaches to teaching. This is a very complex question and it has many facets. You can simplify the approach by framing your answer around a few dimensions that center on motivation.

> *"Keeping my class from becoming boring or routine requires daily attention. As I think about this problem, it seems there are four areas where what I do as a teacher influences the way students will view my class. These items include 1) a statement of strong purpose for all that students must learn, 2) the use of innovative teaching strategies wherever possible, 3) the use of technology to bring dimension to the class and 4) the building of strong relationships between me and my students."*

You may have different views on the topic, but it is important to identify three or four central issues around which you will develop a complete answer. The above are just some ideas to help move your creative mind in the right direction. Read the following discussion to see how the items can be presented in a well-defined sequence.

The purpose of learning is a logical place to begin helping students gain enthusiasm for learning. When students are unaware of why they are learning something, "being bored" is a natural extension of that ignorance. The connection of classroom teaching to the real world of students is essential. The more purpose a student perceives, the more motivated he or she becomes. Outside speakers, field experiences, career connections, and personal anecdotes can enhance the students' sense of purpose.

The next aspect of creating meaningful classes is the use of strong lesson designs and innovation. Look over your lesson plans. In your day's plan, try to include three or four different formats and learning activities. The active involvement of the students is essential during every class. By the way, one student at the board while the others are supposedly critiquing the answer _does not qualify_ as active involvement. Changing class routines will help maintain what Jon Saphier calls "learning momentum." Select a few of your favorite lesson designs that incorporate high student involvement and have them ready to share with the committee. A brief anecdote to amplify your answer can be a compelling punctuation to this portion of your answer. It is vitally important that you include one or two high impact teaching strategies at some point in your answer. Here is a novel approach to the practice of checking for student understanding.

> *"One strategy I employ from time to time in my class is the use of chalk slates during the discussion. I ask questions and have students respond on their slates. When they are ready, I say 'up slates' and look at the responses they have written. The students find this somewhat novel and we have a lot of fun with it. For me, however, it is very effective in quickly finding out who knows what."*

How about the use of technology to add high interest and innovation to your class? Do you know of virtual or on-line learning opportunities for students who demonstrate advanced ability or interest? If you can provide the names of good Internet sites, this significantly increases the strength of your answer. Even if the school does not have computers in your class, include this information in your answer.

You may wish to consider a discussion of what will your room look like. Will there be current and interactive bulletin boards? Will there be learning centers that target a variety of purposes? Will there be displays of student project work, career information or other interesting topics? The feeling tone in your class can have a strong influence on interest, motivation and student learning. Bland classrooms can significantly contribute to the boredom of students.

My final element, and one many candidates tend to omit, is the power of strong personal connections and mutual respect between teachers and students. At some time you may have heard a teacher say, "I'm not running a personality contest." I have heard the comment more than once and believe me when I tell you that such statements represent a totally bankrupt attitude. When you hear such pronouncements, you almost always find that they come from a teacher who has minimal human relations skill with his or her students. Moreover, such teachers rarely enjoy the respect and affection of the children they serve. Do not underestimate the importance of the student/teacher bond to motivation and the learning process. There are numerous ways to build a strong, healthy relationship with students. Consider Jon Saphier's suggestions and see which of them fit your style and can be used in crafting your answer.

WAYS TO BUILD POSITIVE RELATIONSHIPS WITH STUDENTS

- **HUMOR** is an excellent way to build ease and comfort into your dealings with students. This does not mean you need to be a comedian or tell jokes all day, rather just learn to laugh and keep things light. If you can have a sense of humor about yourself and some of your mistakes or idiosyncrasies, that is even better. Let the students know you are a *real* person who enjoys their company and a good laugh at the right time.

- **PERSONAL ANECDOTES** that tell students a little about the inner you help establish good relationships. This doesn't mean to explore your entire personal life, just let students know about hobbies, trips, or other things that are important in your life. When the time is right, listen to some of their stories as well. Young people like to know their teacher.
- **POSITIVE BODY LANGUAGE** has a tremendous influence on student perceptions and positive relationships. One of the most important of these is a <u>smile</u>. Affirmative nods, gestures of approval like a thumbs-up, proximity, and the welcoming body language that is so much a part of positive communication can be employed. Be very sparing with closed stances, frowns at wrong answers, scowls and other communication patterns that place barriers between you and the students.
- **AVOIDANCE OF PUT-DOWNS AND HURTFUL COM-MENTS** is absolutely essential. When a student undergoes a public put-down and the attendant humiliation, a large part of the personal relationship is diminished. In addition, the tense climate during such exchanges affects everyone in the class who may also hurt for that student. Some teachers think these comments can be delivered in "good fun" and as comedy. Unfortunately, here is the fact, put-downs hurt – no matter what the context.
- **PERSONAL INTEREST IN STUDENT ACTIVITIES** is a great way to build positive relationships. If students are in a play, on a sports team, in a recreation event, at a church function, in the band, sing in the chorus, or involved with some other noteworthy activity, take notice. When you are at the door or in the hall, you can ask how things are going. If you know the student did well in an event, why not extend a compliment. Take my word for this, students know which teachers care about them and this characteristic is a hallmark of those individuals.
- **RECOGNITION OF RESULTS OR EFFORT** is so important to your relationships with students. They need to know you cared enough about them to take notice when they tried harder, to take notice when they improved, to take notice when they made a good grade. Do not lose these opportunities. Positive strokes work.

Madeline Hunter lists a phenomenon called "with-it-ness" as one of the intangibles that can make a class an exciting place for both students and teachers. Success in cultivating sound connections to the students can only arise from your consistent attention to the many interactions you have with students over time. Teachers <u>must</u> make it a point to reach out to every student, every day. Discuss this important teaching philosophy in your answer. Others will leave this dimension out and that omission provides you an opportunity to say something special.

In conclusion, look back at your teaching as well as the good teaching you experienced while you were a student. What made the classes you have taken more memorable? Include elements of your background and experience that you believe will make your class one of those students see as memorable and worthwhile.

 Keys to Your Response:

- Form your answer around three or four dimensions of motivation that will define your teaching stance.
- Cite the dimensions individually and give examples of how you will address each one in your class.
- End with a discussion of the importance of human relations in creating classes where students feel respected and valued.

> *Our curriculum and current standards require that students be able to use mathematical tools such as calculators. Explain how you use and teach students about calculators and other mathematical tools to increase their ability to think and solve problems.*

There is more than one part to this question and in such situations you should clarify the parts. 1) Explain how you teach students to use calculators or other mathematical tools and 2) describe how this increases their ability to think mathematically and solve problems. These explanations are quite straightforward and you need not spend an exorbitant amount of time on the answer.

Begin with an explanation of where and how you allow students to use calculators. Exponents, roots, long lists of calculations, trigonometry, calculus derivatives, graphing equations, and other high level functions all need explanation. You should tell the committee how you approach the teaching of at least one of these advanced functions because, unless the classes you plan to teach are primarily remedial math, instruction in four-function calculations will fail to impress a high school committee. If you have an anecdote about an innovative lesson where calculators were used, share it with the committee. Most principals and supervisors like to know about your actual work with students. The only caveat is to watch your time. Stories have a tendency to run long unless you make an effort to be brief. A good rule of thumb is to limit less complicated answers to two or three minutes.

The question also asks you to describe how you would "increase their ability to think and solve problems." This goes beyond just using the tools. To frame your answer, consider employing Bloom's Taxonomy to describe how you can use calculators to extend student thinking through the analysis, synthesis, and evaluation levels of complexity. If you have designed projects or class activities that promote high order thinking, provide a brief description. Do not forget the question asked about problem solving and application. If you have an authentic task or problem-solving activity, this is a perfect place to insert that information. As we have repeatedly said, the specificity of examples adds power to your answer.

 Keys to Your Response:

- Identify the parts of this question so that they can be approached separately.
- Provide details about how you would teach advanced calculator functions and provide at least one example.
- Use Bloom's Taxonomy to discuss how calculators or other

tools can be used to extend student thinking through the higher levels of thinking.

- If you have an authentic task or problem that requires calculators, describe that to the committee.

> **What will you do to help students master the content and process skills that will be necessary to perform well on the SAT or ACT?**

WARNING: *This question can be a deal-breaker.* If you are applying to a high expectation district, SAT results are an important concern. Principals need to feel confident you are aware of this and can provide the kind of instruction that will lead to strong test performance. The irony in this question is a good answer will not carry the day, but a poor answer can badly damage your viability.

If Algebra or advanced math classes are in your projected schedule, this question or one of its relatives can be expected at some point during the interview. If you are not familiar with the requirements of the SAT math section, learn all you can about the central skills and test items students must master. Most bookstores have test-preparation manuals by the ton and a brush up might be in order. The information contained in these sources should provide a reliable entry to your answer.

There are many things a teacher can do to help students ready themselves for the SAT or ACT. Describe some of the test's formats and how you will mirror those designs in class activities or homework. Explain how you will employ mastery lesson designs to teach some of the more frequently tested concepts. You might consider the use of an SAT or ACT preparation program as a learning center in your room. You can have an "SAT Question of the Week." The idea is to consistently provide learning opportunities that cultivate and reinforce strong mathematics skills. This coupled with distributed practice and sample test formats will sharpen student proficiency and deepen their test management awareness.

An important point to make is that whatever SAT/ACT preparation is done, it will be a part of the regular curriculum and not discrete units of study. Principals do not want the core curriculum supplanted by a "teach to the test" agenda. There are numerous ways to help prepare students for these tests and you need only choose a few that show how you will approach the concerns identified by the question.

 Keys to Your Response:

- Begin your answer with an overview of what you deem to be critical areas students must understand.
- Identify a variety of classroom strategies you will employ to teach and sharpen those skills you identified as essential to student success on the SAT or ACT.
- Catalog outside enrichment experiences that will be available throughout the year.
- Let the committee know that test preparation will be a part of the class and not a stand-alone unit of study.

 What interdisciplinary connections do you see for mathematics and other content areas?

Interdisciplinary or integrated instructional patterns are becoming more prevalent in secondary education, especially grades six through nine. The literature has increasingly recognized how concepts in one discipline can enhance student understanding and skill in other subject areas. The synergy created from teaching interrelated, complementary skills and knowledge is an important relationship every learner can appreciate.

If you have had experience designing interdisciplinary units, this is a place to describe that experience. Middle school teachers often plan integrated instruction during their team meetings. High school teachers have less structured planning times and you will need to reflect on occasions when you may have worked with members of different departments or independently to create cross-disciplinary connections.

There is no need to worry if you have not previously been part of this type of planning. You can talk about how you would use and reinforce concepts from other subject areas in your mathematics class. Examples of how math can be used by other disciplines include 1) the use of logic and mathematics in making legal arguments, 2) mathematical reasoning in the science of genetics or forensic medicine, 3) or the use of mathematics in the world of advertising. You can describe how mathematics is a part of music composition, military battle plans, art, or any of a thousand other connections. Present four or five innovative ideas on where other disciplines could enhance the teaching of math concepts in your class. As long as you demonstrate a few novel and innovative connections, you have answered this question well.

 ### Keys to Your Response:

- Provide a short overview of what you know about integrated instruction and why you see it as important to the students in your class.
- Give examples of cross-connections you can make in your teaching. A good anecdote will work well.
- Describe any ways you would work with other departments or teachers to develop interdisciplinary connections.

CONCLUDING THOUGHTS

When applying for a mathematics position, understand that the committee is looking for a candidate who possesses a strong understanding of the discipline, uses innovative classroom instructional strategies, and has an ability to engage students at all levels. Deliver your answers with feeling and energy because enthusiasm is contagious. In this chapter's discussion, sample questions identified a number of places where you need to pre-think an answer and fashion your best thinking. It is insufficient to merely "think" through possible answers. Write the key points of your response down on an index card or piece of paper. You may think of a great example, but if you do not have it in writing, you are likely to later forget an important detail. Prepare ahead by reviewing the response keys at the end of each sample question and you will be ready to establish a strong candidacy. Deliver those good answers and step right to the front of the candidate line!

A Teacher's Story

One thing I do as a teacher is to make my classroom a place where mathematics is honored. When students walk into my room, they see a rich mathematical place with posters of people who do mathematics, activity centers where they can play with some cubes or tangrams, problems of the day, and daily activity sets. I wear math ties upon occasion and share with them my enthusiasm about mathematics. I consider myself a salesman for mathematics and strive every day to "sell" my students on the joys of math. "A day without math is a day without sunshine!" is a phrase they often hear from me because I believe that they shouldn't leave school without it.

JOHN D. PUTNAM, RETIRED SEVENTH THROUGH NINTH GRADE MATH TEACHER: RECIPIENT OF THE MILKEN NATIONAL EDUCATOR AWARD

Reprinted from McGuire and Abitz, <u>Best Advice Ever for Teachers</u>

12
SCIENCE QUESTIONS

GENERAL INFORMATION

In secondary education, you may interview for a position in the area of science. Within this category there are a number of sub-disciplines such as general science, earth science, biology, chemistry, physical science, physics, and specialty areas. This chapter cannot possibly provide an in-depth analysis of each discipline area, but you should expect to hear questions related to content understanding in the area for which you are applying. This is especially true if a supervisor or department head is part of the interview committee. To address content questions for each area would likely become redundant and confusing. Instead, this chapter provides examples across a variety of areas to provide a flavor of how science questions are framed. The questions are designed to illuminate your knowledge of a few basic themes, general teaching practice, or specific skills required to teach science.

SAMPLE QUESTIONS

> **Current pedagogy speaks to the necessity of constructivist learning. How often do you include laboratory activities and what role do these experiences have in your teaching?**

In the past, laboratory investigations were held once a week whether we needed them or not. This was primarily due to scheduling constraints and the fact that most laboratory lessons did not neatly fit into one standard period. Additionally, there was a higher emphasis on content mastery and less focus on what we now call "hands-on" learning.

In the last ten years, science teaching and curriculum design has made substantial moves forward. We now recognize that the "doing of science" produces deeper and longer lasting student understanding than just the "hearing" about science. This change has been a central tenet of the "constructivist learning" movement in science. Constructivism suggests students should "do and construct" their ideas about science as opposed to "hearing" about science. A good place to begin your answer to this question is with a discussion of this trend.

The philosophical shift to constructivist learning has prompted publishers to produce more activity-rich curricula and laboratory-centered teaching. Time innovations like block scheduling and flexible modules have improved the constricted timeframes of the past. Ask the committee what kinds of time arrangements are available for laboratory courses.

In your answer to this question, describe how you will manage time and describe a few innovative class activities that will transform your class into a hub of science experimentation. Speak to the central issue of experiential learning as a means to create genuine understanding and appreciation for the work of scientists. You might also describe how your laboratories capitalize on the natural interests of students and generate excitement for the topic. Give the committee a view of how you will organize the room and materials to facilitate lab-oriented learning. Look at the following example.

"In each unit of study, I include a mixture of hands-on activities and formal laboratories to extend the concepts we are studying through practical applications. I make a point of having at least one activity that students "do" during each class period."

This discussion is a sound start, but remember to add an example or two of these exercises to make the answer complete. You must use your own background and select examples that illustrate how this concept will look in an actual class. The following provides direction as to how you might phrase this portion of the response.

"For example, students might study a unit on rocks and minerals. As we explore this unit students will engage in several hands on activities. One such activity might have students study how to name and classify rocks by identifying their unique physical characteristics such as hardness and acid sensitivity. When students have internalized classification procedures, they move on to a full laboratory experience that requires them to identify local rocks or minerals."

Once you have provided this brief example, you can list a wider variety of classroom activities that might take place. These additional activities could include lab reports, oral sharing, demonstrations, projects, science-fairs, learning centers, cooperative learning, and other varieties of student involvement. Review innovative ways you have created interactive atmospheres in your class and stimulated student discussion in the past.

Now it is time to "kick it up a notch" and add something other candidates may overlook – the use of technology. You can choose technology such as laser discs, computer simulations, on-line explorations, and interactive laboratory experiments. An ever-growing parade of Internet connections can link you to museums, other classes, scientists, universities, and almost any resource you need. If you are not familiar with specific websites, get the book, <u>netStudy, Get Online for Better Grades</u>, by Michael Wolf. Ask someone on the committee if your school has on-line services capable of providing supplemental courses of study or satellite hookups. Talk about these powerful tools and your expertise. Let the committee know you can create extended and innovative opportunities for students to enjoy. Only the very best candidates will describe this teaching dimension. Do not miss your opportunity to shine!

 Keys to Your Response:

- Begin with a <u>concise</u> definition of the constructivist movement and the way that philosophy will influence your teaching.

- Suggest how you will manage time and include a variety of hands-on science activities in your classes. Remember to provide a specific example.
- List a few ways beyond laboratories where you will involve students in the "doing" of science.
- End with a strong statement on technology and its potential applications in your room.

> *In our school we have a greenhouse. Describe how you would use this facility with your classes.*

Unless someone has had specific greenhouse experience or given the idea previous thought, this question can easily catch a person off guard. The topic could just as easily center on nature trails, planetariums, or some other unique feature of the school. The question's purpose is to explore a candidate's familiarity with distinctive resources along with his or her creativity in crafting exciting learning experiences in the target facility. The question can also reveal how a candidate thinks under pressure.

The perfect **WRONG ANSWER** would be,

> *"Gee, I haven't given that much thought, I'd have to look into what could be done, but I'm sure it would be something."*

Mercy. Try not to laugh, but that answer has been offered a number of times. We need to improve on such a weak response.

Even if you have had *no* experience or background in the area, you should have enough general knowledge about such facilities to identify a few ideas. Stay calm, take a deep breath and begin with a few general uses while your creative ideas begin to take shape. Perhaps you can discuss conducting a standard bean plant experiment, organizing a class project with holiday plants, holding a botany club, or establishing a project area. The committee wants to know that you have sufficient science background to put good resources to work.

Add technology ideas to give this answer a boost. There are experiments on-line, agricultural resources, and books that provide excellent project ideas. The Internet provides networks of schools already involved in greenhouse research. If you do not have a wealth of practices on hand to share, you should at least give the committee an idea of where you will go to expand your knowledge. Committees do not expect a complicated and intricate answer. Your goal is to provide a sufficient number of ideas to suggest you will make use of the facilities.

 Keys to Your Response:

- Do not get flustered if you have not had experience with a greenhouse. Just begin with a general discussion of the purposes for which such a facility might be used.
- Discuss projects, special enrichment ideas, lab experiments and other teaching ideas.
- Add technology-based designs and receive a "plus five" on your answer!
- Identify resources you will use to expand your knowledge and use of the facility.

> *Science can be a difficult discipline for special needs students. How can you adapt your class so these young people can enjoy a sound science experience?*

Science is a subject where special education students are often included as a part of the regular class. This is particularly true in general and earth science, but it can occur in college prep courses as well. You need a specific plan for modifications you might use with included students.

The chapter dealing with general questions contained ideas on how to teach mainstreamed special education students. However, that discussion did not speak about the unique problems related to science teaching. Open with a short affirmation of your enthusiasm to teach learning disabled students and a commitment to make these students a full part of your class. It is important that the committee see you are not reluctant to work with special education students.

An excellent resource when designing instruction for special education students is the student's case manager. This person knows the student's Individualized Educational Plan (IEP) and learning history. Outline how you will use that person as a resource for your class planning. Address ways you might adapt science experiments so special students can be involved in the laboratory portion of the class. Be sure to cite any additional safety practices you might recommend and how they will be monitored.

The question specifically asks about which modifications you will consider. Candidates must offer sound ideas on this subject. You might employ adaptations such as special grouping arrangements, modified laboratory report requirements, or compatible activities for times when material is not at the right level of difficulty. With your discussion, let the committee know you are a person who recognizes the value of a science experience for special needs students.

There is one last point you should make to the committee before you conclude your answer. Assure everyone that you will take deliberate steps to create a science experience that is both successful and stress-free. Describe how assessment strategies will be varied to allow students to demonstrate their understanding through more than just one means. Notify everyone that you will adjust and not eliminate curriculum. It is essential the committee understand you will maintain consistent content expectations and educational experiences for everyone.

Keys to Your Response:

- Open with a short affirmation of your enthusiasm to work with special needs students.
- State your intentions to work with the case manager and collaboratively develop a sound program of study.
- Catalog specific classroom modifications and support mechanisms that will promote each student's success.
- End with a commitment to make the class as stress free as possible but still maintain a curriculum similar to that of the other students.

> ***Tell us what you know about current assessment practice and describe how you would use this knowledge to determine grades in a general science class.***

WARNING: *Any question that asks you to explain how you grade students is important and you want to insure the committee is left with a good impression of your practice.* A "wrong impression" would be that you use tests and quizzes as the primary determinant of grades and have an inflexible system of making grade decisions. Obviously, no one is likely to make such direct statements or admit this is their practice, however, principals will read between the lines of what you say and develop their own perception. I say this because you need to consider your answer carefully. Below is a portion of an answer I once received. Think about what these ideas might say to you.

"I give two quizzes for each chapter and a test at the end of each chapter. Since I use a point system, homework counts 20 per cent, grades on laboratories 20 per cent, and tests and quizzes make up the remainder. I total up the points a student has and justify the sum with the school grading **scale to determine everyone's grade."**

This answer did not sit well with me or the other committee members, yet this candidate obviously thought it demonstrated good practice since he described a system so commonly in use in today's classes. Although we wish those days were left far behind, many teachers continue to use this outmoded procedure to determine grades. The trouble with this process is its preponderance of weight on paper and pencil tests as the method of identifying student mastery. Yes, tests and quizzes will let us know some important things about what students know, however, they do not tell the entire story. There are numerous other performance assessments that can allow students to demonstrate their understanding equally well. When you have a wide variety of students, learning styles and abilities, the wider assessment band gives better information and promotes greater student success. Better teachers now recognize this wider role of assessment and use it in a far more sophisticated manner.

We need to examine the elements of grading practice that will make a more favorable impression. Take a moment to analyze what this question is designed to uncover. The two basic concerns the committee wants resolved include 1) your knowledge of current trends and 2) your grading practices for students.

The teaching decisions that involve student grades are complex and you need an organized response. If you fail to organize your thinking on this topic, your answer can easily wander through a maze of unconnected ideas and lose power. Candidates who offer meandering responses that lack clarity will fail to impress their committee. An excellent theme around which to organize a clear response would be the *purposes* for which assessment can be used. Assessment purpose provides a clear focus and will allow you to link your assessment objectives to specific daily practices. For example, you might initially establish two general assessment goals. The first goal would be the **use of assessment to diagnose student learning and plan future instruction.** The second goal might be **the use of assessment to determine student achievement and grades.**

*"This is a very important question because assessment
is the basis on which I determine the effectiveness of my*

teaching. Although there are many uses of assessment, my two main purposes are first to diagnose the progress of student understanding and second to decide on the grades a student should receive."

This statement gives you two defined centers around which you can build the rest of your answer. Both ideas are consistent with what the question asks and you can provide strong ideas on how you will attend to these goals.

Move directly from your discussion of assessment goals to the specific ways you use evaluation strategies to diagnose student learning and design daily instruction. Consistent assessments provide the feedback about student progress on the day's objectives. Based on these results you can then decide exactly what concepts or skills need further attention and what has been learned. In the final analysis, it is assessment that determines how your teaching will proceed and what instruction must be designed. You can add ideas on how you teach students the value of peer and self-assessment so they can monitor their own progress. Through a process of self-analysis, students can exercise consistent quality control over their own learning.

This question offers an excellent place to discuss where and how rubrics will be used in your class. Rubrics are excellent assessment tools because they clearly identify the critical characteristics required for exemplary student performance. (See Appendix A) By identifying the exact performance characteristics required for exemplary performance along with their concrete benchmarks, students can make judgments about their work and determine what must be done to improve the overall quality. Science labs, projects, oral presentations and written essays are all places where a good rubric is of value. Place emphasis on your intention to help students produce exemplary work through an ongoing set of teacher, peer, and self-assessment opportunities.

The second part of the question asks how you determine student grades. I suggest you list a wide variety of measurement methods along with their importance to grade determination. The archaic design that relies heavily on tests, quizzes and homework will not represent a strong answer. A central issue in student grades must be the legitimate attainment of the learning objectives. Did the student master the content for that marking period? How did you make that determination? The greater the variety in the ways you allow students to demonstrate their mastery, the more assurance you have of sound decision-making on their final grade. You undoubtedly have many evaluation strategies in mind and you must weave those into a sound tapestry of grading practice.

> *"When I think about student grades, I consider two basic things. First, has the student demonstrated mastery of the goals and objectives set out by the lessons. I like to provide a wide variety of ways for students to accomplish this, but in the final analysis, I really must know if they have met the standards. To make these decisions I employ . . . . (list your methods). Second, I look at how much growth has occurred and what level of effort has been put forth. Students who extend themselves to learn the material and exerted every effort to succeed should be rewarded for such efforts."*

You can phrase your ideas differently and every good candidate should be able to provide a reasonably good account of him or herself in this part of the answer. I provided the above example because it embodies an element of grading practice not often seen. Did you notice the last two sentences? *Students should be rewarded for effort and growth.* This idea can be very powerful if you can articulate a clear way to accomplish that goal. Lets explore that possibility further. When you provide an objective way to credit a student's academic growth to his or her grade, you provide a totally unique dimension to the grading process. Because you are suggesting a system that awards credit for academic growth, you need to consider how such "growth" can be quantified. Some students have a great science background and aptitude while others start from well behind. The use of pre and post-tests, beginning and ending work samples, rubric growth, or other ways to identify student attainment over time can provide a foundation for this practice. You need to consider how your own system might be adapted to measure student development, but what a powerful dimension this would be to add! Believe me, it is the rare candidate who ventures into this territory. Think about whether that candidate should be you.

As you conclude your response to this question, be sure you have emphasized that success and mastery of essential learning is the most important factor. Insure that everyone is aware there is a dual purpose in your evaluation process and variety in the ways you determine student grades.

 Keys to Your Response:

- Organize your response around the main purposes of your assessment plan.
- Provide an overview of how assessment can be used to diagnose student progress and assist you in designing future instruction.
- Talk about your use of rubrics and self-assessment in your evaluation model.
- Outline how you determine student grades and include a wide variety of ways students can demonstrate successful mastery of objectives.
- End by describing how you will reward students for their growth and significant improvement.

> **When you assign students a science project, what are its design elements and how do you determine successful student performance?**

The committee obviously thinks projects are worthwhile or this question would not have been asked. Begin the discussion with your views on the importance of independent research and the elements of a good science project. Describe a project assignment you have made in the past or tell about one you might use in the future. In your answer, be sure to address the committee's central question regarding the critical "design elements." Consider how students will choose their topics, the level of required experimentation, the research format, the report's length, and any specific writing requirements. Will oral or visual presentations be required? Will there be interdisciplinary connections to other areas such as English or Math? If you address a variety of these considerations, you will have your answer moving in the right direction.

Regarding the determination of grades, include a description of any rubrics you will use to help students critique their work. Tell the committee about the handouts you intend to provide. Identify which elements of the project are graded and outline a broad-based assessment plan. Make clear how class time will be used to complete the project and specify how you will monitor student progress. You will add power to the answer if you identify provisions for students who submit work that is not up to the desired quality. As part of your assessment design, consider the provision of opportunities for students to bring sub-standard work up to the exemplary level.

A mistake many candidates make in answering this question is to omit the identification of specific objectives for the research. Avoid this error by telling the committee exactly what students are expected to learn from their work on the project? If you include a few high power learning outcomes in your answer, you will be a step ahead of most other candidates.

DON'T FORGET: *If you have a great class project you have used in the past, include a one-page overview of that project in your interview portfolio!* This, along with work samples or pictures of students at work, will add two exclamation points to your candidacy.

 Keys to Your Response:

- Begin with a discussion about why science projects are an important part of your teaching.

- Identify a project you have assigned students and categorize its critical elements and desired learning outcomes.
- Discuss how you will grade the assignment. Be sure to define any rubrics you will use.
- Close with a brief description of what students will learn from completing this project.

> **How is your instructional approach for an Advanced Placement (AP) course different from your approach to a college preparatory course?**

This question is sometimes asked of candidates who are expected to teach advanced level courses. Your answer should focus its attention on two specific areas, the AP test and the difference in quality of expected students. College preparatory classes are designed for what the name implies, to prepare students to enter college. As such, you will want to provide a fair level of academic rigor and move students towards more independent learning opportunities. This may mean research papers, field assignments or other work commonly attendant to the college experience.

The AP class is somewhat different. The two main reasons students take AP classes are the possibility of receiving college credit and Grade Point Average (GPA) enhancement. The latter has no bearing on your answer, but the issue of college credit is important. Usually, students enrolled in AP courses take a spring examination administered by the Educational Testing Service (ETS) in Princeton, New Jersey. Students are scored from one through five with a five being the highest rank. A grade of three is considered passing, but many colleges will not award credit unless the student's score is four or five. As the AP test adds a higher level of accountability for both you and the students, your answer should focus on strategies to prepare students for the AP exam. Consider how you might use sample questions from previous AP tests to improve essay writing. You may use "back-loaded" information from old tests to align your curriculum, provide needed test-taking strategies, devise practice tests, and promote a strong content background. Provide the committee with clear evidence that you understand the importance of your role in preparing students for the AP test.

The student who takes an AP class is generally very strong. Some schools even limit enrollment to a select few. This suggests you can introduce a higher level of course rigor than you might for the college preparatory sections. Discuss ways you will challenge students and stretch their thinking.

 Keys to Your Response:

- Begin by providing a *brief* overview of why the AP course should have a different approach than a CP course.
- Highlight the classroom experiences you provide in CP courses that will transfer to college level work.
- Highlight the specific test-taking skills you will teach and how examination of earlier versions of the exam will impact on your teaching.
- Stress the need for a very strong content background in both classes.
- Conclude with a description of how you will add rigor and academic stretch to the curriculum.

Students often ask why they have to learn this "stuff" or why is what they are studying important. How do you answer those questions?

How many times have we heard the phrase, "Why do we have to learn this stuff, anyway?" This is another way of saying, "I don't see any purpose to what we are doing." A science lesson's purpose can be lost unless the teacher provides activities to help establish a clear connection to the world of students. Principals want to know that prospective teachers understand this obligation and they will create lessons that communicate a clear purpose.

You can begin your answer with a statement that establishes your intention to provide a consistent rationale for the units and concepts defined in the curriculum. Make it clear that you intend to link instruction as closely to the real world of students as possible. By providing meaningful class experiences, you hope to decrease the frequency with which this question is asked.

"When I hear this question from students, I immediately know they have failed to see the purpose of the lesson. In my classes we will spend time to establish the purpose of each study area — before we begin the teaching. In my daily teaching, I will need to make the lesson components as meaningful as possible. There are specific ways to do this. Let me describe a few to illustrate what I mean."

The use of a specific example or story will be sufficient to give the committee what it requires. Think about your classes and identify a lesson where you provided a purpose that resonated with your students. Specific ways teachers can establish purpose and meaning include the use of outside speakers, videos, career connections, field trips, Internet sites, or models. There are others and you should choose those that best fit your style of teaching.

Another effective way to establish a strong sense of purposeful learning is through the use of a principle of learning called "meaning." Meaning is the level to which students see the material as related to them. Many education journals cite specific variables that will help students derive meaning from a lesson. Madelin Hunter was one of the earliest to point these out.

Hunter's Variables that Lead to Increased Meaning

- The new learning has **high interest examples** the student understands.
- The lesson has **novel or vivid activities** to capture interest.
- The lesson helps students **solve a problem** they see as important.

- There is a **structure and organization** the students find easy to follow and understand.
- *The new information is **closely related to something students already understand**. (You must help make such connections.)*
- *There is a relationship between what is taught and its **application to real world** around students.*

When giving your answer, you do not need to tick off the entire list of variables. In fact it might be best to confine your approach to just a couple of the variables. Power will come from your ability to provide examples illustrating your use of such variables.

> *"One way I like to create meaning in the lesson is to show students that what they are learning in the current lesson is related to something they already know. For example, when I teach students about inertia in Physics, I explain that we all know what happens when a large object strikes a large immoveable mass. But, once we get that large object moving in one direction, it is sometimes hard to stop. Consider the Titanic. She was cruising along and all of a sudden there is an iceberg dead ahead. Her "inertia" is what killed her. If we are to learn anything from this tragic event, we must know what factors contributed to Titanic's inertia and why this was such a problem. In fact we also need to know why inertia might even be a problem for you!"*

This is a great example of creating meaning because it combines several variables. It relates the concept of inertia to something with which students are familiar. It has a high degree of interest and pictorial vividness. It poses a problem that students might be interested in solving. It involves them in hands-on activities. WOW. The committee should like an example like this!

Close with your recognition of the fact that no single strategy can fit all students. Individuals have unique perspectives and interests. For that reason, you intend to establish a strong purpose and use as many variables of meaning as possible. Trust me on this; if you include the key elements of the response outlined above, you will have nailed this question to everyone's satisfaction.

Keys to Your Response:

- Begin by defining the real problem – a lack of perceived purpose.
- Catalog the ways you will establish clear links between what is taught and the world of students.
- Cite the ways you will enhance "meaning" in your teaching.
- Conclude by noting that a variety of methods are required to establish purposeful teaching.

> *Safety is always a concern for laboratory science. How do you keep this important matter a priority for students?*

This is a straightforward question and science candidates can usually count on a safety question. Liability concerns need to be addressed at the interview stage of any teacher search. A complex answer is not required. The principal and committee just want to know you will take standard precautions and make good judgments to insure everyone's safety.

Let the committee know you will consistently assess any safety features in your lab to be sure they are fully operational and ready for use. You will post and teach clear safety instructions. Specific investigations may require additional safety procedures and those will be taught. You will model good safety practice yourself. You might also administer a safety test or quiz to be sure your students know and understand the rules before they begin work. Talk about how you will deal with students who violate safety standards. If you address these areas, the committee will be well satisfied by your answer.

 Keys to Your Response:

- Do not overcomplicate the question when a simple answer will do.

- Talk about the various pieces of safety equipment you will want in you laboratory and their importance.
- Underscore a few general safety concerns and announce your intention to teach safety measures, not merely recite the rules.
- Conclude with a strong statement that good safety will be consistently modeled in the room and students will be expected to follow acceptable procedures.

> **Tell us how you determine that a student understood the science concepts you taught and did not merely memorize content for the test.**

I include this question because it raises an important issue called "understanding." The question poses an interesting dilemma for candidates. How does the committee define the term "understood?" Some interviewers will simply define the term as the ability of a student to re-explain concepts or ideas in his or her own way. Others may have a slightly higher requirement and suggest that students must also be able to apply the knowledge to a new situation. These ideas are based on explanations originally provided by Benjamin Bloom back in 1955. Many candidates will answer this question by using the Bloom definitions. He is an excellent source and his definition serves the purpose but we can do better – a lot better!

The last 45 years have brought significant advancement to our appreciation of how students come to understand. For our discussion, we will use an expanded description of this term as outlined in the book, <u>Understanding by Design</u> (Wiggins and McTighe, 1998). You should consider this information in designing an answer for any question that involves teaching for understanding. Wiggins and McTighe describe six interrelated variables that make up mature understanding. Even if this precise question is not posed, these ideas can be used in many ways and it will be well worth the time spent to internalize this expanded description of the term "understanding."

WIGGINS AND MCTIGHE'S
VARIABLES OF UNDERSTANDING:

1. **EXPLANATION**: *Apt explanations of theories that provide knowledgeable accounts of events, actions and ideas.*
2. **INTERPRETATION**: *Narratives and translations that provide meaning.*
3. **APPLICATION**: *The ability to use knowledge effectively in a new situation and diverse context.*
4. **PERSPECTIVE**: *Critical and insightful points of view.*
5. **EMPATHY**: *The ability to get inside another person's feelings and worldview.*
6. **SELF-KNOWLEDGE**: *The wisdom to know one's ignorance and how one's patterns of thought and action inform as well as prejudice understanding.*

Fashion your answer around a description of teaching practices that foster the development of these abilities in students. An excellent approach is to describe a designed activity that promotes one or more of these variables. You might suggest the use of discussion techniques, independent study projects or "think tank" activities that promote student understanding. Your goal is to outline a wide vision of the term "understanding" and match strategies to produce those results in students.

> *"Guiding students to truly understand the material is critical to good teaching. Memorization only brings information to short-term memory and will usually not last longer than the day of the test. Two of the ways I know students "understand" is when they can apply the knowledge to a new situation or if they can provide different or unique insights that use the information."*

Here we included two of our definitions to exemplify ways we can identify student understanding. This, however, is not quite enough. We must also take the answer to the next step and supply a practical example. This may be difficult to do on the spur of the moment and I suggest you take the extra time to pre-think a response.

"I can draw an example of this from when I teach tax-onomy in the Biology class. After I conduct my lesson on the ways we classify living things, I show students a few ex-amples of dichotomous keys and we work together to iden-tify a few sample organisms. From this point, I give stu-dents a variety of new items to classify and they have to construct their own key. If they can do this – I know they understand the concept of taxonomy. They have now shown both insight and application."

You possess many strategies of your own and the best ap-proach is to choose those with which you feel most comfortable. Be assured, if you employ this broader definition of understanding and clearly show how you measure it in your teaching, your answer will be a winner!

    Keys to Your Response:

- Study the broader definition of the term "understand" as pro-vided by Wiggins and McTighe.
- Choose two or three of the variables and discuss them.
- Provide at least one practical example from a lesson you have taught.

Science "literacy" is a topic that has received a great deal of recent atten-tion. What will students do in your class to enhance this skill?.

Literacy involves both the reading of science and the ability of students to communicate their knowledge and understanding of science. Once upon a time, literacy was confined almost entirely to the language arts domain. Now, however, many discipline areas are concerned with teaching literacy skills and almost all states have requirements for literacy development across the curriculum.

The only way to increase science literacy is to have students read science, discuss science, and write about science. Therefore, begin with a quick outline of various writing opportunities you might include in your course. These can consist of such things as journals, lab reports, projects, research papers, book reviews, or reflection pieces where students have to communicate their understandings of science. Talk about how you will teach students about the reading of science and list any required readings that might be a part of your class. These readings can consist of books you will discuss in-class or reading the student must undertake independently. Indicate how you will provide ongoing opportunities for students to express scientific viewpoints or information. Student expression of scientific ideas is a very important element of literacy.

> *"I think it is important for every student to be a consumer of good scientific literature and be able to express his or her ideas in a coherent way. In our genetics unit, the entire class will read 24 pages of the book, <u>The Double Helix,</u> by Watson and Crick. We will discuss this reading in class and write a reflection piece on the real world of scientists. Some students will present their ideas to the class for discussion."*

Literacy activities can and should be a part of every unit. It does not have to be an "extra" concern. With thoughtful development of class activities, it can be an integral part of the normal teaching process.

 Keys to Your Response:

- Identify where you will incorporate writing and scientific literacy in your regular teaching.
- Give an example of an outside reading that will extend student experience into the literature of science.

CONCLUDING THOUGHTS

Prospective science teachers should understand that the most important part of selling themselves to the committee rests in their ability to produce classes that will be exciting places for students to learn. These classes must be full of interesting activities, discussions, experimentation and dynamic interaction.

Interviews for science teachers will focus on several key areas such as content knowledge, laboratory investigations, assessment practice, safety, instructional practice, and planning. Additional relevant questions to a science interview are identified in other chapters and I urge you to read those sections as well. Read the questions provided by this chapter a few times and prepare your best thinking on the topic areas we have identified.

You will notice that the names of significant educators and books are sprinkled throughout this book. For example, this chapter focused attention on ideas presented by Wiggins and McTighe. Where possible, mention such individuals and references by name. When you are able to quote the ideas and works of significant others, a message is conveyed that you are someone who knows the important philosophies and educational leaders of our profession. This perception can only help your candidacy. Once the principal realizes you have great answers to his or her questions and a commitment to children, you become a player! You are ready, so attack this interview with enthusiasm and – GET HIRED.

13
SOCIAL STUDIES QUESTIONS

GENERAL INFORMATION

If you are applying to a middle or high school, you may be seeking a position in the social studies. The middle school curriculum is primarily devoted to World and U. S. History, but high school positions might also include courses such as Economics, Sociology or Psychology. As with the other discipline areas, this chapter provides advice to prepare you for interview questions that explore both your general content knowledge and instructional methodologies. Narrow questions in a particular subject are not included because of their limited scope of relevance for all readers.

Candidates for a social studies position must be prepared to demonstrate how they will relate the key elements of a school's curriculum to the contemporary world. Because History is often a required course for all students, class management, your ability to teach heterogeneous groups, and human relations are areas the committee is likely to explore. History often has classes composed of a variety of ability groups and the demand for sound management is a common concern.

As you prepare for the interview, spend time to identify a few innovative lesson ideas from your past teaching. The area of social studies is one that can be interesting, exciting, and highly relevant to the students. It can also be painfully boring and uninspired. The difference is not in the content, but in the teacher's skill and you must provide clear evidence you are the inspirational teacher the school needs.

Review the sample questions included in this chapter and consider how your background and skills fit the suggested response. As you consider the information offered by each question, you will need to reflect on your background and experience before you finalize an answer.

SAMPLE QUESTIONS

> **Describe the opening activities and lessons you might use if you were beginning a 6th grade unit on the Civil War.**

The purpose of this question is to determine how you use the important first days of a unit to initiate activities that will lay the essential foundations of study. The teaching topic in this question is not especially important as one could substitute any long-term area of study. What is important is the way you will lay the groundwork for a productive learning experience. The critical first days of a unit must capture the interest of students and establish a framework on which to construct the key ideas you wish to convey.

You will need a strong hands-on activity to capitalize on the initial enthusiasm of students and provide a good overview of the lesson concepts to be featured. I like to think about ways to make the opening class experience novel and memorable. For example, a social studies teacher once collected several days of classroom trash in a large barrel. At the opening of the unit on anthropology, he had everyone move their chair to the back of the room. The teacher then proceeded to empty the trash barrel onto center of the floor while students were instructed to sift through the material and reconstruct the history of that room as far back as possible. The next two hours were spent sifting, categorizing and hypothesizing. This was a great start to the archaeology topic. The novelty of the approach had the interest of the students and set the stage for future discussion. Your answer need not be quite this innovative, but you can see how a well-designed opening lesson can generate enthusiasm for learning. A strong teaching segment that includes active student participation will immediately move the class in a positive direction.

A good answer to this question will also identify how you will provide students meaningful reasons to study the Civil War. Underscore any exciting special events you plan such as speakers, artifacts, video clips, or other high-interest items. Since the question centers on the Civil War, you might describe class activities that help students identify the unique aspects of this war. This may be done through role-playing or skits, scenario analysis, or public debates. Such activities help students empathize and mentally connect to the important issues that fueled the conflict. Add your own ideas to those offered here, but a good answer will demonstrate imagination and innovative lesson designs.

KEY STRATEGY: *Whenever possible, make the ending of your response as powerful and memorable as possible. The last thing a committee hears should be something worth remembering.* Student learning often depends upon an organized and structured presentation of the material. An excellent way to end this question is with a description of how you will provide the students a structured, written framework around which the activities and requirements for the unit can be organized. Visual organizers can be valuable tools to help students focus on important learning and concepts they must master. You *and* the students must be guided by a clear understanding of the important concepts and objectives to be learned. Your description of a system to organize the unit might sound something like the following.

> *"Before we actually begin the instruction, I like to provide the students with an "advance organizer" of what they must learn and any important tasks they must accomplish during the unit. To achieve this goal, I take six to ten central themes or objectives, write them in student language, and arrange them in a sequence everyone can follow. I write everything on the overhead projector and students follow along on a compatible handout as we progress through the unit. As important information or ideas unfold, I refer students to their organizer. The central ideas are also posted around the room and we refer to them as the unit unfolds. This guide helps keep everyone on track."*

You may take a different approach, and the above is only a suggestion. The important message to convey is that students will clearly know your expectations and the important elements of the unit. The use of **advance organizers** allows everyone to coordinate their thinking and approach to the unit of study. It is an extremely powerful tool and one that most candidates will not identify. That is why your answer will be remembered!

 Keys to Your Response:

- Start your answer with a brief discussion on how you will establish initial student enthusiasm.
- Outline your strategy to introduce course goals, objectives, and purpose.
- Select a few key ideas or concepts you will teach about the Civil War and describe an innovative way to teach each.
- Identify the key elements of the unit and how you will provide an **advance organizer** that alerts students to what they must learn.

> *One of the better-known statements regarding history is, "Those who cannot remember the past are condemned to repeat it." What would you do in your class to illustrate this maxim and help students internalize its meaning?*

This is an interesting question because it allows you an opportunity to demonstrate how you will tie the student's knowledge of history to contemporary policy making. According to the author of this question, it was designed to assess three things; 1) the candidate's general history knowledge, 2) his or her ability to craft an objective that would continue through the full semester, and 3) his or her ability to use current events as a regular part of the classroom.

When addressing this question, you might want describe how you would open the unit with an anticipatory set that asks students to analyze an incident in which history has influenced current policy.

This can be done with an example or two where history has evidenced two similar events or where a historical figure blundered because he or she was ignorant of history. For example, most military leaders study the lives of great generals and battles of the past. It has been suggested that Hitler's failure to study and recognize the significance of Napoleon's failed Russian Campaign contributed to the undoing of Germany's entire eastern campaign during the Second World War. Had Hitler considered the logistic nightmare that a harsh Russian winter could create, a different plan might have been considered. An anticipatory set that uses this information might be structured as follows.

> *"I would ask students to consider this question. What happened to the German army when they tried to invade Russia during WWII? List some of the major obstacles that confronted them.*

Advise the committee that you expect the brutal winter conditions of Russia to be among the answers students would provide. From this point, you can set the stage for the coming lesson.

> *"Yes, the winter was a huge factor. Now, does anyone remember what happened to the army of Napoleon when he tried to invade Russia? Would it have helped had Hitler taken heed of the history of that campaign? How might that reflection have affected German military policy? In the coming days we are going to look at a variety of occasions where history could have influenced an important decision. More importantly, we are going to look at what is going on in the news today and identify historical precedents that might be useful in crafting contemporary policy.*

With this beginning, you can discuss how you would make the relevance of history to today's world an ongoing theme in your teaching. There were numerous times throughout history when this maxim was significant. As such important past events are reached in the curriculum, historical connections to later events can be drawn and reinforced. If you have examples or your own, be sure to add one or two and strengthen your point.

Take the last few moments of your answer to cite where history may be influencing current policy-making. World leaders often use their knowledge of history to craft treaties and agreements with other nations and individuals. Be sure to explain how students will be required to analyze where current world events are being influenced by historical events. An extremely poignant example is the terrorist attack on the World Trade Center. Were there historical pointers the United States missed? How was this attack similar or different than terrorist attacks in the past? How did Desert Storm influence the decisions in the design of the United States response to the WTC atrocity? Stress that analytic ability is a process skill you intend to cultivate in each person over the year. Specific examples will add impact to the answer. However, if you do not have a good example at just that moment, the general discussion will suffice. You can be confident that if you offer an overview of the ideas presented in this discussion, you will be one step further than most other candidates!

   Keys to Your Response:

- Begin by describing a teaching set that uses an important historical event that connects to today's world. Explain how this will establish the foundation to teach the concept described by the question.
- Underscore your intention to make this concept an ongoing theme that runs through the curriculum over the entire year.
- End by citing an example of current day policy making that you would use to drive home the importance of this concept to students.

A criticism made of current high school graduates is they do not have a fundamental understanding of democratic citizenship and the operation of our government. If you were to teach a 9th grade social studies class, how would you fashion a unit of study to minimize this perceived learning gap?

Whether the lack of citizenship on the part of young people is a real or perceived problem is not the issue. The mere presence of the question provides license for you to assume the committee feels it is a concern in need of attention. Although the ninth grade history program can vary widely from school to school, the question allows you to assume citizenship is a legitimate part of this school's curriculum and, as such, a logical place to include a unit on this topic.

Entire books have been written on civics and you obviously do not have time to address the matter to that level of detail. Include only a few critical points in your answer and deliver a brisk, concise response. Because the essential concepts of a participatory citizenry are such an important part of every community, you have an opportunity to use your creativity. Be sure you do not just outline the information students will be taught. Add some activities, outside experiences, and other more innovative lesson design features.

Open with a few civic concepts you feel are essential for students to understand such as the Constitution, the rights and responsibilities of good citizenship, democratic participation, and government organization. Be sure to indicate your intention to teach a lesson or two about the organization and function of the students' local government.

Once this discussion is complete, illustrate the activities and interest-building experiences you intend to provide for students. For example, talk about how the Internet and other technology could be used to extend learning. Most local and county governments have a website and students can learn a great deal from just a few visits. If field experiences are available, take advantage of those. Propose guest lectures, enrichment topics, research projects, on-line courses, video or videodisc programs, and any other innovative strategies that link what you are teaching to the real world issues surrounding students today. You might consider an outside project that involves student attendance at a town council or planning board meeting. These high impact experiences lead directly to participation in the democratic process and drives directly to the heart of the question.

The key to this answer will be your description of meaningful lessons that include hands-on activities to show students how and where their democratic participation is necessary. **TIP:** If you are not sure you have a great lesson on <u>any</u> topic, go online and logon to <u>www.taskstream.com</u>. (Appendix B) This site has "best practice" lessons from all over the country and you are sure to find one that fits your style. You want to help students enjoy this unit as it may establish positive transfer to future action. By creating this more comprehensive vision, you will rise above the usual dry recitation of just what students need to know.

  Keys to Your Response:

- All units begin with a core of knowledge the students must understand. Open with a discussion of a few core requirements.
- Describe a wide variety of hands-on excursions into the ways students can participate in their government.
- End with a short explanation of why you believe the strong activity centered approach will lead to positive transfer of good citizenship habits.

> *Recently, the Columbine incident and a rash of other events have involved school violence. What role, if any, do you as the social studies teacher have in using these events in your curriculum?*

First – if this question is asked, the principal and committee do see a role for the social studies teacher. Today's interviews often have a question that asks how a contemporary issue will be approached in your class. The purpose of such questions is to determine your ability to relate what you are teaching to important issues in the world outside the class. Topics are interchangeable because teachers can structure their response in a variety of ways. Your answer will depend on your teaching stance and general method of handling current events.

Obviously, this question poses a relevant concern for every school-aged person. It embodies a few delicate issues and your awareness of the need for sensitivity may be a good place to begin the answer. Describe the relevance of the topic and an understanding of its highly charged elements. For example, views on gun legislation have sharp lines of division within the country. Columbine has added fuel to this debate and the committee must know you will take a thoughtful approach to your handling of such controversial topics with students. Sketch a picture of what information you will provide for the students regarding school violence and provide an example of a question you might pose to focus a discussion.

"In working with students on the issue of school violence, I would want to identify a set of incidents with which they might be familiar. To do this, I would separate the group into three teams and give them articles, clippings, or other information about separate incidents. Each team would distill only the pertinent "facts" of each incident into a list. These findings will be reported to the class while another student lists the facts on the board. When this is complete, I would ask the group to identify the similarities and differ-

ences between the facts listed by each group. We would then hold a class discussion on these findings."

You might have a different strategy that has worked for you in the past. The above is simply an illustration of an activity that opens student thinking and creates discussion. Whatever approach you choose, it is important that you identify a specific plan to gain initial student interest. Once you have identified an opening activity, move on to the ways you will guide student discussions on issues attendant to the Columbine incident. Make the committee aware of your intention to listen and allow students to express themselves as fully as possible. You will need to be flexible and aware of the potential for emotional reactions to appear.

A great close to this response is a description of the mentorship role teachers can play in their daily role. Tell the committee how every teacher needs to act as a mentor and guide for his or her students. A central concern underscored in many of the reported incidents of school violence has been the sense of alienation and bullying the student perpetrators felt. Expand on that issue and talk about how you intend to take steps to keep your class free of mean-spirited activity. Explain how you and the class will set higher expectations for the treatment of all students. By ending with a comment that emphasizes the necessity for us to learn from these horrible incidents, the committee will see how you are someone who will use your role as a social studies teacher to promote the wider good of the school. Those are BIG points and will move you to the top of the group. Trust me.

 Keys to Your Response:

- Start with a description of the topic's relevance and the sensitive issues that require your attention.
- Describe how you organize the group to study the problem and explain an activity to stimulate student discussion.
- Underscore the important elements of the Columbine incident that you want to review in your discussion.

- End with a statement about how you will use the lessons from Columbine to promote the good of your class and the school.

CONCLUDING THOUGHTS

As you consider the response suggestions provided in this chapter, make every effort to draw upon your daily experiences and personal teaching philosophy. The committee wants to hear how you will bring history to life in the classroom. A key to your success will be the enthusiasm you provide to each response you give. Many good answers lose their impact because they are delivered with no energy or intensity. If you are not passionate about your teaching, your ideas will not come across to the committee. Be creative, demonstrate your skill and make a statement. Good answers delivered with passion almost always carry the day.

My Favorite Teacher

One of my most memorable teachers was my tenth-grade American History teacher. She set the stage for learning history by not only teaching us about the past, but taking us to museums and other historical places. Once, when teaching the Civil War, she took us to two of the battle sites that had been fought in our area. We studied the land formations and the battle strategies employed by both sides. Her teaching made the war more real. I've remained a student of the Civil War ever since.

RICHARD BROCK, INVESTMENT BANKER
DALLAS, TEXAS

Reprinted from McGuire and Abitz, Best Advice Ever for Teachers

14
SPECIAL EDUCATION QUESTIONS

GENERAL INFORMATION

Over the last decade, more and more jobs have become available in special education. Federal and state legislation dealing with the handicapped as well as rising public pressure for services have resulted in significant changes to the way schools manage special needs students. There are now more special education employment categories and job opportunities for prospective teachers. In addition, the working conditions for teachers in the field of special education have been changing over recent years. These changes have placed increased demand on those who would enter the field to stay current in both their knowledge of the law and specific state requirements that impact their teaching.

Institutions for professional training and the workplace have responded to the increased demand for special education professionals by introducing a wider variety of courses, additional fields of study, wider varieties of certification categories, and improved staff development programs. In the past, classroom teachers were not expected to understand a great deal about special education. In many schools it was not unusual for special education classes to be staffed by teachers with only a few extra courses in the field. Today, the requirements for teaching are very different. Certificated teachers and specialized instructional designs are the norm. Even the more traditional mainstream teacher is expected to know how to work with special needs students. If you are applying for a position in the field of special education, interviewers will be anxious to explore your teaching philosophies and instructional skills in working with a variety of learning disabilities.

TEACHER OF THE HANDICAPPED

The teacher of the handicapped has become an extremely important role in public education. Students in today's schools are far different from those of the 1970's and 1980's. In addition, the knowledge base in the field of special education has advanced to a far more sophisticated level. Our ability to diagnose learning problems has risen such that student disabilities are identified earlier and more often than before. Some claim we now over-identify children, but the fact remains that this increase has created a tremendous need for special education teachers.

The combination of increased student numbers and a rapidly rising number of school litigation cases has led to a shortage of certificated special education teachers. Well-qualified, motivated special education teachers are highly sought by school districts across the country. *This is the good news*!! But, the good news notwithstanding, you will still have to do well at the interview to prevail. Keep in mind that Chapter 1 underscored the **FALLACY OF TEACHER SHORTAGES.** *Even when there is a high demand for teachers, a number of excellent candidates are likely to compete for the better positions.* In that regard, you must approach the interview process in a way that prepares you for the competition. Do your homework and construct a comprehensive interview strategy.

TEACHER OF THE HANDICAPPED QUESTIONS

The confidentiality laws are an important part of your work with special education students. If you are co-teaching a class, what information would you want to share with other teachers and what kinds of information should remain confidential?

The area of confidentiality has become an important concern for school administrators because growing legislation and increasing lawsuits regarding student privacy represent a significant school liability. As a teacher of the handicapped, you will be privy to a great deal of sensitive information. It is essential that the interview committee know you will use good judgment when you disseminate student information to other parties. At the heart of this matter is a "need to know" requirement attendant to all confidential information. A difference exists between teachers who have a student in their class and other staff members who have no consistent contact with the student. When there is a teacher who works with a child on a regular basis, you have a responsibility to convey to that teacher any IEP information that affects his or her work with that student. In addition, if there is an anecdotal record pertinent to the student's past school performance, this information can also be shared. Something conveyed to you in confidence by the parent or student should most often remain confidential unless it represents a possible danger to the student or others. Teachers who work with a student only on specific occasions may also need to know background information that can impact teaching practice. Educational concerns such as student reading levels, test profiles, and class performance are important details that can greatly assist a professional. Let the committee know you understand how teachers rely on you to provide relevant information regarding their special needs students.

Before you conclude your answer, underscore your understanding of the need for care and sensitivity about when and *where* confidential discussions or activities should take place. Even when it is appropriate to convey confidential information, it must be done in a place that is private enough to insure that other parties will not overhear the conversation. In a school building, this can be tricky. If you convince the committee you are aware of this matter, you will demonstrate your depth of judgment.

Keys to Your Response:

- Recognize the importance of student confidentiality.
- Use the "need to know" criteria to guide your selection of those to whom you will share confidential information.
- Conclude with your understanding of the need for caution about when and where confidential material is shared.

> *If you were told you were to be a co-teacher next year, what steps would you take to prepare for this assignment?*

As a teacher of the handicapped, expect to be considered for a co-teaching role in any school where there are inclusion classes. In those cases, the ability of the two teachers to plan and work together is essential to the success of the program for all students. For that reason, the committee will want to know your approach to such assignments and how you and the co-teacher will work together.

In instances where special education students are working in an inclusion setting, you are the individual most responsible for the education and success of the special needs students assigned to that class. Critical to that effort is your familiarity with each student's personal requirements and background. Gather as much information as you can about each student in advance and tell the committee how you will share pertinent details with your colleague. You might share with your co-teacher such things as copies of the curriculum to be taught, names of the expected students, information from other teachers regarding earlier inclusion experiences, the IEP's of all included students, and the names of previous case managers.

Describe what you would do to hold planning meetings with your colleague to discuss the educational program for included students and lay out specific recommendations for program designs and modifications. Indicate how you would want to discuss the instructional role each of you would undertake in the class. It is essential that each teacher have vital and well-defined operational responsibility in the class. In cases where co-teaching has failed, a central problem has often been communication and role definition between the two teachers.

A subject many candidates fail to address in their answer is how they plan to alter the room to accommodate special needs instruction. Considerations would include the use of private work areas, learning centers for varied abilities, addition of computer technology, organized places for consumable materials, reference libraries, or other accommodations that facilitate your work with students. Search your teaching background to frame this portion of your answer, but the committee will be impressed by your attention to facilities as an instructional concern.

 Keys to Your Response:

- Describe how you will gather needed information in advance and familiarize yourself with the students.
- Outline how you will work with the co-teacher to organize the instructional program and identify pertinent modifications required for student success.
- Develop an instructional role for each teacher.
- Determine the process for grading the included students.
- Identify any specific room alterations that might be necessary.

 How will your assessment program for included students be structured and what steps will you take to promote student success?

Performance assessment for the special needs pupil is different than for the regular education pupil. At this point in your career it is likely you have already established a system by which you determine student progress and grades. To answer this question you need to clearly articulate specifically what those judgments entail.

Here are a few things you should consider when framing your answer. First, the primary basis for determining the progress of a special education student is his or her Individualized Educational Plan (IEP). Has the student shown growth in the areas identified in the IEP and what is the *specific evidence of progress* towards the established IEP goals? This is the cornerstone of your assessment. Additionally, there will be class expectations applied to all students and you will need to determine each SE pupil's progress along that continuum as well. Such expectations should be fair, but there is no reason to exclude a requirement for success on class objectives unless those objectives are unreasonable or contrary to elements of the IEP. Let the committee know of your plans to work with the co-teacher to arrive at a fair grade for every student based on his or her specific accomplishments.

The second portion of this question asks how you will promote student success. As the thrust of the question concerns class grades, you can assume the committee wants to know how your grading practice will positively affect student performance. There are a number of ways to deal with this concern, but a safe approach is to outline how consistent use of performance feedback will provide students a clear picture of how they are progressing and what areas continue to need work. Keep in mind that special education students generally have a support class with a specially trained teacher. Be sure to describe how you will use this resource to help students stay abreast of their mainstream studies.

The sense of meaningful success is one of the most powerful agents of motivation we know. Talk about how you will build on each student's success to promote continued effort and learning. **KEY STRATEGY:** *A powerful way to enhance your answer is the use of a personal anecdote that describes how you successfully worked with a particular student in the past.* Such success stories live on in the minds of the committee well after the interview has closed. If you can show the committee that you recognize the positive influence of success and specific ways student grading can be used to promote performance, you have answered this section well.

 Keys to Your Response:

- Identify the primary basis of grade determination as fulfillment of the student's IEP.
- For the common class objectives you deem reasonable, progress against a realistically established set of expectations make up the remainder of a student's grade.
- Describe how you will establish an individual assessment program as opposed to the "one standard for all" grade practice.
- Highlight the ways you will work with the support class teacher to maintain student readiness.
- Describe a strategy that uses grades as an indicator of success to enhance student performance.

Special education students often see themselves as second-class students less worthy than their regular education classmates. What can you as the teacher do to minimize such self-esteem problems?

This is an ongoing problem in every school and a concern for every caring educator. The committee wants to insure your sensitivity to the issue and hear about actions you will take to reduce student anxiety. In your approach to this answer, reflect on what you now do on a daily basis to maintain student dignity and self-worth. For example, explain how during class discussions you will include all students and treat them as valuable participants. Underscore reinforcement strategies you will use to promote a high probability of student participation. Let the principal know that you will consistently encourage all students to do their best work.

Describe how you will recognize the good work or efforts of students and reward their successes. Think about your answer to this question because, even if it is not present, there are likely to be other opportunities to cite these pertinent ideas.

In years of working with special needs students, I have seen their enthusiasm for learning decline when the expectations and achievement goals are not accurately set. In many cases, class expectations were so high the student was convinced that legitimate success was well beyond his or her ability. At other times students felt the work was so babyish or simple it presented no worthwhile challenge. For the Teacher of the Handicapped the level of difficulty represented by the daily work is an ongoing issue because students with vastly disparate IEP requirements are present in the same room. Your ability to fashion an answer that recognizes this challenge will demonstrate insight and judgment. If you know how to do a task analysis, you might describe how such a device will help you choose instructional activities that fit each person's unique level of readiness. Describe how you will use lessons that have a clear "purpose" so students see their efforts as worthwhile. This portion of your answer must leave the committee with a clear understanding that you are a teacher who will design daily work at the right level of difficulty for every student.

Lack of confidence and self-worth often come from a long-standing history of failure and poor school grades. Let the committee know how you intend to reverse that trend if it has been a problem to the student in the past. Talk about your plan to build patterns of success by guiding and supporting student work until it reaches an acceptable level. A teacher I once interviewed described her grading system in the following way.

> *"I only give four kinds of grade, A, B, C and Not Yet. If a student has not achieved at least a C, I let him or her continue to work and I add my support until performance reaches at least the C level."*

She knew how to insure student achievement because the "Not Yet" grades received further help until they were elevated to the desired standard. Patterns of success build on one another just as do patterns of failure.

Finally, you can end with a description of how you involve parents and other professionals to reinforce student feelings of self-worth. When all of the adults who touch a student's life work together to promote his or her self-confidence, the chance for negative opinions to flourish in the mind of that student are diminished. Your answer should reflect your own ideas and dimensions, but it is important that the committee recognize your awareness of what underlies poor self-image and your enthusiasm in trying to maximize feelings of self-worth in your students.

 Keys to Your Response:

- Describe ways you plan to maintain student dignity, provide equal treatment, and provide recognition to each member of your class.
- Explain the process you will use to set worthy expectations and establish achievement goals students can attain.
- Articulate how you will establish a pattern of success by insisting that unsatisfactory work be corrected and resubmitted until passing grades are earned.
- Underscore your intention to communicate with the case manager, other professionals and home to enlist support in making each student's experience in your class positive.

 If you are the teacher for a support class with eight students, what steps will you take to assist those students in the completion of work for their regular education classes? How will you work with the regular education teachers on each student's behalf?

As a Teacher of the Handicapped, you are likely to be asked to teach a "Support Class" for small groups of students. In such classes, your role is to work with the student and keep him or her abreast of all work. You will also work with the mainstream teacher to cooperatively create the most effective teaching situation for the included students.

With this question the committee is asking what specific actions you will undertake to work with the student during the time he or she is in your support class. Some issues to consider when framing your answer include:

CLASSROOM ISSUES FOR SUPPORT TEACHERS

- *What materials from the mainstream class do you need in your room to help you assist the student with his or her daily work?* You may want to get copies of all classroom books and materials to keep in your room. It will help if you also have copies of the written curriculum to keep on file. If there are daily handouts or workbooks on which the students will work, you will want copies of these. Any instructional aides to be used in the class will assist you in working with the student.

- *How will you stay abreast of what is taking place in the class and each student's performance?* You must describe how you will communicate with classroom teachers and what information you will need regarding daily student work. If the students maintain assignment planners, you will need to check them on a regular basis. Perhaps the teacher can provide copies of overhead transparencies and handouts you can keep in a notebook or file.

- *What responsibility will you place on the student to stay abreast of his or her work in each class?* You should work with each student to promote his or her personal responsibility for the day's assignment. If the mainstream teacher has informed you of what is taking place in class, you will be in a position to monitor student efforts to stay current. Once students know you are keeping track of their daily effort and have high expectations, their accountability is raised and they are more likely to assume personal responsibility.

In summary, communication with classroom teachers, consistent monitoring of student progress, and ongoing reinforcement of student efforts will promote the success of your support class. If you provide the committee an answer that addresses the central issues contained in this discussion and add your own strategies, you can feel confident the question was well answered and that you have possibly moved a step closer to a job offer!

 Keys to Your Response:

- Describe which materials and necessities the mainstream teacher must provide for your support classroom. Include things that put you in a position to <u>know</u> what is taking place in the mainstream class.
- Define the strategies you will use to communicate with the mainstream teacher and stay abreast of student progress.
- Outline specific measures you will take to make the student responsible for his or her own work.

> *If you were to teach the concept of decimals to students in replacement math, what teacher actions and activities would you plan for that lesson? What steps would you take to assist students who are not successful in meeting the lesson's learning objectives?*

In an interview for a teacher of the handicapped position, you can expect a question on teaching methodologies. I chose one on decimals because the concept often presents a problem to students. To some degree, your answer will include strategies similar to those for other students. *The difference will be in the specific activities you design to diagnose and deal with learning problems.*

A good place to begin answers to curriculum questions is with a description of how you conduct advance planning for units. **KEY STRATEGY:** *When presented with a question that asks how to teach* *a difficult concept, begin with a good **task analysis**.* A task analysis breaks the end-goal into the specific sub-learnings required for mastery. For example:

TASK ANALYSIS FOR MULTIPLICATION OF DECIMALS

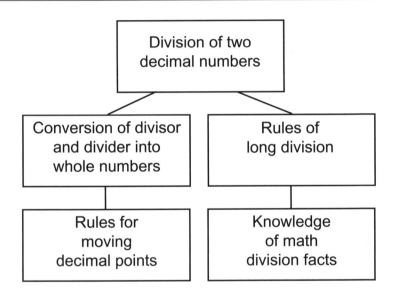

As you can see, the sub-skills must be mastered before the final task can be undertaken. There are other sub-skills you might have to consider in teaching this concept such as knowledge of multiplication facts, setup procedures, terminology, estimation, and so forth. The important element is for you to highlight a few essential sub-skills in decimal computation to the committee and explain why those were chosen. Once you have a set of sub-skills in place, you can use them to diagnose places where learning may have broken down and design *specific* remediation as necessary. If task analysis is not your strength, then discuss what methods you use to check student understanding and determine remedial strategies.

Move from your task analysis directly to the instruction you plan to provide. Obviously, there are numerous ways instruction of a topic can be approached, however there are a few important elements you should consider when you explain your design to the selection committee.

KEY STRATEGY: *Whenever you intend to describe a teaching strategy, you should consider separating your discussion into three separate categories of teacher actions.*

FIRST: List the essential information pieces you will need to teach. Be sure to include all of the items you listed in your task analysis as separate teaching segments. The sub-learning objectives are essential! To spice this portion of your answer, include how you will incorporate a few principles of learning such as modeling, transfer, student participation, and other ideas from your methods class.

SECOND: Outline the kinds of guided practice or teaching you will you carry out and how hands-on tasks will support those teacher actions. Be sure to let the committee know how you will guide students through a few practice problems before they are released to work independently. After guided practice you can move students to a "supervised" practice where they are working independently but under your watchful eye. Students do not own knowledge until they are using it on their own.

THIRD: Describe assessment strategies you will use to monitor learning progresses. Describe three or four different kinds of assessments that will diagnose initial student understanding and proficiency. You might want to begin your check for understanding by soliciting group responses and then move to individual evaluation.

Once you have outlined your instructional design, there is one last area to address – the way you will manage time and remediation. As with any new learning, there will be students who quickly demonstrate mastery while others continue to evidence a lack of proficiency or even total confusion. Be prepared to offer ways to address and alleviate these problems with such things as differentiated assignments based on mastery level, tutoring designs, re-learning centers, technology, or other support strategies. If you hold after-school or before-school help classes, mention them in your answer. This is a good place to provide a specific example of how you have worked with struggling students in the past. Even if it was in a different area of study, the committee will make the logical transfer to how you might help students to succeed with this concept. Remember, practical examples are powerful messages. The following is a good example of a supportive teacher's work with one student:

> *"I recall one of my students was having a great deal of trouble with the set-up for science problems on Newton's Law. Frankly, it was something he had never before been required to complete. I was convinced he could do it and persuaded him to give it a try. We began with two easy problems and wrote out a set of steps on an index card so he could follow them whenever he had questions of this kind. We did our samples together and promised to meet when he had library study. During that time, he did two more questions on his own and I merely prompted him where necessary. We continued this routine for a few days and, to his amazement, he got four of the five quiz questions right on Friday's test! That was a real accomplishment!"*

This answer shows a deliberate process and describes a situation that required extra time and effort on everyone's part. Believe me, this kind of anecdote is remembered by the committee.

An important element of your answer is the way you address the problem of varied learning styles and different rates of student learning. As long as the committee is confident you have the teaching expertise sufficient to present the concept in a clear and understandable way, everyone will be satisfied you can be successful. By adding a variety of methods that will diagnose learning problems and provide directed remediation, you are ahead of most candidates.

Keys to Your Response:

- Describe your planning methods and any specific areas where you need to pre-plan. A good task analysis or some other method of diagnosing learning problems will be worthwhile to include.
- Outline your teaching methodologies and include the three-step method that tells what you will teach, describes student activities, and utilizes an array of assessment methods to uncover learning problems.
- Explain how you will support students who do not master the concept and exhibit problems learning the concept.

 How often should you communicate with parents about the progress of their child and what kinds of information would you want to provide?

This question will often surface during an interview. The difficulty lies in the range of possible answers a committee might find acceptable. Their frame of reference will depend greatly on district expectations and the amount of community involvement commonly experienced. In a school with a very active parent base, you can expect the parent notification requirement to be significantly higher than one where parents are uninvolved and complacent. Here is advice you can use for any question that has a range of answers. **KEY STRATEGY:** *NEVER try to guess what a committee wants to hear. Answer every question with exact fidelity to your true position.*

Reflect on your experience and provide a description of how you maintain regular communications with each home and inform parents of their student's progress. You may have kept a phone log to insure a record of the calls you made and topics that were discussed. Tell the committee of any regular written communications you use. Identify how many contacts you like to make with the family each semester. **KEY POINT:** *A critical point for you to make is that home contacts are <u>planned</u> and made on a regular basis.*

You should move from regular contacts to those occasions when special communication might be necessary. Express your intention to provide phone calls with positive student reports as well as calls to deal with possible problems. Principals are interested to hear of specific experiences candidates have had regarding their home communications so if you have a good anecdote to share, that would be an excellent way to conclude this portion of the answer.

The question also asks what kinds of information you want to share with parents. Again, you have a history to draw on and you should draw on that experience. Most parents depend on the teacher to keep them informed, therefore a regular pattern of meaningful communications goes a long way toward helping families work with their students. The kinds of information you can address in your answer include:

SAMPLE INFORMATION FOR
PARENT COMMUNICATIONS

- ✓ Ways parents can support their student's work at home.
- ✓ Important information provided by mainstream teachers.
- ✓ Notification about important events taking place at school.
- ✓ Teacher feedback on the school performance of their student.
- ✓ Interpretation of test results to help parents understand their meaning.
- ✓ The need for parent involvement at school functions.
- ✓ Provision of pertinent IEP updates.
- ✓ Ways to work with parents on cooperative problem solving.

There are other kinds of information you might regularly communicate to parents and you should discuss these matters along with any you select from the above list. It is not necessary to discuss every element in great detail, a general idea of what you feel is important to convey will suffice. Be prepared to give your reasons for each item of information you intend to include. If you can convince the members of the committee a sound line of communication will be established, you have answered the question well.

 Keys to Your Response:

- Provide an answer based on your own background and **DO NOT** try to second-guess what the committee wants to hear.
- Cite a number of communication examples and assure the committee that your pattern of communication will be consistent.
- Give five or six examples of the kinds of information you feel are important to transmit to parents. Be prepared to provide the reasons for each item you include in your discussion.

THE LEARNING CONSULTANT (LC)

The LC role is essential to every school. In cases where the school is small, one LC may be shared amongst two or more buildings; however, every school should have at least shared services. Principals rely heavily on their LC to organize, monitor, and manage much of the special education activity in their building. In particular, you will be expected to design educational programs, establish consistent communications with parents, be a liaison between families and teachers, serve as a resource for the staff, and assist the administration in working with the special education program. At the interview, you may find there are questions to explore your administrative abilities as well as your knowledge of special education. Your interview questions will be directly related to how the school uses the Learning Consultant.

As an overall goal, you should present yourself as a knowledgeable and reliable resource with excellent management skill. You will need to demonstrate an ability to get along with diverse groups of people who often have different needs and competing agendas. These groups include administrators, teachers, parents, and students. Human relations skill, management, instruction, law, testing, and report writing will be important elements of your background the interview team will want to explore.

In the next section, we will examine specific questions you may encounter. Each example is designed to provide specific insight to a critical issue you might encounter and offer a possible approach to your response. The discussion for each question should provide a framework around which you can later customize a personal response. **KEY STRATEGY**: *The final answer to all questions must include the personal insight you have gained through experience along with those distinctive viewpoints and thinking that make you a unique candidate.*

SPECIFIC QUESTIONS

> ***If you could write your own job description, what elements would you include in your role and why would they be important?***

Since most schools will not let you design your own position, this may seem an odd question. It is not. The intent is to determine what parts of the LC role you prioritize and how you would work with other people in the school organization. More specifically, the principal wants to hear you discuss the working relationship you want to forge with the school child study team (CST). He or she needs to know how you will merge your efforts with the CST to diagnose student needs and design effective programs. In some states there are school committees that review all students prior to any referral. They go by a variety of names and one is a Pupil Assistance Committee (PAC). You should address how you envision your role in assisting with the pre-referral intervention process. A good beginning might sound like this:

"Let me begin this answer by addressing one of the central LC responsibilities: identification of student learning disabilities and the design of programs to meet those needs. I

will need to complete a review of the record, organize testing procedures, conduct interviews, and arrange appropriate professional involvement. To my mind this work would have the highest priority."

You may have a different first priority, but whatever that is, your highest priority item is where you should begin your response. Move down your list of priority functions to address the other areas that you see as important to your role. For example, you may wish to outline ways you can assist the planning of co-teaching or inclusion arrangements, organize parent newsletters, conduct student counseling, or engage in other characteristics of good special education programs. You need only include three or four items. When discussing these, the order is not as important as the rationale for your choices.

Before attending your interview, organize your thinking on the all-important role of communications. **KEY POINT:** *For an LC, communications include both internal and external elements.* The principal will rely on you to maintain a sound line of internal communications with school professionals and external communications with parents and other professional agencies. This is an important area of concern for principals and a well-designed answer that includes this aspect of communication can greatly advance your candidacy.

Discuss ideas on how to maintain the flow of information between staff members. Be prepared to discuss the kinds of teacher meetings you feel are necessary and the frequency with which such meetings should be held. Help the committee understand any methods you will use to communicate with parents about their student. Talk about how you will establish a working relationship with local and state agencies who may be needed to help the school carry out its mission. These actions will help establish your role as a key member of the special education team.

Many good candidates will have addressed the bulk of what we proposed in the above paragraphs. Now add something to make your answer stand out! Get the attention of the principal by adding ideas about roles you might undertake that will assist him or her with the administration of the special education program. For example, you might suggest how you could collegially develop ways to streamline administrative involvement in the annual IEP development process. Identify ways you can help organize and disseminate decisions regarding student programs in time for the spring scheduling process. Offer to sit on an administrative council whenever your participation would be helpful. In short, describe the part you can play in facilitating the decision-making process for special education programs. The help you offer may not be seen as necessary — that is immaterial. The attitude and cooperative spirit is what will be noticed and that will markedly improve your stock!

 Keys to Your Response:

- Begin your answer with a description of the priority areas you see for a learning consultant.
- Describe how you will promote sound working relations with the child study team and other key groups.
- Describe the importance of your role in communications with teachers and parents.
- Conclude with a discussion of your willingness to assist the principal or other school personnel with special education decisions.

 What steps would you take to establish an inclusion class in science that will utilize a co-teacher for the first time?

Generally, this is a responsibility of the administration and principal. The LC, however, can also have a role in facilitating the successful implementation of this teaching design. For that reason a question on co-teaching might be expected. Your role in this task will focus on facilitating the steps necessary to insure teachers are well supported, trained, and informed. In cases where co-teaching was unsuccessful, an underlying reason was often poor teacher se-lection and preparation. An LC can have a profoundly positive in-fluence on this process.

Begin your response with a description of how you will make yourself available to assist with the selection of teachers who might best work together. Describe the kinds of teacher planning meet-ings you would facilitate. Tell how such meetings will help provide the necessary groundwork for constructing a successful teaching relationship. If the teachers are new to inclusion teaching, you can offer to research worthwhile workshops the teachers might attend. Offer to assemble pertinent articles or other print information that can help the teachers prepare for their role. I interviewed one LC who described a handbook she had prepared for all teachers who were participating in the inclusion model. That was a very persua-sive addition to her answer.

The program planning for included students will also need your help. Specify ways you will work with the teachers to assemble program recommendations and design required modifications to be used in class. Explain how you can assist in designing assessment strategies that will promote student success. You are the primary resource for teachers and the committee will be interested to hear how you will organize your support.

Before ending your response, be sure the committee is aware of your willingness to support the administration and teachers in the planning process. The planning and teacher support process are key ingredients for a successful in-class experience. Your role in facilitating that process is the central element of this answer.

 ### Keys to Your Response:

- Outline how you would assist in the organization of a plan-ning process for teachers who will be working together.
- Emphasize how you might facilitate the communication be-tween teachers and the flow of information to all parties.

- Explain ideas you may have about workshops or staff development to assist the teachers in defining their roles.

> *A parent calls <u>you</u> to complain that her son has made no progress over the year. She is frustrated by the treatment he receives in his mainstream classes. The student feels left out, always unsure of what is expected, and completely unhappy. She wants an urgent IEP conference and, if immediate and productive changes do not occur, she will involve her lawyer. How will you proceed on this matter?*

Oh boy, this is one of those hot cases that always seem to crop up at just the wrong time (is there a right time?). It is a situational question designed to see how you handle difficult, volatile conferences. Here is the bad news. This situation is becoming more frequent and you can expect to encounter a similar circumstance at some point in your career. As a result, even if the question does not appear, your time is well spent considering a response.

KEY STRATEGY: *When faced with any questions that involve a hostile parent, begin by analyzing the real concerns that underlie their comments.* Following this advice, begin your answer by identifying what underlies *this* parent's anger. There appear to be three concerns: 1) Student unhappiness and alienation, 2) insufficient communication, and 3) the possibility of instructional inequity. The results of your analysis will help clarify what your meeting goals should be. In this case, your goals must include an effort to reduce parent frustration and anger, conduct an open and objective review of the student's program results, and an identification of what each party can do differently to achieve better results in the future. Before winding up the conference it will be important to explore ways you might improve communication with the home and institute an improved support system for the student. These steps will help reduce the probability that this kind of frustration will reappear. In phrasing your response, it is important that you have provided a specific action to achieve each meeting goal.

Before you begin to draw any conclusion regarding what is taking place, make certain that you speak directly with the teachers involved and hear what they have to offer regarding this student. There are at least two sides to these issues and you will need a complete picture before you design a conference strategy. Parents are reacting to what they hear and see at home which makes it unlikely that they have all of the facts and information. This step is considered essential and its omission can significantly undermine the quality of your answer.

Let the committee know that you have a plan in place before you approach meetings that could be confrontational. The first part of any such plan is to listen, listen, and listen. Explain how you will use your listening skills to allow the parent to fully describe his or her problem BEFORE you begin to respond or problem-solve solutions. The goal of the parents in this meeting is to make the class situation more rewarding and pleasant for their son. Explain that as this is a mutual goal, you see hope for a successful outcome to the conference. The situation described in the question is volatile, but let the committee know that with your good human relations strategies, you feel more than equal to the task.

As the parent mentioned her lawyer and possible litigation, this is a conference that should be brought to the principal's attention. If there is a director of Special Services, he or she should also be informed. The Director may want to be at any planned meetings. Inform the principal you will be meeting with the parents to resolve the matter and will keep him or her advised of any decisions or future actions. During the conference, it is best to remain moot on the subject of lawyers or litigation unless the parent reintroduces the issue.

The last point you want to address in this answer is your intent to insure first-rate documentation. In addition to the conference notes, explain how you will ask the teachers to maintain their own documentation within the class. This record will be important to reduce school liability.

 Keys to Your Response:

- With situation questions, begin by identifying the real issues for the committee.
- Discuss how you will interview the teachers and other school personnel to get the entire picture before you draw conclusions.
- Link the central issues of contention that your meeting goals must address.
- Underscore the need to listen and then find a mutual goal on which all parties can agree.
- Cite your intention to inform the appropriate parties regarding the parent comment on litigation.
- End with a clear statement regarding your intent to document and maintain court-suitable records.

> *As a case manager, what steps do you take to monitor the progress of assigned students and the success of their programs? What alternatives do you consider when programs are ineffective?*

This question was on several of the gathered interviews and, although rather straightforward, it requires the candidate to provide a sound answer. A poor answer on this item can critically damage your candidacy. Recognize the two parts to this question. The first is how you monitor progress and the second is what you might alternatively do when programs are unsuccessful. The response you offer will be based on your past experience and only you can determine what should be included in the answer. Below is a list of ideas around which you might shape an answer.

STEPS TO CONSIDER FOR
MONITORING SE PROGRAMS

Monitoring student progress:

- If there are scheduled planning meetings, decide how often should you attend and for what purpose.
- Recommend a portfolio of student work and ways to link it to the student's IEP goals.
- Include a record sheet at the front of the portfolio to provide a snapshot identifying student progress towards essential skills.
- Identify the informal ways you will meet with teachers or case managers to review progress.

Dealing with the ineffective program:

- Describe how you decide that a student's program is ineffective?
- If you find that programs are ineffective, identify a process to use to determine possible reasons.
- Catalog specific interventions you might recommend when the instructional program is not meeting the student's needs.

  - **INITIAL POSSIBLE ACTIONS:** Consider how you might alter amount of support, utilize PAC intervention, adjust program goals, utilize more technology, adjust class or school time.
  - **LAST RESORT ACTIONS**: Change teachers, adjust IEP with the parent, or re-evaluate the appropriateness of your placement.

You can organize your own thinking on this question because it will differ for each LC. The important concern is that you convey a sense of thoughtful organization to the committee. Your ability to answer this question with precision and authority may well advance you to the top of the class. It is for that very reason that you should pre-think this answer. Even if you leave out an item the committee had in mind, and such an omission is fairly common, the answer will still have its desired impact if it is well organized and concise.

 ### Keys to Your Response:

- Begin with a brief reinforcement of how you see this as a central responsibility of your position.
- Address the steps you would take to monitor each student's progress.
- Highlight a variety of alternatives you might consider when a program is not working.
- KEEP YOUR ANSWER CONCISE AND ON MESSAGE.

> *As special education students must often meet state testing requirements, what steps should be taken to help students prepare and are there special test considerations might you consider?*

The laws that govern testing of special education students vary from state to state and it is important for you familiarize yourself with the laws that govern your state. Student performance on state tests can often affect state sponsored monitoring processes, public perceptions of the school, and evaluations of overall program quality. Because of the importance of testing and the differences from state to state, a definitive approach to this answer is difficult to describe. There are, however, a few factors that seem to have universal application. You should review these and determine which of them might apply to your situation.

STEPS TO HELP PREPARE STUDENTS
FOR STATE TESTING

✓ Insure that any test requirements and modifications are written into the IEP and justified.

✓ Consider whether it is worthwhile to teach students specific test-taking strategies. Decide if this should be done in support classes in addition to mainstream or replacement classes.

✓ If there are clearly identified skills required of students you manage, those skills should be written into your program and curriculum.

✓ If you have past test results that reveal areas of strength and weakness this information can help you focus instruction. If you use this information, consider an individualized preparation program.

✓ Decide how much information you will communicate to the home and what the goal of those communications will be.

✓ If the students are tested in centers outside the class, consider the use of a special education teacher as one of the proctors.

✓ Determine if your state will allow you to establish a center where specific modifications, such as time or oral reading, can be accommodated. If so, this may be an avenue for some students but such accommodations need to be written into the IEP before the test is to begin.

These are only a few of the ideas that may impact your answer and you may well have others. Your goal is to demonstrate knowledge of a few good strategies that will promote student success. As with other answers, a laundry list of ten disparate items is not superior to a concise design with four or five well-constructed elements. You are not expected to be an expert on the state test, but the committee needs to see you as someone who recognizes the test's importance and one who has high-quality ideas to help students give their best performance.

 Keys to Your Response:

▪ Before you go to the interview, be certain you know the laws of your state regarding special education and student testing.

- Look over the ideas presented in this chapter and select those that fit your situation.
- Present three to five tightly crafted ideas to the committee and insure they understand your recognition of the importance.

CONCLUDING REMARKS

Special education has become an important part of every public school. The principal and school committee will want to know you are a person who uses good judgment and understands the various added constraints that bear on professionals in this field.

An important impression to leave in everyone's mind is that you are an empathetic and child-centered person. Convince the principal that you have the adaptability and flexibility to deal with difficult student issues as well as the day-to-day problems that arise. Let the committee see that you possess the human relations skills necessary to successfully work with a wide variety of people. It is very important the principal see you as a genuine team player on which he or she can rely.

You have chosen a demanding field, but by the end of this interview the committee will see that you have all the skills necessary to meet this challenge. Be upbeat and optimistic. Stay positive and believe in yourself. Showcase your dedication and persistent pursuit of student success. Accomplish this and you will emerge as a top candidate. Now go for it and let people know what you can do!

15
HANDLING YOUR OFFER

GENERAL INFORMATION

The highlight that concludes any job search is notification you have been chosen for the position. You prepared an excellent cover letter and resume, presented a professional image, answered the interview questions with insight and enthusiasm, closed the deal with a knockout portfolio, and now you have been offered the post. What do you need to know about the next steps?

At first glance, there seems to be an easy answer – one gratefully accepts the offer and asks when to report. In some cases, that may be just what you will do. Other circumstances and concerns, however, will require your consideration. For example:

- *At some time after the interview, should you make follow-up calls to determine your status in districts where you have high interest?*

- *What should be done if you are a finalist in more than one district?*

- *What if you receive an offer that is not your first choice and you are awaiting a decision regarding a more attractive position?*

- *What if you accept one of your second choice positions and your first choice school later offers a contract?*

- *What if you have decided this is not the job for you, how do you gracefully refuse?*

- *What if the offered position is different than the one for which you applied?*

- *What problems occur when you are currently employed in another position with a due notice requirement?*

- *What should you put in a letter of resignation?*

- *Once you accept a position, what steps need to be taken prior to beginning work?*

These are all issues that quite commonly arise and it would be worth our time to look at each of these questions and develop some advance thinking with regard to each.

At some time after the interview, should you make follow-up calls to determine your status in districts where you have high interest?

This seems a reasonable and innocuous thing to do. After all, you are simply showing interest. Should you not have the right to know where things stand, particularly if you are an applicant in other districts? I have spoken to many principals and superintendents on this matter and there seems to be unilateral agreement – follow-up calls are not always well received. Let me say that again, "not always well received." There are many reasons cited as to why these calls are less than welcome, but the most frequent is that the process has to have sufficient time to run its course before feedback is available to candidates. Principals generally advise that you be patient and wait to be contacted after a decision has been made. Unless special circumstances exist, it is preferred that candidates refrain from appearing to force the issue.

Most principals have had experience with candidates who call two or three times in a week to ask when the results will be available. In those cases, you can be sure each call has weakened the candidate's viability. Secretaries develop a patience deficit for those who call too often and one should not underestimate the influence of the principal's or superintendent's secretary. Understand that interviews may include ten or more candidates and you should consider the impact if each person called two or three times. The line between "interest" and "pest" is very fine and best left untested.

There are exceptions to this advice. During the interview, your candidacy in other districts may be discussed. At that point, the principal may ask that you contact him or her before you make any decision to accept another position. If this occurs, then the candidate can be sure he or she is under serious consideration and should call the principal's office in accordance with whatever arrangements have been made.

There will be times when you do not hear the outcome of an interview for what seems a long time. At the interview, the school may have indicated they wanted to conclude the process by a specific date. That day passes and you have heard nothing. Should you call? Here is the bad news; if you have not heard, there is probably a reason. The best advice is to continue your job search and let this district continue with what it needs to do. Sometimes the decision was delayed and you are still under consideration. Nonetheless, stay active in the interview process and keep your options open. If you receive another job offer, feel free to call the first district and advise them of your situation. We will discuss what to do with multiple job offers later in this chapter.

What should be done if you are a finalist in more than one district?

First, congratulations on placing yourself in this enviable position, but be careful. Until you have a firm offer of a contract in hand you are still only a candidate. Districts may advise you that you are one of only two they are considering. The principal might convey that he or she is strongly interested in having you on the staff and is about to call your references. Things may look great and you may feel very positive about a school's interest. We offer a word to the wise at this point. **CAUTION:** *Without a definite contract offer, there continues to be at least some potential for this decision to go another way.* Unless you have an agreement to contact a prospective district before accepting another position, it is best to wait for a firm contract offer before you begin the notification process to other districts where you may still be a viable candidate. Consider why this might be the best course of action. When you call a principal or school office to advise them you are a finalist in another district, it is possible they may assume you are more interested in taking the other position. If their process is not yet complete, such assumptions can compromise your viability because of questionable availability. It has sometimes happened that a candidate announced to a district that he or she was a finalist at another school and later had to call back when the position was not offered to renew his or her candidacy. You can easily see how this would undermine a person's chances.

A second, but somewhat less likely, concern is how such declarations might be construed as a subtle way to exert pressure for a decision. Even though this may not be your intention at all, if something in your voice or the words you choose is interpreted as pressure, it will damage your candidacy. Unless there is a compelling reason to take that risk, it is best to avoid.

The final pitfall in prematurely announcing yourself as a finalist concerns the district's pride. When a candidate tells a principal he or she is in the final stages of accepting another offer, an assumption can sometimes be made that your interest in his or her district is not as strong as originally thought. This notion can then lead to a feeling, "if that is all the interest he or she has, maybe we should look harder at the other candidates." This may seem irrational, but it has happened and cost good candidates jobs they would otherwise have had. Proceed as you feel best, but be cautious in your approach.

What if you receive an offer that is not your first choice and you are awaiting a decision regarding a more attractive position?

It is likely that good candidates will find themselves in this position at some time in their career. It is one of the most sensitive and difficult decisions a professional may face and you need to pre-think what you will do should that circumstance present itself. You may have you heard the maxim, "A bird in the hand is worth two in the bush." That goes double in a professional job search. Be aware that the window of opportunity is open ever so briefly. In interviewing numerous principals and superintendents, they are generally unimpressed by candidates who receive their offer of a position with reservations. Requests such as, "I am continuing to look at other offers, can I have the weekend to think this over" can make principals or superintendents question their decision. If they sense a candidate is stalling, they may assume he or she is waiting for a "better position." No matter what you may think or how you rationalize the delay, realize it is not helping your situation. In fact, there have been occasions when principals have withdrawn an offer after a candidate hesitated too long. It has happened that good candidates with multiple possibilities have ended with no job because they mishandled the offer. I must add that many principals and superintendents feel a few days to consider an offer is perfectly reasonable, but unless you know this is the case, you may be taking a chance.

With these thoughts in mind, only you can decide whether you want to risk losing one position to possibly win the prize position. No one can answer this question for you. If you have thought the issue through in advance and developed a clear course of action, it will help you deal with the call when it arrives. The advice is – have a game plan already in mind.

Should you decide it is best to take the first position offered, then do that. When the call comes, be upbeat and enthusiastic. Remember, it was *you* who applied for the position and told the committee all the great things you would bring to their school. When the principal calls to offer the position, he or she expects to hear that same great candidate on the other end of the phone – BE THERE!

Here are a few final insights on accepting jobs that may not have been your first choice. A teaching position will be exactly what you make of it. Often that "must have" job in the great district will not turn out to be what you envisioned, while those "second-tier jobs" become much more than you had ever hoped. So, if you decide to take the first position on the table, you did not make a mistake. Congratulations and go make a difference to every child you teach!

What if you accept one of your second choice positions and your first choice school then offers a contract?

This is another problem that can present itself and is closely related to the last question. In this case, however, you committed yourself to one district and the first choice was offered at a later date. There are two possibilities regarding your current circumstance. One possibility is that you have made a formal commitment to the first district and have a signed contract for the coming year. The second possibility is that you have only made a verbal agreement with the principal or superintendent to accept the first position. We will deal with these separately.

If you have signed a contract, you are legally committed to the first district. If you call them and ask to be released from your contract, it is unlikely you will be successful. Understand, the other candidates who they might have employed have been notified of the decision and are no longer available. The school will not want to reopen the entire search process because you now have a "better offer." This request will also be negatively received and place an unnecessary shadow over your employment at the school. Avoid starting in a new school with negative baggage whenever possible. Once you sign a contract, you should consider yourself committed and proceed with enthusiasm and energy.

In the second case, you do not have a signed contract and a clear legal bind has not yet occurred. Again, however, you have given your word and the district has probably acted on that by notifying the other finalists of the school's decision. Should you withdraw to take a better offer, be aware it will be considered a violation of your professional ethics. Whereas there may be no *legal* recourse for the district, you place your professional reputation at risk. You need to decide how important that is as compared to the prospects of the new position.

These are not easy decisions and should not be taken lightly. Keep your overall goals in mind, weigh the relative strengths and weaknesses of each choice, and make your decision. Most importantly, do this before the calls arrive. If you try to make such decisions over the phone when an offer is made, you will place yourself at risk of making a costly mistake.

What if you decide this is not the job for you, how do you gracefully refuse?

This can happen and it is not unexpected by the interviewing districts. The important issue in this decision is its timing. If you complete the interview process and come away with the feeling this may not be the right school, you should take immediate steps to clarify those thoughts. If you choose to withdraw, the best time to act is prior to the district's selection of final candidates.

The withdrawal process is reasonably simple. First, call the district and attempt to speak with the principal or head of the interview committee. This is a professional courtesy that most school leaders appreciate. The principal may ask you for a reason so be prepared to offer an honest but diplomatic response to the question. There is no need to burn any bridges. If the principal is not available, it is perfectly acceptable to leave a message with the secretary. You may or may not receive a follow-up call from the principal, but you should be prepared for either event.

Although you have advised the school by phone, you are not quite finished. You should write a short letter of withdrawal and extend your appreciation to the principal and committee for their consideration. Address your letter to the principal of the school. In this letter, it is not necessary to cite reasons for withdrawing although some candidates do. The importance of the letter is its ability to demonstrate your professionalism and courtesy.

Take a look at what might be contained in this letter. **NOTE:** *Use the sample letter as a starting point for what you will write, but use your own words.* The model is intended to give you some ideas as to how you might structure your own document.

Mr. John Hopeful

23 Brandon Lane
Anytown, PA 55555

Dr. Robert Pollock
PS 101
Brighton, PA 55520

May 2, 2001

Dear Dr. Pollock,

I would like to thank you and the interview committee for providing me the opportunity to see your school and interview for the position of Science Teacher. I found the time we spent together to have been both informative and enjoyable. The steps taken by your staff to make me feel comfortable and welcome were most appreciated.

In light of a number of issues now before me, I must regrettably ask that you withdraw my application from further consideration. I would like you to know that this decision is not predicated on any dissatisfaction with your school or our time together. There are other matters that make my continued candidacy impractical at this time.

In closing I wish you the best in finding the right candidate for your 5th grade science position. I am honored to have been a candidate.

Sincerely,

J. Hopeful

As you can see from the model, there are three separate paragraphs. The goals of the first paragraph are to identify the position for which you applied, demonstrate your appreciation for their time, and set a pleasant tone to the letter. It need not be long or gush about how wonderful you found the school. Remember, you are withdrawing from consideration.

The second paragraph withdraws you from further consideration. As mentioned before, a specific reason is not necessary, however, you want to make clear you have thought this through and made your decision based on reason. If, unlike the model, your reason for withdrawing is specific to the interview or some perceived shortcoming of the school, you are not obliged to provide those details in your letter. Most often, it is best to remain moot on the subject and move on to other opportunities. There is nothing to be gained by risking antagonizing the school principal or committee. If, on the other hand, you feel obligated to include your reason, be diplomatic.

The last paragraph is a simple closing you will find in most letters of this nature. It wishes the district well and restates your appreciation. As in the first paragraph, it should not be overdone.

A final word on the subject is to keep your letter short and to the point. The entire text should fill no more than one side of a single sheet of paper. If it exceeds one side, it is probably too long.

What if the offered position is different than the one for which you applied?

This happens from time to time and can be disconcerting if you have not given the idea advance thought. There are a number of changes that can occur to prospective teaching assignments between the time of your interview and the time of your offer, but a few seem to predominate. The most common changes include an amendment from a tenure-track contract to leave replacement, an alteration of grade level to be taught, or a revision of the subject areas to be taught. We will treat each individually.

There are times when you believe you are applying for a tenure track post and later find the position is for a teacher who is on leave. Ads in the newspaper usually indicate a position is for "leave replacement" when that is the case. On other occasions, a change may have occurred after the posting and you will not find this out until the interview or later. You need to realize that teachers on leave often return to reclaim their position. While it is also true that some teachers do not return, you cannot count on such good fortune. Therefore, if you have a tenure-track offer from another district, you may be best advised to accept it and leave the replacement position for someone else. If you have no other offers, then by all means consider the replacement position. Should you perform well, the school may take steps to try and keep you even if the original teacher returns. At worst, you have one year's experience and a good recommendation for your next search.

Elementary teachers are sometimes faced with a change in their grade placement. They applied for what they believed was a 1st grade position and were later asked if they would be interested in teaching 4th grade. The best advice is to accept the position if it is offered and disregard the grade level change. Once you are on the staff, the principal has the prerogative to change you to any grade within your certification. Again, if you provide good service, a transfer to your preferred grade level may be made later. In the meantime, you have a fine position in a good school.

With secondary teachers, changes to the teaching schedule can easily occur. You originally thought you would teach 3 classes of sophomore English and 2 Honors English. When the job is offered, you are told your schedule will include two freshman composition classes instead of the Honors English. As with grade level changes, principals can assign you to any subject for which you are certified. Once you join the staff and show everyone what you can do, schedule changes can be requested. Unless there is a very good reason to object, subject changes in the offered position need not be deal killers. You can often improve your standing with the principal by demonstrating your flexibility and utility in accepting these changes and making them work. In sum, do not let class assignments stand between you and a good school.

What problems occur when you are currently employed in another position with a due notice requirement?

This is often the case when teachers are changing positions at times other than the end of a school year. It can also occur when a candidate leaves the business field to enter teaching. In such cases, it is customary to provide notice to employers at the time or your resignation.

Teachers have an almost universal 60-day notice clause in their contracts. As such, there are some precautions you will want to take. **CARDINAL RULE**: *Never submit a resignation until you have a signed contract in hand.* Many districts will suggest that their "verbal offer" is good and you can provide notice. If you follow such advice, do so at your own risk. Boards of Education have been known to reject the hiring recommendation of the superintendent and a candidate who thought he or she had a firm job offer was left in a very awkward position. You need to have a written confirmation that you were appointed by the Board prior to any formal action to resign your current position.

Your new district will likely want you to start as soon as possible and you can make a request of the current district to provide an early release. As a general rule, principals and districts are unlikely to grant an employment release until a suitable replacement is found. If your resignation occurs in June or July, the possibility of early release rises dramatically because schools do not usually like to start the year with a temporary teacher. Prospective employers understand the 60-day clause and, if they are prepared to hire you, this impediment should not present a problem.

If you are a long-term substitute or occupy a position that is other than a regular contract, examine your agreement and determine the length of any "due notice" arrangement. Even if there is no formal clause to govern your release, you should notify the current school as soon as possible and give them time to provide a replacement for the children in your classes. If you are a daily substitute, no notice is required other than to inform the substitute caller of your last day of availability. That is just courtesy and good professional conduct.

What should I put in my letter of resignation?

Once you inform the principal that you intend to resign, you will be asked to submit a letter of resignation for Board action. In all matters concerning a job change, the best policy is to leave your district or position on the most positive terms possible. Even if you are leaving because of dissatisfaction, be professional and gracious in your exit. The good impression you leave can only assist you in the future.

Your letter should be positive and brief, less than one page. There is no need to detail your reasons for leaving the district. The Board only needs to know that you plan to leave and the termination date you request. Look at this sample letter and you will see that there are only a few important items included.

Mr. John Hopeful

23 Brandon Lane
Anytown, MA 55555

Dr. John Topp, Board President
York Valley Schools Board of Education
100 Main Street
York Valley, MA 55520

December 2, 2001

Dear Dr. Topp,

This letter is to advise the Board of Education that I will be resigning my position as 7th grade Science Teacher at the Valley Middle School effective Friday, December 8, 2001. I fully understand that my continued service for 60 days is required to insure a smooth transition for my students.

I would like to thank the Board of Education and the community of York Valley for the opportunity to have worked in such a fine school with so many wonderful children. I have many happy memories to cherish.

Please accept my best wishes for the future. It has been a privilege to teach in this district.

Sincerely,

J. Hopeful

As you can see, the only required information is the resignation date and your understanding of the 60-day clause. The remainder of the letter consists of pleasantries and appreciation. Feel free to make adjustments that suit your situation.

Once you accept a position, what steps need to be taken prior to beginning work?

The first step will be to make an appointment through the superintendent's secretary to go to the board office and sign the necessary paperwork required for your employment. Usually the superintendent's secretary will provide a time and date for this along with a list of items you will need. You will generally need an original copy of your teaching certificate, a social security card, and possibly a set of college transcripts if you are a new teacher. If you have not already been fingerprinted and had a background check, that is likely to be required and can be arranged by the district. Some districts also require a physical examination and you should be prepared to make arrangements with either the school doctor or your own physician. The secretary will advise you of any additional requirements and you should rely on her for guidance.

Try to arrange a visit to your new school through the principal's office. Do this as soon as possible so you can obtain copies of any materials you need to begin planning for your classes. If possible, you might want to meet with the person who will be supervising you or helping to direct your efforts. This could be a grade-level leader, team leader, department head or supervisor. Even if you met this person at the interview, now that you are hired, a more detailed conversation regarding your role can be held.

If you are fulfilling a 60-day clause, touch base with your new school on a regular basis. If there are monthly bulletins or other announcements the school regularly provides, you may want to read those and keep abreast of school news. If there is an evening performance, it is a good idea to attend if at all possible. These small steps will help you to garner necessary knowledge of your school and ease the transition. When you arrive for your first day, you will want to be as fully prepared as possible.

Congratulations on your selection and good luck!

16
PUTTING IT ALL TOGETHER

Congratulations on completing this book and taking the initiative to secure a great new position in teaching! With the information you now own, you will be a formidable candidate in any selection process. You have no doubt realized these pages contain too much information to memorize, but that was not the goal when we began. What you now have are critical understandings on how to get noticed, prepare for the tough questions, and avoid costly mistakes. These larger issues and insights will stay with you while you formulate an interview style that is uniquely yours.

At this point we must turn our attention to assembling all our information into a winning strategy to get hired. When I was a young naval officer, my captain used to say something that has rung true over the years. "It is one thing to have the knowledge but still another to put it to good use. Many people may <u>know</u> but only a few <u>act</u>." Now that we have the knowledge, we need a deliberate, well-formulated plan to place you in the right school. The best way to accomplish that goal is to break our task into manageable parts. These parts include the search, preparation, interview, and follow-up.

It is likely that you will need to go back and reread certain chapters or passages during your preparation. During that process you will discover new ideas and additional insights you may have missed the first time. Re-reading may also stimulate response ideas you had not originally considered. Allow this creativity free reign and jot these good ideas down as they appear. New thoughts are very perishable and when we try to remember them later, they can be difficult or impossible to recall. If you wrote a few notes, your ideas will spring back instantly.

THE SEARCH PROCESS

This task is often done in a way that lacks thinking and planning. Graduates simply scan the newspaper for jobs that fit their title and send off their resume. One can occasionally be lucky, happen on just the right position, have a successful interview, and receive a job offer. More often than not, however, a haphazard search has an unsuccessful ending.

Since this decision carries such importance, take your time and do it right. Remember, school districts are looking for you; it was they who placed the advertisement. Avoid the temptation to "blanket" the marketplace with resumes. Be deliberate and selective.

In your selection process, consider the following questions.

In what community or location do I want to live?

This is a very important question and you need to be honest with yourself. If you have family commitments and strong ties, you may wish to draw a radius circle on a map that identifies the geographic region you want to target. You must decide if you like rural, suburban, or city lifestyles. If you like the arts, theater and shopping that are available in the larger cities, you need to think about schools within a reasonable distance of those amenities. If you are married, you need to discuss the matter of location thoroughly with your spouse to make sure the place you select is one where you will both be happy.

What would be the ideal school for me?

I remember one of my college classmates at the University of Tennessee who answered this question by saying, "Any district that has a job and will hire me." Even then I thought that to be a shortsighted approach to establishing a professional career. Unfortunately, that philosophy continues to predominate in many young teachers looking for positions. This is due in part to the fact that new teachers may still be somewhat insecure and uncertain as to their market demand. Let me assure you, the profession has a high demand for skilled teachers and good candidates like you. You do not need to take the first opening that comes along the way.

A district's pay scale is another reason candidates choose a school, but overemphasizing salary also lacks the broad-based thinking that will bring you to the right decision. I will share the advice I once received from an outstanding superintendent. "Never leave or take a position on the basis of money alone. You almost always regret it." I found that advice to be extremely valuable and I hope you will as well. Within a geographic area there are some salary differences, however, most districts are reasonably competitive and the money differential is unlikely to make much difference in your lifestyle. To illustrate, let us take District A that pays a starting salary of $37, 500 and District B that pays only $34,100. Adjusted for taxes and other deductions, the difference will be in the range of $100 per bi-monthly check. Of course finances are important and, with all other things equal, you would be foolish to ignore salary in your decision-making. The point is money should not be the primary reason for choosing your school. It makes more sense to focus on districts that offer you the kind of position and working conditions you seek.

To identify schools that meet your criteria, you need to investigate. Once you have identified a geographic area, find out what school districts are in that region. There may be a county education office that can supply all the information you need in one stop. Get copies of annual school reports, brochures, state report cards, websites, and other items that will provide insight into the school districts. As you review these materials, certain schools will begin to emerge as a good match for you. Keep each district's materials in a file because it will be important if an opening exists and you decide to apply.

How do I go about finding the right vacancy?

Now that you have identified the area and types of schools to which you will apply, it is time to look for a vacancy. The first obvious place to look is the newspaper. There are generally at least two papers that service a particular geographic area and you should get both papers on a weekly basis. The Sunday paper will often carry the ads you need, but there may also be ads in the daily paper. This varies from location to location and you should check yours.

Check with the county education office. They may receive school vacancy listings that are posted. Professional magazines such as <u>Education Week</u> and other periodicals also run ads, but in my experience, they are not always as current as those in local sources and you may find yourself entering the selection process late. A last method is to call districts where you are interested and ask for a list of their vacancies. The best time for this inquiry is mid-April through early-May. **CAUTION:** *Do not make a pest of yourself by calling every week to ask if there is an opening yet.*

A final word on this matter is to extend your search over a four or five week timeframe. As stated above, the spring is the best time, but there are numerous jobs all through the summer and school year as well. In particular, there will be leave replacements, recently added positions, permanent substitute positions, and other more temporary employment opportunities. Stay informed of the vacancies in your field.

If a temporary vacancy appears in a district where you have high interest, be sure to investigate its possibilities. Go to the school and speak with the principal or someone who is in charge of the search. Often, teachers will accept a temporary position and establish a valuable avenue for future full time employment. In short, do not overlook the possibilities presented by some of these less than ideal positions.

What if there are no posted vacancies in the geographic areas and schools I have selected?

This can happen; especially if you are applying during the academic year when most good schools are fully staffed. In this case, there are two avenues you might want to consider. Perhaps you can think about a job outside your desired travel range or a school that is not exactly the type you want. In these instances, you need to decide how important the experience is that you will gain. Keep in mind that any teaching skills you acquire in this school will make you a more attractive candidate in the future.

An alternative many others have successfully used is substitute teaching. I finished my MA degree at Indiana University in January. When I arrived home there were no jobs in my subject so I accepted a substitute teaching position. Within five weeks, I learned of a science teacher who was going on maternity leave in a neighboring district. I applied, attended an interview and voila, I was in the door. Many teachers take this route and it is an excellent way to gain valuable experience. There is another benefit. If you are substituting in a school where you would like to someday work, you are gaining exposure and an inside track to the next position. You will know about the vacancy well ahead of everyone else and the administration will be acquainted with you and your work. It has happened where a substitute teacher was offered the position before it ever reached the paper. We all recognize the life of a substitute teacher has its shortcomings, but do not overlook its positive features.

THE PREPARATION

1. **RESEARCH**: Once you have selected a few districts to which you will apply, you need to prepare a plan of action. First, go back to your files and retrieve the information you gathered on each district. If this has not yet been done, do it now. Study each school and prepare a short list of facts regarding its demographics, programs, district initiatives, and other items that may be used in an interview.

2. **COVER LETTERS:** Write a separate cover letter for each district to which you will apply and include the executive summary to match your background with the school's stated requirements. Those requirements may be listed directly in the advertisement and you should be sure to hit each one. If the ad is not specific regarding the district or school needs, then go back to your research and choose one or two items that you feel will promote the reader's interest.

3. **SHARPEN THE RESUME:** In the section outlining your experience, tailor the bullet items so they meet district needs or initiatives. Look in the newspaper to see if the same district has placed ads for co-curriculum positions. If they have and you can fulfill one, be sure to highlight that in your cover letter and resume.

4. **PREPARE THE INTERVIEW PORTFOLIO:** I suggest you use a large loose-leaf binder that will lay flat. Put documents and pictures in page protectors. Place marked dividers between each section so that you know where everything is located. There is nothing more frustrating than looking through twenty or thirty pages for a document or picture while saying, "Gee, I know it is here somewhere." By the time you reach it, the impact is greatly reduced. Tailor your portfolio to what you know the district is seeking!

5. **PUT YOUR INTERVIEW ATTIRE TOGETHER:** This means having garments cleaned, shoes shined, hair freshly cut or styled, nails, and so forth. If you are not sure of what you want to wear, reread the chapter on this subject. Have someone who can be objective check your selections.

6. **ASSEMBLE YOUR BRIEFCASE:** The day before the interview, assemble your briefcase. It should contain a file folder with additional resumes, pad, pen, and the interview portfolio. Leave out anything that is not pertinent to this interview.

7. **PREPARE FOR THE INTERVIEW QUESTIONS:** Prepare a few index cards with points you would like to make during the interview. There are numerous places in the book where I suggest you pre-think an answer. There are **KEYS TO YOUR RESPONSE** sections for every question to help you organize a clear answer. In addition, numerous **KEY STRATEGIES** are spread throughout the book to offer sound advice on general interviewing techniques. These big ideas are handy in streamlining the review process. Some candidates like to place the prepared questions on one side of an index card and a few bullet-type comments on the opposite side. **WARNING:** *Do not show the index cards at the interview.* Some teacher candidates leave this step out because it seems to be more work than they want to expend. Believe me, it is not a lot of work and the little extra effort this takes will pay big dividends at the interview.

THE INTERVIEW

The day of the interview is always one with added stress. For that reason, do all the preparation beforehand. If it is a morning interview, get up in plenty of time and leave the house a little early. Traffic, road construction, and other unforeseen problems can crop up and turn your trip into a nightmare. Oh, once you are in your interview outfit, do not eat or drink. That cup of coffee or jelly doughnut is just waiting to get on your jacket or blouse. Besides, you will enjoy it more after the interview is over. I always treated myself to a nice lunch or dinner after I had completed an interview session.

Before you leave the house, flip through your cards one last time, check your briefcase and insure yourself that you have everything. You probably do, but the ride is more relaxing if you know everything is ready.

Try not to arrive at the school more than ten minutes early. If the interviews are not on schedule, they are almost surely running late. Ten minutes gives you time to go the men's or ladies room and check yourself one last time. When you go into the office, announce yourself to the secretary and tell her you are there for the interview with Mr. or Ms. Jones. Then take a seat and patiently wait for your turn. DO NOT PACE IN THE OFFICE LIKE A CAGED TIGER!

Also, secretaries are generally very busy so resist the temptation to engage in casual conversation unless initiated by them. Smile and use courtesy remarks such as thank you and please. You may be offered coffee or a drink. In most cases, it is best to gracefully decline.   The cup can be a nuisance if you are invited into the office and you are not finished. There is also another chance for spillage.

When you are invited into the office, offer everyone a **smile** (did I make my point?), handshake and greeting. A simple, "pleasure to meet you" is sufficient. Keep it professional and upbeat. The principal or designee will generally tell you where to sit, but if they do not, it is customary to ask if "this chair will be all right?" Once in your seat, you can retrieve a pad and pen from your brief case. Leave everything else alone unless it is needed. You might ask if anyone would like a copy of your resume. Most often copies have already been made, but occasionally someone will say yes. In either case, it makes a good impression that you were planned enough to bring extra copies.

Now sit back and just do your best on the questions. If you read the chapter on general questions, you already know the first one they are likely to ask. This should get you off to a great start and you can build from there. Do your best to smile, relax and be yourself. As was said many times in this book, your enthusiasm and demeanor can offset any small omissions or technical errors. After you have answered the last question, remember to ask the committee if they would have just a few minutes to look at the portfolio you have put together for them. Phrase it that way because you want them to know you made special preparations just for them. This knowledge increases the probability they will give your material some attention and adds to your stature as a serious candidate. Now close the sale!

Once the portfolio review is finished there will be a signal that the interview is over. Sometimes the principal or committee stands and at other times, someone will simply say, "If there are no more questions, I think we are concluded." Stand, shake hands again and thank everyone for the time you have had together. On your way out, remember to thank the secretary and say goodbye.

FOLLOW UP

Many candidates like to write a short letter to the principal thanking him or her for the opportunity to meet. This is a nice gesture and generally appreciated. The only advice is to keep such notes simple and to the point. Do not try to resell yourself by telling the reader how you are such a perfect match for the school. The letter is a thank you and should be left at that.

While you are waiting for the results, keep your search activities alive and active. Do not be impatient. Know that you did well and are receiving full consideration. When the offer arrives – and it will – be ready with your answer.

CONCLUSION

The last advice I can offer is to be positive and believe you will be successful. You have all the information and skills necessary to find and get the position you want. By the very fact that you took the time to read this book and follow its advice, you have made yourself into an extremely formidable candidate. Even if you remember only a small portion of what you have read, you will be ahead of the many other candidates who just showed up hoping to do well.

I wish you nothing but the best and look forward to hearing about the successes you are sure to find. I welcome you to one of the noblest professions in the human endeavor as a colleague and teacher!

A Student Teacher's Story

My name is Crystal. I am currently doing my student teaching and everyone who has ever been there knows that this is a difficult time. Day after day I would go and teach my heart out and afterwards I would wait for my mentor teacher to compliment or degrade my actions, but there was never anything. The only thing she ever said for two months was, "If I have a problem with you I will let you know." I guess I was supposed to take this as a compliment, but I didn't feel it was. Just when I was about to give up because I thought my teaching wasn't even changing or helping even one child, my mind was completely changed. I went to school the next week to begin my placement and one of my first grader's parents came to me and just fell into my arms and cried out, "THANK YOU." She had explained that her child had ADHD (I had already discovered that) and no one had the patience to teach or just love her for who she was. She told me that I made a difference in her daughter's life, just by showing I cared and having patience with her. She wanted to learn when she was with me, but her other teachers constantly condemned her because they couldn't control her. What a compliment, needless to say I am continuing on with my student teaching. Never give up, if you teach from the heart, you may not realize it at that precise moment, but you are making a difference in someone.

By - Crystal Anderson

Appendix A
Sample Rubrics

The scoring rubric is an assessment device that provides very specific information about what criteria will be judged and the specific performance factors required. Generally, a rubric has from three to five levels of performance that move from a near absence of quality to exemplary performance. The strength is that specific indicators are listed for each level of performance and both the student and the teacher are clear on the expectations.

Rubrics are used as both formative and summative evaluative tools. As the work is progressing, students can be informed of precisely what level of work is present. By examining the rubric, the student can also see what improvements must be made to reach the exemplary performance level. Peer evaluation is made possible through this tool and small group discussions can often lead to improved performance.

Another strength of rubrics is their ability to focus student attention on just the elements that the teacher sees as important. A simple rubric for a 5th grade short story assignment might list such criteria as: Use of Opening, Story Development, Conclusion, Mechanics, and Overall Story Interest.

The items included would be those the teacher has taught and has a reasonable expectation for student understanding. The teacher can also simplify or sophisticate the rubric by adjusting the number of performance levels. Look at the example on the following page which tries to simplify the short story assignment.

Criteria	1	2	3	Your Score
Use of Opening	Story has little or no opening.	The opening somewhat sets the stage for the coming events. Uses one or two of our devices to wet the reader's appetite.	The opening lays all essential ground-work for the coming events. Uses all three of the devices to stimulate reader interest.	1 2 3

As you can see, the teacher has taught students to provide the story setting and use three specific devices to raise reader interest. Those are the performance issues he or she assesses with the rubric.

Two additional sample rubrics from TaskStream.com are included here for your review. In addition, we anticipate posting sample rubrics, blank forms and other helpful materials for our readers at our web site:

http://advantapress.com

BOOK REPORT

Criteria	1	2	3	4	Your Score
Brief Plot Summary	Inaccurate plot summary	Incomplete plot summary or re-telling of entire story	Adequate plot summary without drawing attention toward significant events	Complete plot summary with attention focused on significant events	1 2 3 4
Main Characters	Incomplete description of main characters	Adequate description of main characters, but no sense of character comparison	Descriptions of main characters including some character comparison	Complete descriptions of main characters and full comparative analysis	1 2 3 4
Mechanics	Frequent errors in spelling, grammar and punctuation	Errors in grammar and punctuation but spelling has been proofread	Occasional grammatical errors and questionable word choice.	Nearly error-free which reflects clear understanding and thorough proofreading	1 2 3 4

BOOK REPORT (continued)

Criteria	1	2	3	4	Your Score
Originality	Report displays no evidence of original thought	Basic information and plot summary with little or no evidence of new insight	Report demonstrates a clear understanding of the book's content and offers some original insight	Evidence of high level reading comprehension demonstrated through description, originality and fresh insight	1 2 3 4
Setting	Incomplete or weak description of setting	Adequate description of setting, but no apparent sense of its relation to events and/or characters	Description of setting with basic sense of its relation to events and/or character motivations	Thorough description of setting and its relation to the plot, theme, and/or character actions	1 2 3 4

ORAL PRESENTATIONS

Criteria	1	2	3	4	Your Score
Attention to Audience	Did not attempt to engage audience	Little attempt to engage audience	Engaged audience and held their attention most of the time by remaining on topic and presenting facts with enthusiasm	Engaged audience and held their attention throughout with creative articulation, enthusiasm, and clearly focused presentation	1 2 3 4
Clarity	No apparent logical order of presentation, unclear focus	Content is loosely connected, transitions lack clarity	Sequence of information is well-organized for the most part, but more clarity with transitions is needed	Development of thesis is clear through use of specific and appropriate examples; transitions are clear and create a succinct and even flow	1 2 3 4
Content	Thesis is unclear and information appears randomly chosen	Thesis is clear, but supporting information disconnected	Information relates to a clear thesis; many relevant points, but they are somewhat unstructured	Exceptional use of material clearly relates to a focused thesis; many supported materials	1 2 3 4

ORAL PRESENTATIONS (continued)

Criteria	1	2	3	4	Your Score
Creativity	Delivery is repetitive with little or no variety in presentation techniques	Material presented with little interpretation or originality	Some apparent originality displayed through use of original interpretation of presented materials	Exceptionl originality of material and interpretation	1 2 3 4
Presentation Length	Greatly exceeding or falling short of allotted time.	Somewhat exceeded or fell short of allotted time	Remained close to the allotted time	Presented within the allotted time	1 2 3 4
Speaking Skills	Monotone voice; speaker seemed uninterested in material	Little eye contact; fast speaking rate, little expression, sometimes inaudible.	Clear articulation of ideas, but not always confidenct with material	Exceptionml confidence with material. Displayed. poise, clear articulation, eye contact and enthusiasm	1 2 3 4

Courtesy of TaskStream.com

Appendix B
Online Resources

TaskStream.com

This website is listed as a separate appendix because it is one of the most valuable online resources a teacher can use. It is located at ***www.TaskStream.com*** and can be accessed with that address or through almost any search engine using the keyword box. When you get to the site, you will find that there is an annual subscription fee, however, if you use "Guest Registration" and supply some pertinent information, you can get about 3 weeks of trial membership at no cost. Even if you do not choose to subscribe, the information you needed for your interview will have been retrieved and ready for use.

In order to obtain information regarding the proficiency standards for your state, you should proceed to the bar marked "Standards Wizard." When the page appears, you will see a dialog box that is marked "Select a Region." If you type in the name of your state, all of the various standards that apply to your area will appear. Click on the item of choice and you can read or download the information as necessary. For example, if you go to Illinois, you will see the Illinois State Standards. If you click on this, the discipline areas will appear and you can select your subject area. If you click on "English Language Arts," this breaks down into a variety of subjects such as Reading, Literature, Writing, and so forth. You can continue this process all the way down until you reach specific learning proficiencies.

Another great feature of this site is its "Cybrary." In this area you have the Lesson Database, Links, Software, Standards and Tutorials.

LESSON DATA BASE allows you to view and download lesson plans submitted by other TaskStream subscribers. If you need a great lesson on a topic, go into this feature, select a subject area and type in a topic name. If there are lessons, they will appear. By simply clicking on the lesson name, a complete lesson plan with objectives, activities, student products, time allotment and step by step procedures are displayed. In addition, there is information on assessment, how the lesson links to the state standards, scoring rubrics and how to contact the author. This is an excellent resource for outstanding lesson designs.

LINKS provides a list of websites that fit a particular topic you are studying. These can be accessed directly from this site for preview purposes. If you like it, bookmark it for future use.

SOFTWARE is a list of free downloadable software that you can receive. Some very good programs are available.

STANDARDS is the Standards Wizard referred to earlier in this discussion. You can also access the feature through this area.

TUTORIALS will help you to use various learning tools and tutorials to create task-based lessons.

As you can see, this site has many features for the teacher. There are many others as well and you should take the time to visit this web-page. Even if you choose not to subscribe, there is valuable information you can use at any interview.

NJPEP Virtual Academy
http://njpep.org

NJPEP is a state-of-the-art New Jersey Professional Education Port. A major goal of this professional development site is to support teachers and the entire educational community in the understanding and implementation of the New Jersey Core Curriculum Content Standards and their related statewide assessments at fourth, eighth and eleventh grades. It offers courses and opportunities for teachers to learn more about the standards and develop ways to more effectively teach students the required skills for mastery.

For example, this year course listings included: *October 29: Teaching to New Jersey Standards; November 15: Developing Multiple Choice Questions in Support of Competency-based Standards; November 15: Support for Novice Elementary Language Arts Literacy Teachers; November 15: Steps from NJ Standards Assessment.*

Whether you teach in New Jersey or other states, websites like this one provide a wealth of information that can be used in any interview. In addition, the "Great Ideas" section at this site offers a host of "best practices" any teacher can use. A sampling of the items included such things as The Explorer Project, The Shrewsbury River Project, and the Ocean County Lesson Center with tested lesson plans on a variety of the content standards. You can reach this website at, http//*NJPEP.org*. or by typing NJPEP into a search engine. It will be worth the time you spend.

Improve Learning
http://improvelearning.com

This resource for teachers continually receives updates to its collection of themed web sites. Teachers who want to acquaint themselves with an overview of ways to use technology for instruction will find sites about Ancient China and Ancient Egypt, Birds of the World, Black History, the Civil War and Reconstruction, Libraries and Museums, Webbed Schools, Women in History, and World War II.

Those who want to learn more about using a word processor, spread sheet or data base will find tutorials that work with middle school students through adults. Some online quizzes that are scored instantly are also provided.

Topics of provided tutorials include evaluation criteria for websites, using search engines, and SQ3R/wT (reading strategies for technology). Teachers have used the strategies of Survey, Question, Read, Review and Recite for a long time. Now, they can adapt these ideas to web pages.

Brain-based research has confirmed what many teachers believed for a long time about ways students learn. It also offers many suggestions for teachers to consider and implement as part of their classroom management and lesson planning. The Improve Learning web site provides a host of resources to introduce the ideas generated by those studying brain-based research.

Before going to an interview in a school where teachers and students use technology (almost every school in the United States), a candidate might want to complete a technology self-assessement. Just go to http://improvelearning.com and click on Professional Development. Fill in Teacher Interviews as the name of your school; you will receive the results back via email.

References Cited

Armstrong, T. (1998). *Awakening Genius In the Classroom.* Alexandria, VA: ASCD

Barth, Roland (2000). *Learning By Heart.* San Francisco, CA: Jossey-Bass

Beatty, R. H. (1996). *175 High Impact Cover Letters.* New York: John Wiley and Sons.

Carnegie Council on Adolescent Development: Task Force on Education of Young Adolescents. (1989). *Turning Points: Preparing American Youth for the 21st Century* : *The Report of the Task Force on Education of Young Adolescents.*

Cummings, C. (1986). *Managing to Teach.* Edmonds, WA: Teaching, Inc.

Dungey, J. (1989). *Interactive Bulletin Boards.* Washington, D. C.: National Education Association

Freid, Robert, (2001). *The Passionate Teacher: A Practical Guide.* Boston: Beacon Press

Hunter, Madeline (1982). Mastery Teaching: Increasing Instructional Effectiveness in Elementary, Secondary Schools, Colleges and Universities. :Corwin Press

Kimeldorf, M. (1994). *Creating Portfolios for Success in School, Work and Life.* :Free Spirit Publishers

Lortie, D. C. *Schoolteacher: A Sociological Study.* Chicago: University of Chicago Press

McTigue, J. and Wiggins, G. (1998). *Understanding By Design.* Alexandria, VA: ASCD

Purkey, W. W. (1998). *Inviting School Success: A Self-Concept Approach to Teaching, Learning and Democratic Process.* Wordsworth Publishing

Saphier, J. & D'Auria, J. (1993). *How to Bring Vision to School Improvement.* Carlisle, Massachusettes: Research for Better Teaching

Saphier, Jon & Gower, Robert (1997). *The Skillful Teacher: Building Your Teaching Skills.* Acton, Massachusetts: Research for Better Teaching

Rogers, S. & Danielson, K *Teacher Portfolios: Literacy Artifacts and Themes.* New Hampshire: Heineman

Watson, J. D. & Bragg, L. *The Double Helix: A Personal Account of the Discovery of the Structure of DNA*

Wolf, M. (1996). *netStudy:Your Guide to Getting Better Grades.* New York: Wolf New Media

Yate, M, (2002) *Knock Em Dead 2002,*

CONTRIBUTORS

Lynn Caravello, Principal, Bernards HS, Bernardsville, NJ

William Clarke, Superintendent, Roselle Park Schools,
>   Roselle Park, NJ

Chris Campisano, Camden County Education Specialist,
>   NJ Dept. of Ed.

Anne Evangelista, Superintendent, Milltown Schools,
>   Milltown, NJ

Jim Hyers, Assistant Principal, Tinton Falls ES,
>   Tinton Falls, NJ

Glen Lampa, Bedwell ES, Bernardsville, NJ

William Librera, Superintendent, Allamuchy Schools,
>   Allamuchy, NJ

Linda Palumbo, Principal, Allamuchy ES, Allamuchy, NJ

Archie Pollock, Assistant Principal, Clifford Scott HS,
>   East Orange, NJ

Susanne Reilly, Past Superintendent, Millstone Schools,
>   Millstone, NJ

Arlene Roth, Director of Special Education,

James Thompson, Principal, LeRoy ES, LeRoy, NY

Quick Order Form

Fax orders: from Advanta at (732) 302-2585
or from Atlas at (800) 247-6553

Online: www.atlasbooks.com or **AdvantaPress.com**

Postal Orders:

> Advanta Press
> 1982 Washington Valley Road - PMB 344
> PO Box 309
> Martinsville, New Jersey 08836-0309

Or Atlas Books

Please send the following books:

_____ copies of <u>Teacher Interviews: How to Get Them and How to Get Hired!</u>

Sales tax: Please add 6% to books sent to New Jersey addresses.

For free information on seminars, workshops or speaking:

> Dr. Robert Pollock
> 38 Linberger Drive
> Bridgewater, New Jersey 08807
> (732) 302-2585

Please mail information on _____ to:

> Name: _____
>
> Address: _____
>
> City: _____ State ____ Zip _____
>
> Telephone: _____
>
> email: _____

Or complete our request form on **AdvantaPress.com**

Shipping: Please add $4.50 for up to first two books and $2 per additional two books. For larger orders, specific freight will be included in the invoice.